EVERYDAY INNOVATORS

Computer Supported Cooperative Work

Volume 32

Everyday Innovators

Researching the Role of Users in Shaping ICT's

Edited by

Leslie Haddon
University of Essex, U.K.

Enid Mante
Utrecht School of Governance, The Netherlands

Bartolomeo Sapio
Fondazione Ugo Bordon, Italy

Kari-Hans Kommonen
University of Art and Design Helsinki, Finland

Leopoldina Fortunati
University of Udine, Italy

Annevi Kant
ITC User Research HB, Sweden

 Springer

A C.I.P. Catalogue record for this book is available from the Library of Congress.

ISBN-13   978-90-481-6887-3 (PB)
ISBN-13   978-1-4020-3872-3 (e-book)

Published by Springer,
P.O. Box 17, 3300 AA Dordrecht, The Netherlands.

www.springeronline.com

Printed on acid-free paper

Contents

Chapter 1.   Introduction   1

**Frameworks: The Social, Unpredictable, and Innovatory
Use of ICTs**   17

Chapter 2.   Beyond User-Centric Models of Product Creation
Ilkka Tuomi   21

Chapter 3.   Following the Emergence of Unpredictable Uses?
New Stakes and Tasks for a Social Scientific Understanding
of ICT Uses
Alexandre Mallard   39

Chapter 4.   The Innovatory Use of ICTs
Leslie Haddon   54

Empirical Studies: Users as Innovators and Critics   67

Chapter 5.   Supporting Creativity – Co-experience in Mobile
Multimedia Messaging
Katja Battarbee and Esko Kurvinen   71

Chapter 6.   The Social Shaping of New Mobile Devices Among
Italian Youth
Fausto Colombo and Barbara Scifo   86

Chapter 7.   Creative User-Centered Design Practices: Lessons
from Game Cultures
Olli Sotamaa   104

Innovation and Artistic Users 117

Chapter 8.   Artistic Deviance and Innovation in Use
Emmanuel Mahé 121

Chapter 9.   The Mobile Multimedia Phone and Artistic Expression:
A Case Study of Moby Click
Heli Rantavuo 136

Problems of Researching and Involving Users in Design 151

Chapter 10.   Questioning the "Rural" Adoption and Use of ICTs
Rosemarie Gilligan 155

Chapter 11.   Dealing with Dilemmas in Pre-competitive ICT
Development Projects: The Construction of "The Social" in
Designing New Technologies
Sander Limonard and Nicole de Koning 168

Chapter 12.   Test Scenarios and the Excluded User
Jarmo Sarkkinen 184

The Politics of User Involvement in Programes of Innovation 201

Chapter 13.   The Construction of "Equal Agency" in the
Development of Technology
Marja Vehviläinen 203

Chapter 14.   Community–Technology Interfaces in Participatory
Planning: Tool or Tokenism?
Somya Joshi 218

Chapter 15.   Conclusion 233

Chapter 1

INTRODUCTION

This book brings together a selection of papers from the conference *The Good, the Bad and the Irrelevant: The user and the future of information and communication technologies*, organized by the European COST269 network at the University of Art and Design in Helsinki in September 2003. The previous few years had seen regular conferences devoted to particular ICTs, especially the mobile phone and the Internet. However, there were still relatively few events, and indeed publications, that looked more generally at the various telecom-, computer- and media-related technologies encountered in everyday life.

Yet there are lessons to be learned from looking across studies of a range of ICTs. We can ask more generic questions about the insights provided by different research tools and theoretical concepts. For example, we can consider the problems and issues involved in studying the actual and potential users of these technologies and services, or imagining how they might be used. How innovative are users and in what ways? When have and how could their actions had a bearing upon design? When should we focus on individuals versus more collective social processes? But this is only half of the story. Since the 1990s, there has been a growth of a literature dealing with the adoption, use and experience of ICTs (summarized in Haddon, 2004). But there is far less written about the process of innovation in this particular field of ICTs. When and in what capacity are (potential) users involved in the design process? What dilemmas does this entail? What factors serve to limit user contributions? What types of interaction take place amongst design teams or amongst those stakeholders dealing with certain types of innovation? This book addresses both the dimensions outlined above, exploring both the issues involved in anticipating ICT use and the nature of the innovation process.

To return to its origins, this book took life at an event, a conference, that was interdisciplinary not only in terms of those attending but also in terms of its goal – to create a dialog. The organizers were interested in achieving a degree of conceptual integration among the many different disciplines studying ICTs and felt the need for inspiration from different approaches in order to enrich our tools of analysis. But the conference was also interdisciplinary at a second level in that it addressed the divisions between the communities who study

Leslie Haddon (ed.), Everyday Innovators, 1–16.

these innovations and users and those who develop and build technologies. The approaches of these communities are very different, and they tend to have separate events, making it difficult for members of one community to get to know and meaningfully debate the approach of the other (but as an example of one attempt to do so, see Haddon and Kommonen, 2002).

These two cultures often have different concerns, use different methods and speak a different language. Technology developers tend to be pragmatic, their everyday life concern is to build something that did not exist before and that can be said to work. Those who study technology and users sometimes consider the practical development processes to be speculative without exhibiting enough scientific rigor. For developers, technology studies can be interesting reading, but they often find it hard to even begin to apply the insights in their work. For social scientists who are concerned, for example, that technology development is not a democratic process, it may be hard to point out what kind of design or technology architecture could in a specific development project help to change that situation.

Extending the interdisciplinary theme still further, the conference also encouraged reflection on the contribution that artists could make to ICT development. This community often brings a completely different point of view to the technology and tends to push the limits of available possibilities while striving for high quality of expression and end-user experience. The inclusion of artists in the innovation cycle could also introduce a useful element of serendipity into the process. Historically, technology has always attracted artists, as in the technical configurations signifying Modernity that were built in the laboratory of the Bauhaus. And, as is demonstrated in later chapters, many of the practices artists invent open possibilities for mainstream products by using new technological tools, ICTs included, in an innovative way in order to create new languages, styles, and meanings. Unfortunately, industry has not generally understood the value of this kind of work and has not been able to tap into this innovation potential.

The original conference aimed to build grounds for a dialog that can help to bridge the gap between these various communities. The participants were specifically asked to consider that their audience may not be from their discipline and use language and explanations that could open up their position to the non-initiated. This approach was developed further in this book as the contributors were asked to clarify concepts and provide examples as appropriate.

While generally adding to knowledge in this area, the book also self-consciously addresses current and potential practitioners who have a common interest in the subject matter but who come from diverse disciplinary backgrounds. Since the editors were requested to bear in mind that these various audiences also approach books in different ways, the introduction to each section summarizes the key points of the following chapters. While each chapter can be read as a stand-alone contribution to the field, the cross-referencing and summaries are intended to demonstrate their shared underlying themes.

There are five sections to the book:

a) Frameworks: The Social, Unpredictable and Innovatory Use of ICTs.
b) Empirical Studies: Users as Innovators and Critics.
c) Innovation and Artistic Users.
d) Problems of Researching and Involving Users in Design.
e) The Politics of User Involvement in Programs of Innovation.

The remainder of this introduction sets the scene in two ways. It provides an overview of the major traditions upon which the individual authors draw. And it summarizes the basic underlying themes that cut across but also unite the various chapters.

1. An Overview of Relevant Literature

The contributors to this book draw upon a wide range of theoretical approaches and to an extent these are introduced within specific chapters. However, in some cases it is useful for readers unfamiliar with these frameworks to have more background information, especially when several of the authors refer to shared concepts. This first section provides a brief, though not exhaustive, description of some of the relevant literatures to which the chapter authors refer.

One such literature is that dealing with the social shaping of technology. But here we need to appreciate the notion of technological determinism that it critiques. Technological determinism as a theory of society is reflected in claims that the arrival of new technologies has "impacts" on society, i.e. they have social consequences, as in McLuhan's (1964) arguments that electronic media are changing our perceptions of the world. Technological determinism as a theory of technology is of more relevance to this overview. This is the view that technologies emerge from science and/or evolve from their own technical logics so that particular paths of technological development are inevitable. While product developers may be skeptical of this through a behind-the-scenes appreciation of the countless decisions involved in any innovation, this is nevertheless a popular understanding of the nature of technology. The social shaping of technology tradition has challenged this view by showing the many social factors at work influencing how technologies emerge in a particular form (e.g. MacKenzie and Wajcman, 1999).

There are variations within this tradition such as the social construction of technology approach (SCOT) and Actor-Network theory, references to which appear in some of this book's chapters. What they share is the idea that technologies emerge out of processes of choice and negotiation between "relevant social groups" (SCOT, described in Pinch and Bijker, 1984), "socio-technical constituencies" (Molina, 1989) or "actor-networks" (Latour, 1986; Law and Callon, 1992), which have different degrees of power to influence outcomes. One concept within the SCOT tradition is that of "interpretative flexibility," which means that different groups of people involved with the development of a technology can have very different understandings of its role and purpose. We can appreciate this process in the chapter by Mallard on uses drift or that of Colombo and Scifo on different users' interpretations of MMS.

Within this broader social shaping tradition, Mallard's chapter describes how those involved in product development will necessarily formulate ideas about who the users will be and how they will use the technology – and act on this in making design decisions. This has been referred to in terms of "configuring the user" (Woolgar, 1991; discussed in Silverstone and Haddon, 1996) or the "scripts" built into design (Akrich, 1992) that contain or embody visions of the future use and users (see also Fortunati, forthcoming). These assumptions shape innovations, inviting users to develop some practices but sometimes making others more difficult.

A different literature focuses on what happens to technologies after acquisition in some form, when they start to be used. The implication is that we should not see innovation as somehow ending in the design phase. This gives rise to a key theme of this book: that users are in various senses innovators. One framework mentioned in some chapters is that of domestication (Silverstone and Haddon, 1996; Silverstone *et al.*, 1992). This has tended to focus on what users do with technologies in the home, although in principle it could be widened to consider how we interact with ICTs in other parts of our everyday life, such as how we deal with portable technologies (Haddon, 2004). But the point of significance here is that this framework asks what users do to and with technologies in order to fit them into their lives, to make them acceptable. Returning to the first sense of technological determinism, as a theory of society, such an approach questions whether it is appropriate to characterize technologies as simply having impacts, if users are seen to be active in this whole process.

To understand the domestication framework, but also the themes of some of the empirical and historical studies outlined below, it is important to appreciate that technological objects are, like any other object, symbolic. They mean things to people. This emphasis has been developed in anthropology (Douglas and Isherwood, 1980) and cultural studies (Hebdige, 1988). It has also been important in the more recent field of consumption studies (McCracken, 1990; Miller, 1987), which has itself drawn upon numerous academic disciplines (Miller, 1995) and in those psycho-sociological studies looking at the social representations of ICTs (Contarello *et al.*, 2003; Fortunati and Contarello, 2002a, b; Fortunati and Manganelli, forthcoming). The domestication framework applied some of these ideas to ICTs. Hence, one of its interests is in the meaning people give to technologies, how they perceive and talk about them, as discussed, for example, in the Colombo and Scifo chapter.

Furthermore, if technological objects have meanings, then at one level they can be seen as being like texts – like books to be read (as discussed further in Vehviläinen's chapter). One can note the limits of this metaphor by pointing to ways in which technologies are not like texts. But this perspective does enable a connection with a strand emerging within media studies and captured in the notion of "encoding" and "decoding": that text producers may encode meanings into texts, intending them to be read in one way, but audiences may decode them differently, creating their own interpretations of what they mean. Battarbee and Kurvinen develop this line of approach in their chapter on the meanings of MMS images, looking at how ordinary people encode multimedia texts, and how the recipients decode them. The more general point from this textual metaphor is that audiences (or text readers) are very active and creative in interpreting texts. There are clear parallels with the ways in which users are innovative, including by using technologies in ways unintended by producers.

In addition to the above theoretical frameworks, there are particular historical studies of how technologies developed, sometimes dealing with the part played by users in this process (some of which are discussed in the chapter by Haddon). These studies included ones covering several innovations (Flichy, 1995; Marvin, 1988), particular studies of early radios (Douglas, 1986; Johnson, 1981; Moores, 1988), early telephone (de Sola Pool, 1977), and early television (Spigel, 1992; Williams, 1974). In more recent times, we have histories of video (Keen, 1987), the home computer (Haddon, 1988; Lally, 2002), interactive games (Haddon, 1999), mobile phones (Fortunati, 2002), and parts of the Internet (Rommes, 2002). Some of these studies draw upon wider theoretical frameworks more than others. But they can all be used to illustrate different points about the innovation process, showing its complexity. Many of these histories show how technology could have been developed in different ways, how they sometimes evolved through multiple trajectories. A number of them deal with representations of early technologies, including the hopes and fears surrounding their arrival. And many deal with the "experience" of these technologies, which encompasses more than use. A parallel interest in experience is now emerging amongst the design community, as discussed in the Battarbee and Kurvinen chapter.

The role of users in the innovation process has constituted a small field of study in its own right (e.g. Coombs *et al.*, 2001; McMeekin *et al.*, 2002). The literature includes a few, but relatively few, studies of innovation in the area of ICTs. For example, Cawson *et al.* (1995) looked at home automation, multimedia (CD-*i*) and electronic messaging. This study explored a range of issues: where developers' ideas about users, their wants, their interests, their problems, etc. came from; why, to what extent, and in what ways potential users were involved in the ICT innovation process (e.g. in focus groups, usability testing); and how user feedback was evaluated as a source compared to other influences on developer decisions. A later EC-funded study looked, in addition, at how and why consideration and involvement of users varied across different types of ICT industry and what types of users were considered (Haddon, 2002; Haddon and Paul, 2001). One subsequent study of mobile phone innovation focused on the growing influence of users on design in this particular area. Mobile phone user's consumption patterns prompted a lower degree of design, allowing for more user experimentation and in the process involved a "reconfiguration of telcos" (Fortunati, forthcoming).

Within this small literature on users in the innovation process, there are also discussions of the limitations of different particular ways on involving users. For example, product developers can learn about the effectiveness of a certain technology for achieving a particular goal, as when electrical car experiments could show how users responded to particular features of the technology (Hoogma and Schot, 2001). The authors of this study refer to this as "single-loop learning." In contrast, "double-loop" learning would go a stage further to involve users in exploring and questioning the assumptions, values, and worldviews that are built into innovations. Here, the authors argue for giving users more chance to construct their own meanings and preferences during the innovation process and allowing them to be more active and creative, along with designers, in formulating new products that could satisfy their own needs. So rather than involving users late in the innovation process as "a source of information about a pre-conceived product" (Hoogma and Schot, 2001, p. 3) there would by a process of "mutual learning by both producers and users about the possibilities for use of the technology" (Hoogma and Schot, 2001, p. 2). These discussions provide some context specifically for the projects outlined in the Limonard and de Koning chapter, but they are also relevant for several other chapters.

Innovations do not only take place in the realm of the individual user but also in organizational or institutional settings, as when policy makers or management decide on a program of institutional or social change in order to reach certain goals. Examples from this book would include the implementation of a national information society program (Vehviläinen) or a city regeneration project with an ICT component (Joshi). To ensure the acceptance of the change and its fit with the specific target population, there have been writings arguing that it is important to ensure that the potential users participate in the change program.

In fact, there is now a substantial organizational and management literature on the involvement of different stakeholders in organizational change programs. Going back to the discovery of the role of informal groups in setting work standards and ethics (McGregor, 1960; Roethlisberger and Dickson, 1956), various strands within organizational science have emphasized the importance of intrinsic motivation. (Herzberg *et al.*, 1959; Maslow, 1964). These ideas were later incorporated in those management science approaches stressing the importance of making use of the creativity generated by employee participation in such change (Morgan, 1988). Various writers have noted how differences in interests as well as power between stakeholders can hamper such participation (Morgan, 199; Tannenbaum, 1968). As both Vehviläinen and Joshi outline in this book, numerous stakeholders can be party to change programs. They need to be informed, they need to be able to have an input but their participation also needs to be managed (de Bruyn, 2003).

Social learning theory, referred to in Tuomi's chapter, draws attention to how learning is embedded within the historical and cultural context of the community in which the individual lives (Elbers, 1993). The key point is that individuals derive the meaning that artifacts have in their life from the perspectives they share with other social beings in their world (Goodman, 1978; Saljo, 1996).

> *The community in which the child grows up, the community wherein the individual participates communicates implicitly and explicitly basic skills and competences to enable him to share the responsibilities of daily life. (. . .) The community provides the meaning and the perspectives in which technical constructs are perceived and are institutionalised* (Saljo, 1997).

Moreover, this happens not only during childhood, but also throughout adult life. The interest people have in learning new practices is enhanced or hampered by their pre-conceptions and the perceptions about what has to be learned (Thijssen, 1996) and these perceptions are influenced by significant others. Learning is also a process through which knowledge is actively created by experience through experimentation and reflection on the result. Social learning models have been developed to capture this, for example by Dewey (1991) and Engeström (1999). Tuomi's chapter shows how these models work in the case of the adoption of technological innovation.

2. Themes of the Book

Four underlying themes are addressed throughout these chapters. They can be expressed through the following questions:

- How do, or could, teams developing ICTs imagine users and uses? What tools, in terms of methods and concepts, are helpful? What aspects of everyday life do they consider? What problems do they encounter?
- How do users take part in the innovation process? In what ways and at what stages are users involved? What are the issues that arise from user participation? What are its limitations?

- When and why is it useful to focus on the collective rather than individual use of ICTs? What counts as communities of users?
- What issues emerge around interdisciplinary collaboration during the innovation process? In what ways can different disciplines make a contribution? How could the relationships between disciplines be managed?

2.1.   Imagining Users and Uses

Both the chapter by Limonard and de Koning and that by Mallard deal with the innovation process, examining the role of the social scientist operating within teams designing ICTs. However, other literature suggests that some of the points they raise can apply to others besides those with a social science training and sense of identity. Sometimes the role of representing users passes to certain types of designer who can therefore have a similar experience of trying to represent and imagine users (Haddon and Kommonen, 2003). Sometimes it can apply to some product managers whose initial training was more technical but who have subsequently taken on the need to consider users.

Both chapters in their own way characterize the problems faced when it is important to know about potential users, when they as social scientists are often the ones expected to supply that knowledge, but when user reactions to technologies remains fundamentally unpredictable – a point also alluded to from an artist's perspective by Mahé. Mallard shows this by looking at the history of a number of innovations, while Limonard and de Koning do so through considering particular projects in which they have been involved. Both chapters offer advice to social scientists involved in ICT product development, reflecting upon the relations between team members. In fact, Limonard and de Koning, make links with the question of user involvement in design and the nature of interdisciplinary collaboration – to be discussed in later sections. They see ways in which these may not be discrete issues but are sometimes interconnected, which might be a fruitful avenue for further reflection. Lastly, both chapters in effect argue that understanding users is only one consideration: a sociological appreciation of the dynamics of the wider project is also required.

Tuomi discusses the frames of reference that designers use when innovating. He encourages them to look beyond the narrow functionality of technical objects in order to consider the social role that technological objects may be playing for users. This involves examining how these objects fit into the interaction between people, how, at different levels, they are used to communicate. In this instance, his example of the coffee cup is striking because it is such a common taken-for-granted "technology," and yet it is possible to look at it in completely different ways, over and above being a vessel for containing a certain type of hot liquid. This way of conceptualizing uses has potential design implications.

Finally, a number of other chapters focus on more specific dimensions of imagining uses and users. Gilligan's chapter draws attention to the processes at work behind the statistical assessment of ICT use. In other words, she reflects upon one of the tools used to imagine users by showing the problems with measurements of rural uses, and in so doing highlights difficulties with the very concepts being used. Colombo and Scifo illustrate how we can understand people's reactions to new ICTs, in this case the camera phone, through looking at how they perceive this innovation in a wider context. They also suggest how we might understand the role of users as innovators. Battarbee and Kurvinen do this through looking at users co-producing multimedia messages with camera phones. Sotamaa, examines the different ways in which games enthusiasts are creative and how this also influences the design process. Meanwhile, Haddon reflects more generally upon the various ways in which users of ICTs can be innovative.

2.2.   *Involving Users*

ICTs firms, more so the larger ones, have for some time collected various forms of information about users and potential users at various stages during the in-novation process. Of course, this research can be constrained by considerations of time and money. And companies vary in their ability to put to good use the feedback that they do receive. One further qualification is that the input about or from users is by no means the major factor shaping product design decisions – although in the field of mobile phones, there is some evidence of user influence (Fortunati, forthcoming). Other research has shown that companies can often attach more weight to other considerations. These include the views of other firms, including competitors' plans, their own interpretation of trends and industry lore, i.e., beliefs widely shared within the industry about what types of product strategies can and cannot be successful (Haddon, 2002). Moreover, in the case of many complex innovations there may well be a number of potential stakeholders, only one of which is "the user." This may have a bearing on later discussions of how powerful, or "equal," a role users can play in the innovation process.

That said, a number of the contributors to this book have raised issues concerning user participation in the design process. The first of these is the very nature of that user involvement: on what terms are users contributing, what is their role? For example, Sarkkinen's chapter looks at how feedback from people involved in usability testing is steered in certain directions by the nature of what is asked of them. In the projects described by Limonard and de Koning, the role of potential users is sometimes to respond to product ideas from company staff while at other times they are invited to be co-developers. How much of their input is actually taken in account by technology developers remains open to question. In Joshi's paper, users from the "community" (to be discussed below) were asked to provide feedback, but her research shows how difficult this can be and, as in Sarkkinen's chapter, she suggests ways in which potential users need to be empowered in order to be able to provide a better input. Ultimately, both Joshi's and, especially, Vehviläinen's chapter question how significant an influence users can have, asking whether they can be more "equal" partners in the design process, what this could mean in practice, but also what factors and frameworks mitigate against this happening.

A second, though arguably related, question concerns the timing of when users become involved in the innovation process. Limonard and de Koning show projects where this varies. Although they provide one example of a project that tried to start from (particular) users' daily lives, other research shows that it is relatively rare for users to be involved in the genesis of product ideas (Cawson *et al.* 1995; Haddon, 2002). Users are more likely to be involved at later stages, such as evaluating products ideas/concepts, evaluating prototypes, usability testing, and user trials. That said, there are exceptions, as shown in Sotamaa's chapter, where the games industry looks to the gaming community, the fans, for certain types of innovative ideas.

Then there is the, again related, question of which users are involved. Joshi raises this point when asking who is consulted within a "community." Moreover, are these users somehow supposed to be representing other communities as well, i.e. are they simply a test bed for something that may have wider applicability? Or are they supposed to be giving feedback just about their own particular use of these technologies. To refer to a concept from Vehviläinen's work, if users' knowledge is very "situated," reflecting their own particular experiences and situations, then this well may be useful for understanding how they will take up an innovation in the case of the "local" or "small-scale" experiments and initiatives that she and Joshi describe. But how does that relate to ICTs that are intended for a much wider user base, when different users' situated knowledge may lead them to provide conflicting suggestions? Is there a type of "expertise" to reconcile these that is inevitable in such cases?

Finally, there is what Limonard and de Koning refer to as the dilemma of user involvement. In some cases, users cannot themselves predict what they will do with ICTs (as noted also be Mallard). Certainly Limonard and de Koning show that there are cases when users can find it relatively more difficult to articulate their responses to innovations. Although users can provide useful feedback for the better design of things which they already know and use, radically innovative thinking about possible ICTs often comes from designers who are able to conceive almost limitless possibilities in the far future – or artists, as argued by Mahé. Other research has shown that some product developers are wary of consumer responses to more radical innovations for this very reason (Cawson *et al.*, 1995).

2.3.   *Collective Use and Communities of Users*

There are traditions in user research that focus on individuals – the "uses and gratifications" framework would be a key example. Some other approaches, as exemplified in the second part of Haddon's chapter, have looked at a different unit of analysis. The domestication framework has been used to examine the relationships between individuals within households in order to understand their perceptions and use of technology. Other researchers have looked at forms of interplay in public spaces, between people who do (and do not) know each other. For example, Goffman's approach has proved popular in some cases (particularly when looking at mobile telephony, Ling, 1997). And ethnographic methods have been used to observe interaction around technologies as a basis for making design suggestions (Taylor and Harper, 2001).

This collective dimension of use and innovation, as opposed to individual creativity, is a key theme of quite a few of the chapters of this book. In their empirical study, Battarbee and Kurvinen show how the creative use of multimedia does not reside solely within the individual. They use the concept of "co-experience" to reflect upon the ways in which people collectively interpret experience through interaction, and in this case learn how to use a new technology.

Mallard points to the importance of collectivities in terms of the well-established concept of network externalities – i.e., in the case of ICTs involving communications in particular, the usefulness of the product increases with the number of users. However, he adds a qualitative dimension to this, arguing that the more one's social network uses certain ICTs the more likely it is that they will develop different ways of behaving. Mallard gives the example of the emergence of new ways of arranging meetings, and indeed we can see this in the mobile phone literature. Here, there is evidence that this device has enabled younger people to meet more spontaneously (e.g. Ling, 2004). Hence, Mallard notes the importance for product managers of building upon such collective dynamics by integrating new ICTs into pre-existing communities.

Tuomi addresses a related point within a more general, theoretical argument. People's behavior is only meaningful if we see them acting within a wider social world, in parallel to the way that languages only exist if there are communities of speakers. Similarly, people's use of technologies only makes sense if we see them as being parts of communities of users, which is particularly visible when they use ICTs, perhaps symbolically, to communicate. Tuomi then emphasizes how we socially learn to use ICTs within communities of practice, exploring the different ways in which these communities interrelate.

Haddon's chapter details various ways in which particular "communities" have innovated, such as radio hams or early microcomputer users. They did so partly to gain the appreciation of their peers and in the knowledge that those peers were also exploring the technology. This chapter documents ways in which innovation occurs at various levels, including innovation in terms of new practices – similar to Mallard's example of new ways of arranging meetings. Battarbee and Kurvinen may focus on the moment of creation of a new experience with multimedia, but they go on to argue that we need to look beyond this in order to see how both personal styles and collective practices emerge around a technology in the longer term. We can see this in the case of early computer gaming noted in Haddon's chapter, while more contemporary details of this phenomenon are provided in Sotamaa's one.

One word of caution, though, is that it has long been recognized within the social sciences that "community" is also a problematic word with multiple meanings. This is demonstrated in Joshi's work, one of the two chapters that looks at efforts to "involve the community" in ICT development. She points out that what counts as a community in this instance is often specified by the spatial boundaries of a particular geographical area. Obviously, this is different from defining communities in terms of "communities of shared interests and practices around which people interact." The media studies literature talks about other communities being "imagined" – the important point is that people have a sense that others are doing the same thing as them (Scannel, 1988). So while talking about communities is useful in terms of making us think beyond individuals, there is still scope for reflecting more upon the nature of those communities and where to place boundaries around them.

2.4.   Interdisciplinary Issues

Before considering issues of interdisciplinary collaboration, it is important to point out that the boundaries around disciplines may themselves be somewhat flexible and there is diversity within them. In many of the writings in this book, whether by those who would consider themselves to be designers, social scientists or artists, we see a process of borrowing from a variety of different theoretical traditions. Sometimes the concepts are used for very different purposes: in Colombo and Scifo the idea of bricolage is referred to, and criticized, as a description of the behavior of users, whereas Mahé uses the concept to characterize the role of the artist in innovation. In addition, a number of the contributors, such as Tuomi and Mallard, have themselves drawn upon elements from different literatures when developing their arguments. This variety indicates that we should be a little wary of overstressing disciplinary distinctiveness.

Turning to the process of interdisciplinary collaboration, Limonard and de Koning describe different forms of team interaction. One example entails a division of labor where social scientists make authoritative claims, speaking as "experts" about or "spokespeople" for users. The problem here is that how those claims are arrived at is not visible to other team members – the authors describe them as being "blackboxed," just as the way in which a technology works can be made invisible to users, hidden away in a box. And indeed, partly because of this, those claims may turn out to have little influence or, as in one project, be actively resisted by technical staff. The checklist offered by Mallard provides one way to address this problem by trying to make visible to the rest of the team what is being considered and why.

However, Limonard and de Koning note other ways of collaborating, for example, when social scientists interact with other team members' ideas about users, raising more and more issues for the others to consider when developing innovations. This is the social scientist as "facilitator," sometimes "agent provocateur," although arguably this role could apply equally well to others, such as some types of designer. The authors suggest that, like any approach, as implied by their use of the term "dilemma," this too has its pitfalls.

Compared to the above authors, Sarkkinen's chapter focuses on a much more specific contribution that a social scientist, or someone with a humanities background, can make. Here, the role is one of reflecting on what implicit assumptions are being made and how they could they be otherwise if the tasks and questions asked of users were different. In this particular study, the research was conducted by an outsider who was invited to make observations. But if we think about product innovation teams, this role implies one team member commenting on, and potentially challenging, the frameworks of another. While certainly interesting and worth following up, there are questions about the way the interpersonal dynamics of team interaction can be managed in such situations.

Finally, we have the contribution of the artistic disciplines, as argued and illustrated with past and contemporary examples by Mahé and discussed in relation to a particular project by Rantavuo. Mahé makes the case for the artist's contribution to innovation. It is certainly one at the more speculative end of the spectrum of roles discussed by Limonard and de Koning and arguably goes beyond this, thinking less about users and more about exploring the technology's potential. However, Mahé draws attention to a principle that the Rantavuo chapter examines in more detail – that any discipline, including art, has its own frames of reference that influence any evaluations and decisions. So while artists might feel a particular responsibility to be creative users, their explorations can nevertheless be channelled by artistic conventions and values in certain directions rather than others. For example, Rantavuo shows how the particular artistic values of her students shaped how most of them chose to use camera phones. It was within this framework that they also evaluated the technology and its limitations. Hence, just as with other disciplines, and indeed with end users as demonstrated in Colombo and Scifo, the wider understandings that people bring to the technology have a bearing on how they are viewed and how they are used.

In the Rantavuo case, so too did the context, the "definition of the situation." Here, we have students who were very conscious of passing the test of their first exhibition, which is a very different context from an established artist having the freedom to experiment with technological media. It is different, too, from the context of working in companies looking for innovative ideas. The final message we can take from the chapters on artistic creativity is that the extent to which professional and personal life interweave varies. While Mahé provides particular examples of an artist whose use of a technology in artistic ways was also a very personal experience, Rantavuo's students only thought in terms of their discipline when "on duty" as artists. In their personal everyday life, the picture phone was thought about in very different ways.

References

Akrich, M. The description of technical objects. In Bijker, W., Law, J. (Eds.), Shaping Technology/Building Society: Studies in Sociotechnical Change; 1992. MIT Press, Cambridge.

de Bruyn, D., De kunst van het implementeren; 2003. van Gorcum, Assan.

Cawson, A., Haddon, L., Miles, I. The Shape of Things to Consume: Bringing Information Technology into the Home; 1995. Avebury, London.

Contarello, A., Fortunati, L., Gomez, F., Mante, E., Versinskaya, O., Volovici, D. Social representations of ICTs and the human body. A comparative study in five countries. In Haddon, L., Mante-Meijer, E., Sapio, B., Kommonen, K.-H., Fortunati, L., Kant, A. (Eds.), The Good, the Bad and the Irrelevant: The User and the Future of Information and Communication Technologies; 2003. Media Lab UIAH, Helsinki: 56–62.

Coombs, R., Green, K., Richards, A., Walsh, V. (Eds.) Technology and the Market: Demand, Users and Innovation; 2001. Edward Elgar Publishing, Cheltenham.

Dewey, J. How We Think; 1991. Prometheus books, Buffalo, NY.

Douglas, M., Isherwood, B. The World of Goods: Towards and Anthropology of Consumption; 1980. Penguin, Harmondsworth.

Douglas, S. Amateur operators and American broadcasting: shaping the future of radio. In Corn, J. (Ed.), Imagining Tomorrow: History, Technology, and the American Future; 1986. MIT Press, Cambridge, MA: 34–57.

Elbers, E. Leren door interactie; 1993. Wolters, Groningen.

Engeström, Y. Innovative learning in work teams: analyzing cycles of knowledge creation in practice. In Engeström, Y., Miettinen, R., Punamäki, R.-L. (Eds.), Perspectives in Activity Theory; 1999. Cambridge University Press, Cambridge: 377–404.

Flichy, P. Dynamics of Modern Communication. The Shaping and Impact of Modern Communication; 1995. Sage, London.

Fortunati, L. The mobile phone: towards new categories and social relations. Information, Communication and Society, 2002; 5(4): 513–528.

Fortunati, L. Understanding the mobile phone design. In Pertierra, R., Koskinen, I. (Eds.), The Social Construction and Usage of Communication Technologies: European and Asian Experiences; forthcoming. Singapore University Press, Singapore.

Fortunati, L., Contarello, A. Internet–mobile convergence: via similarity or complementarity? Trends in Communication, 2002a; 9: 81–98.

Fortunati, L., Contarello, A. 2002b Social representation of the mobile: an Italian study, Paper given at the conference 'The Social and Cultural Impact/Meaning of Mobile Communication'; July 13–14, 2002b, Doosan Resort, Chunchon, Korea.

Fortunati, L., Manganelli, A. The social representation of telecommunications. Personal and Ubiquitous Computing; forthcoming.

Goodman, N. Ways of World Making; 1978. Hacket Publishers, Indianapolis.

Haddon, L. The home computer: the making of a consumer electronic. Science as Culture, 1988; 2: 7–51.

Haddon, L. The development of interactive games. In Mackay, H., O'Sullivan, T. (Eds.), The Media Reader: Continuity and Transformation; 1999. Sage, London.

Haddon, L. Information and communication technologies and the role of consumers in innovation. In McMeekin, A., Green, K., Tomlinson, M., Walsh, V. (Eds.), Innovation by Demand: Interdisciplinary Approaches to the Study of Demand and its Role in Innovation; 2002. Manchester University Press, Manchester: 151–167.

Haddon, L. Information and Communication Technologies in Everyday Life: A Concise Introduction and Research Guide; 2004. Berg, Oxford.

Haddon, L., Kommonen, K.-H. Interdisciplinary explorations: a dialogue between a sociologist and a design group, Report for COST269; 2002. Available at www.cost269.org.

Haddon, L., Paul, G. Design in the ICT industry: the role of users. In Coombs, R., Green, K., Richards, A., Walsh, V. (Eds.), Technology and the Market: Demand, Users and Innovation; 2001. Edward Elgar Publishing, Cheltenham: 201–215.

Hebdige, D. Hiding in the Light: On Images and Things; 1988. Routledge, London.

Herzberg, F., Mausner, B., Snyderman, B. The Motivation to Work; 1959. Wiley and Sons, New York.

Hoogma, R., Schot, J. How innovative are users? A critique of learning-by-doing-and-using. In Coombs, R., Green, K., Richards, A., Walsh, V. (Eds.), Technology and the Market: Demand, Users and Innovation; 2001. Edward Elgar Publishing, Cheltenham: 216–233.

Keen, B. Play it again Sony: the origins and double life of home video technology. Science as Culture, 1987; 1: 7–42.

Johnson, L. Radio and everyday life: the early years of broadcasting in Australia, 1922–45. Media, Culture and Society, 1981; 3(2): 167–178.

Lally, E. At Home with Computers; 2002. Berg, Oxford.

Latour, B. Science in Action; 1986. Open University Press, Milton Keynes.

Law, J., Callon, M. The life and death of an aircraft: a network analysis of technical change. In Bijker, W., Law, J. (Eds.), Shaping Technology/Building Society: Studies in Sociotechnical Change; 1992. Routledge, London: 29–52.

Ling, R. (1997) One can talk about common manners! The use of mobile telephones in inappropriate situations. In Haddon, L. (Ed.), Communications on the Move: The Experience of Mobile Telephony in the 1990s, COST248 Report, Farsta: Telia: 73–96.

Ling, R. The Mobile Connection. The Cell Phone's Impact on Society; 2004. Morgan Kaufmann, San Francisco.

MacKenzie, D., Wajcman, J. (Eds.) The Social Shaping of Technology, 2nd edition; 1999. Open University Press, Milton Keynes.

McCracken, G. Culture and Consumption: New Approaches to the Symbolic Character of Consumer Goods and Activities; 1990. Indiana University Press, Bloomington.

McLuhan, M. Understanding Media; 1964. Routledge and Kegan Paul, London.

McMeekin, A., Green, K., Tomlinson, M., Walsh, V. (Eds.) Innovation by Demand: Interdisciplinary Approaches to the Study of Demand and its Role in Innovation; 2002. Manchester University Press, Manchester.

Marvin, C. When Old Technologies Were New: Thinking About Communications in the Late Nineteenth Century; 1988. Oxford University Press, Oxford.

Maslow, A. Motivation and Personality; 1964. Harper and Row, New York.

McGregor, d.M. The Human Side of Enterprise; 1960. McGraw Hill Book Publishers, New York.

Miller, D. Material Culture and Mass Consumption; 1987. Blackwell, Oxford.

Miller, D. Acknowledging Consumption: A Review of New Studies; 1995. Routledge, London.

Molina, A. The Social Basis of the Microelectronics Revolution; 1989. Edinburgh University Press, Edinburgh.

Moores, S. The box on the dresser: memories of early radio and everyday life. Media, Culture and Society, 1988; 10(1): 23–40.

Morgan, G. Riding the Waves of Change; 1988. Jossey Bass, San Francisco.

Pinch, T., Bijker, W. The social construction of facts and artefacts: or how the sociology of science and the sociology of technology might benefit each other. Social studies of science, 1984; 14: 399–441.

Rommes, E. Gender Scripts and the Internet: The Design and Use of Amsterdam's Digital City; 2002. Twente University Press, Enschede.

Saljo, R. Mental and physical artifacts in cognitive practices. In Reimann, P., Spada, H. (Eds.), Learning in Humans and Machines; 1996. Pergamon, Oxford: 83–96.

Saljo, R. Learning and sociocultural change. Research paper 4 Onderzoeksschool Arbeid, Welzijn, Sociaal Economisch Bewustzijn, Utrecht University, Utrecht; 1997: 11.

Silverstone, R., Haddon, L. Design and the domestication of information and communication technologies: technical change and everyday life. In Silverstone, R., Mansell, R. (Eds.), Communication by Design. The Politics of Information and Communication Technologies; 1996. Oxford University Press, Oxford: 44–74.

Silverstone, R., Hirsch, E., Morley, D. Information and communication technologies and the moral economy of the household. In Silverstone, R., Hirsch, E. (Eds.), Consuming Technologies; 1992. Routledge, London: 15–33.

Scannel, P. Radio times: the temporal arrangements of broadcasting in the modern world. In Drummond, P., Paterson, R. (Eds.), Television and its Audience: International Perspectives; 1988. BFI, London: 15–31.

de Sola Pool, I. (Ed.) The Social Impact of the Telephone; 1977. MIT Press, Cambridge.

Spigel, L. Make Room for TV: Television and the Family Ideal in Postwar America; 1992. University of Chicago Press, Chicago.

Tannenbaum, A.S. Control in Organisations; 1968. McGraw Hill, New York.

Taylor, A., Harper, R. The gift of the gab? A design oriented sociology of young people's use of 'MobilZe!' Working Paper; 2001, Digital World Research Centre, University of Surrey, UK. Available at http://www.surrey.ac.uk/dwrc/papers.html.

Thijssen, N. Leren, leeftijd en loopbaanperspectief; 1996. Kluwer, Deventer.

Williams, R. Television: Technology and Cultural Form; 1974. Fontana, London.

Woolgar, S. Configuring the user: the case of usability trials. In Law, J. (Ed.), A Sociology of Monsters; 1991. Routledge, London: 57–99.

FRAMEWORKS: THE SOCIAL, UNPREDICTABLE, AND INNOVATORY USE OF ICTs

These three papers raise a number of issues that are later followed up in chapters with a more empirical content. Ilkka Tuomi and Alexandre Mallard look at the design or innovation process more generally, taking a designer and social scientist perspective respectively. Leslie Haddon focuses more specifically on the nature of innovative or creative use, a theme nevertheless touched upon by the other two authors. All three papers, in their different ways, address the theme of collective use. They ask what social dimensions of use, of the user's context and of use-related behavior we need to take into account. And they discuss implications for managing the innovation process.

Tuomi aims to develop a more complex view of users than is captured even within the human–computer interface (HCI) tradition. The chapter starts with a short history of technological design, where consideration of users was initially minimal given the focus on the artifact's functionality. Later usability studies were more user-centric and developed beyond looking at individual technologies to consider the user's experience of complex systems. The main emphasis of this chapter is that users cannot be considered in isolation from the wider social context in which they operate and, indeed, in which they socially learn ways to behave, ways to work and ways to use technologies. In other words, it is important to pay attention to the manner in which such artifacts are used within wider social practices, within shared patterns of behavior and shared understandings. In this sense, "uses" are not simply the creative inventions of individuals – they only make sense when we stand back to see these individuals interacting with the rest of their social world.

Tuomi stresses the fact that artifacts, including technologies, are also symbolic. Hence they can be "used" to communicate, for example, through displaying them, perhaps giving a message about the type of people we are. Tuomi gives the example of how the covers of mobile phones or the ringer tones chosen work at this level. But all artifacts are "communicative" in this sense. Design needs to take this into account, looking not only at functionality but at the social meanings that can be built into technologies and then the further implications for social interaction that these can have.

The central example explored to illustrate some of these arguments is the practice of having a cup of coffee at work. Tuomi shows how the potential "use" of the coffee cup is not what it seems – in fact, there are multiple social roles for this "technology," especially as this artifact is "used" socially in organizing or managing relations between people. Taking this perspective opens up new challenges for design, because once we say that there is far more happening when we have a cup of coffee than merely drinking a particular hot liquid then this raises the question of what else could be designed into that object.

The next section returns to the importance of thinking about collectivities rather than individuals. Tuomi examines the specific ways in which different social groups, for example, different types of worker, utilize technological artifacts or require different designs. But we also see here some of the dynamics involved. Changes in design, or innovation more generally, can influence how people organize their lives. Yet some designs have such an inertia that they act as a constraint on social change. Conversely, some innovations fail because of the inertia of the social institutions within which they have to operate. Here, Tuomi provides the example of expert systems for medical diagnosis.

After providing a critique of simplistic attempts to understand use in terms of work tasks, Tuomi returns to the emphasis on collectivities, referring to the literature on "communities of practice." He provides further examples of the interaction between changes in design and changes in the practices of these communities and outlines how these communities influence each other. Sometimes this interaction can limit the degree of change in practices that may need to take place to accommodate new innovations. Finally, drawing examples from the "social learning" literature, Tuomi argues how successful products, most visible in the case of ICTs, have often allowed users a space to experiment with new social practices. Hence social learning models need to be taken into account in the product development process so that they support innovation in user communities.

Mallard argues that the unpredictable ways in which ICTs come to be used represents a paradox and challenge for social scientists involved in innovation projects. Using recent historical examples, the author demonstrates ways in which the uses made of various ICTs were unexpected. He discusses the notion of the creative user, providing examples, and refers to the theoretical framework of von Hipple. Mallard argues that this theory of creative users is not sufficient as a general explanation of the unpredictability of use. Such a theory underrates the role of other actors. It refers back to market-pull theories of innovation of which there are few examples. And both the degree of user creativity and when users are creative varies widely.

Studies of the innovation process often see use as a factor to be predicted. If it is not done accurately enough this represents a failing within the project. However, within this tradition, there are some writers who do acknowledge Mallard's position that use can never be fully predicted. Meanwhile, in another literature, those researchers who study users stress how active a role the latter have in creating uses. Mallard argues that both approaches ignore each other, when really it is necessary to see the whole process as a continuum from design into use. In fact, his overall argument is that nobody has control over the way products will be used, because, to use the analogy of a boat subject to multiple forces that are pushing in different directions, "uses drift."

Mallard focuses on four factors at work. The first is the stage of configuring the user. Designers have to make decisions about what they think future users will do with ICTs. They then act on those decisions, building their assumptions into the design parameters. The expertise of the social scientist, representing the user, can be called upon at this moment. However, uses are still not totally fixed at this point in time, since other stakeholders in the innovation process can have an influence at later stages. Hence, the envisaged uses of products can drift over a longer "production" phase, and this slippage continues into consumption. Second, Mallard turns to the literature on users, outlining several relevant theories. The material on lead users, de Certeau's work on tactics and strategies, work on appropriation and domestication, and a structurationalist approach emphasize, in their different ways, the active role of users. Third, like Tuomi, he deals with the collective take up and use of ICTs. The dynamics that this involves, including the influence of "network externalities," is yet another factor in its own right influencing how uses will evolve. Lastly, the experience of ICTs takes place within a wider environment that can itself influence usage. The role of such environments is discussed in the cognitive sciences and ergonomics, in writings about different rules and understandings within different social contexts, and in thinking about how the presence of other objects can itself affect use (as in "systems effects").

Because of the above factors this drift in use is not pathological. Instead, it is the norm. Appreciating this process and reflecting upon the above checklist of influences can help social scientists working on innovations and facilitate cooperation between them and designers.

Haddon examines the variety of levels at which the use of ICTs can be "innovative" or "creative," making connections with the work of a number of the other chapter authors. Using the example of early home computing in particular, Haddon starts by describing the innovativeness of technically competent hobbyists in terms of developing hard- and software, noting also the technical conditions that allow this. Here, at the more technically sophisticated end of innovativeness, we sometimes see a blurring of the role of user and designer. The examples, especially one showing how early ham radio amateurs pioneered broadcasting, also revealed the nature of the innovativeness that these same enthusiasts have sometimes shown in terms of helping to create new practices using the technology.

But innovative use of a different kind can also be seen in the types of creativity revealed by a much wider band of users, either in designing websites for others to see or in projects for more private enjoyment. As was also the case with hobbyists, some of these forms of innovation are actually encouraged by companies. However, certain types of innovation reside not in developing the ICTs themselves or creating new applications, but rather it occurs as groups of users create new practices when using these technologies. Sometimes these are complex and unanticipated, and to make a link to the work of Tuomi, Mallard and others, such social innovation around ICTs is often a collective process.

The second half of the chapter moves on to consider the creativity that people routinely show in everyday life, but which can lead to unexpected uses. People are creative in the very basic acts of interpreting texts (and making sense of technologies) as well as in communicating – as shown in Battarbee and Kurvinen's camera phone study. This is relevant for design if too much creativity is demanded when learning to use ICTs. The next section provides illustrations of the everyday individual innovatory use of ICTs that may never become widespread – once again using the camera phone example. Finally, the section focuses on the strategies that people employ to manage ICTs on a daily basis. This can involve arranging for ICTs to "fit" into social spaces like the home and personalizing them. It can entail trying to control other people's use of ICTs, as when parents try to influence their children's use. But this in turn can lead children to develop strategies to resist this. The chapter also provides examples of the ways in which people manage their communications and deal with mobile phone calls in public spaces. The conclusion of the chapter is that we need to consider all these levels of innovativeness, and hence expand our notion of "use" when trying to anticipate people's experience of new ICTs and when trying to get feedback from potential end users involved in the design process.

Chapter 2

BEYOND USER-CENTRIC MODELS
OF PRODUCT CREATION

Ilkka Tuomi

1.   Introduction

Historically, the creators of technical products have emphasized functionality. In the traditional division of labor, product development was often separated from industrial design. The latter was sometimes delegated to a role where its task was to design packaging for already designed products. In practice, "lack of design" was indicated by gray paint and robust boxes. This "engineering" approach to design often prioritized functional design and separated it from the "packaging" of products.

More recently, the engineering approach to design has been extended to manufacturability, quality, and usability. Design for manufacturability and quality typically focus on production and product life cycle economics, and pay little attention to the user. Usability design, in contrast, has invited the user to the center of the stage. Usability research has informed product developers by studying human–machine interaction, first as a problem of user interface design and later by studying the use of products and product prototypes in both simulated and real user environments.

The traditional approach to human–machine interaction research was a cognitive one. Case and laboratory studies commonly focused on information presentation in fighter cockpits, nuclear power plants, and data entry terminals. Such studies constructed "use" as a relationship between humans and designed objects. Instead of focusing on the designed object, they emphasized the role of the subject. Human–computer interaction research and, before that, man–machine interaction research have typically been informed by this "subject-centric" view.

Many contemporary products are elements in complex systems. For example, a mobile phone or a computer has to be connected to a network before

Leslie Haddon (ed.), Everyday Innovators, 21–38.

it becomes a fully functional product. This has led to a more system-oriented view of human–machine interaction. Whereas the traditional design task was viewed as a problem of creating an essentially independent machine that perhaps interfaced with other machines in a relatively static configuration, modern technological products are combined and configured with components and infrastructures that are constantly changing. Interaction, therefore, is now at least in theory understood to extend beyond a simple relation between an individual user and an individual technical artifact.

The networked nature of many modern products highlights the point that machines are actually media that connect systems of social activity. We do not simply use new products independently of the rest of the world. Instead, we plug them into a complex system of existing technologies and social relations that make these new products operative and meaningful. Usability, therefore, is not only about human–machine interaction. "Independent" products are social artifacts that become usable only in a context of social practice. On the factory floor, machines reify specific work practices that are organized for productive purposes. More generally, technical artifacts acquire their meaning in relation to social systems of activity.

Modern products are also becoming increasingly "intelligent". Their functionality can often be programed and it can change according to the context of use and across time. Traditional everyday objects and the lived environment are becoming networked and embedded with information and communication technologies (Ducatel *et al.*, 2001; Norman, 1999).

The "object-centric" view on product design focused on product characteristics. The "subject-centric" view, in turn, started from the user's characteristics. Conceptually, both these approaches are inadequate. Product functionality is a phenomenon that exists as a relation between the product and its user. The phenomenon of use, therefore, needs to be conceptualized as a relation between the user and the artifact, where the user and the functionality of the artifact mutually construct each other.

Below I shall propose that even such a "mutual construction" approach is not sufficient when we study modern information and communication technologies or products that embed information processing functionality. In addition, we have to reconsider the way in which we describe the users. Although users are commonly understood to be individual human actors, on a more fundamental level they can only be understood as agents that express socially rooted meaningful action. Technical products are used by human actors who act in a complex but highly structured field of social practices. The fact that individual human actors implement socially meaningful acts is in this view somewhat of an accident. The fact that their actions gain meaning in the context of social and socially learned activity, is not. Without existing social context, individual acts would remain random and meaningless behavioral noise, and the concept of technical functionality would remain incomprehensible.

To understand the "usability" of a device such as a computer or mobile phone, we therefore have to penetrate through the interface and study the underlying social processes that drive the use of technical artifacts. In a conceptually rigorous analysis of design, we have to move beyond object- and subject-centric approaches toward a more relational analysis where users and functional artifacts mutually construct each other. We also have to reconstruct the user so that the social basis of meaningful use can be made visible. This conceptual strategy may at first appear counterintuitive and perhaps excessively theoretical. The distinction between the subject and the object is one of the most central distinctions in our modern views of the world. When we start to talk about users and uses of objects, we immediately rely on this distinction and take it for granted. In a conceptually rigorous analysis "users," however, need to be conceptualized as social patterns of meaningful action. In this view, individual human users simply provide the "substrate" for the social life, in a similar way as individual humans are needed to make language possible, without being able to create languages on their own. Similarly, individual human actors use functional products, but the uses and functionalities of products are not reducible to individual behavior, needs, or characteristics.

Information and communication technologies make the social dimension of technologies increasingly visible and important in practice. This chapter outlines some challenges for design in this emerging world and proposes some theoretical starting points for a social and communicative theory of design.

The chapter is organized as follows. The next section discusses the social character of material and functional objects. To make the theoretical concepts introduced here more concrete, the subsequent section shows how an ordinary everyday object, a coffee cup, implements – and could implement – social and cognitive functionality. The next section then moves beyond the user-centric view and discusses users as social practices. It points out that the redesign of product functionality, in general, implies the redesign of social relations. The following section discusses the traditional way of doing this: task-based abstractions of use, which, for example, provided the foundation for the division of labor in mass manufacturing. The next section will then introduce the concept of "communities of practice" and argue that it can provide a starting point for understanding the social contexts of product functionality, product use, and the adoption of new products. The following section introduces learning models that could be integrated into product design methodologies and product concept definitions so that the resulting products would support social change and learning. The chapter ends with a short summary and some concluding remarks.

2.   Social Objects

The "social" character of designed objects becomes particularly visible in communications products. Communication is inherently social, and understood to
be so. In everyday usage, we associate communication with speech and text.
On a more fundamental level, however, communication is a specific form of
social interaction. The different functionalities that a communication device
provides are functionalities that connect the user with others and which enable
social interaction.

This view of communication extends beyond the conventional view, which
focused on linguistic interaction.[1] Although in this chapter it is not necessary
to discuss the theoretical issues that relate to communication and language,
it is important to note that as soon as humans start to operate on the level of
language – in other words when they operate as social beings – objects and
actions become meaningful and culturally constituted. We do not only speak
into a mobile phone to communicate, but we also change its cover and ring
tone to communicate at a different level, and to be able to talk about it. Objects
become defined as elements in social interaction, which itself is structured
by culturally and historically accumulated stocks of meaning. Technological
tools are no exception here. The essence of technology is functionality, and the
essence of functionality is that it enables some social activity. In this sense, all
technologies are communication technologies.

Cultural objects, including technologies, are appropriated, they are brought
into our lives, through being somehow used within meaningful social practices,
and they do not exist in any meaningful way outside those practices. Moreover,
material objects and technological tools enter the wider social system as elements of social practices that are maintained by communication. Different
technologies afford or enable different types of communication, as we shall
see in later examples below. We conventionally define relatively static artifacts, such as a fork, a coffee cup, a steam engine, or a telephone, as "objects."
They enable us to build relatively permanent conceptual nodes in the system of
communication by linking the immaterial linguistic system of meanings with
material artifacts. This permanency is the essence of their "objectiveness."
Simultaneously, such "objects" enable more transient communication and interaction to be built around these nodes that unite the two worlds of material
and meaning. As long as we do not change our interpretation of the "object," it

---

[1] The fundamental difference between linguistic communication and other forms of communication is not in the use of words. Instead, the difference can be located in the specific self-
referential character of systems of language. (Luhmann, 1995; Maturana and Varela, 1988).
In this sense, social self-referential circulation of signs, money, and meaningful products can
all constitute languages.

stays what it is, and we can keep on talking about it as if it would be independent of our interpretations. When the interpretation is socially shared and culturally learned, the object also becomes "objective" in the interpersonal and cultural sense.

Such a communicative view on material and functional artifacts implies that when we design a product, we actually design structures for meaningful interpersonal social interaction. These social interactions, in turn, become reified, fixed or built into the practices, routines, and institutions that are embedded in material artifacts. For example, when we design a phone with a button that can be pressed to call home or our closest friend, we also define what constitutes a home and what friendship means in modern society.

3. The Socio-Cognitive Coffee Cup

The concepts discussed above are abstract and integrate several theoretical traditions. It is therefore useful to illustrate them using a practical example. I will use a well-known designed object, a coffee cup, to show how the social world is embedded in objects.

The functionality of a coffee cup is commonly taken for granted. We assume that the essence of a cup is that it holds hot liquid. The design of a cup as a container of material is therefore constrained by the characteristics of gravitation, temperature gradients, the shape of the human hand and mouth, and the human digestive system. A cup is there to hold coffee, until the coffee-drinker drinks it.

Mass production systems fulfill the demand for coffee cups. To respond to competition, producers differentiate their products and lower manufacturing costs. Industrial designers, therefore, have for a long time been shaping different forms of coffee cups using different materials. The mass production system has created "individualized" coffee cups by producing large portfolios of different designs, from which the consumer can choose a particular one.

An important design factor for coffee cups is how they feel. This relates to the material characteristics of the cup and its shape, but also to the emotional aspects of the cup. Designers have tried to attach emotional content to coffee cups, for example, by choosing colors, non-functional shapes, and by adding symbols, text, and pictures to the cup.

In such approaches, the functional character of the coffee cup is taken as the starting point. Typical coffee cups do not need engineering. The designer therefore focuses mainly on the "non-functional" aspects of design, in an attempt to add layers of meaning to the basic functional container of hot liquid.

If the functions of a coffee cup are not taken for granted, a completely new space of opportunities emerges, however. We can try to observe coffee cups in real use environments and try to understand what they are about. Such an "ethnographic" perspective reveals that coffee cups are complex social and cognitive objects.

The first simple observation is that the liquid that is put into the cup contains alkaloids that interact with the human brain. Specifically, caffeine adjusts the level of alertness. The coffee cup, therefore, is a cognitive tool that humans use to control their mental processes.

Coffee cups also need to be filled. This often requires walking. People grab the cup, take a break, and go for coffee. Coffee cups, therefore, are used to organize time and space.

Coffee cups are social objects. People walk to a coffee machine to meet other people and have a chat. They go to coffee shops to meet friends. Coffee cups are often used to organize random meetings and to exchange information. In fact, in many knowledge-based organizations, coffee cups have an important role in the management of information flows. They are extensively used to share unstructured information and tacit knowledge. Coffee cups are often among the most important information technology tools in many cultures and organizations.

The social role of coffee cups also extends to the symbolic and institutional sphere. Events are celebrated by lifting coffee cups. People are invited to join meetings with coffee cups. Trust is built by talking over coffee cups.

Cultural variations exist, and in some parts of the world cups are bigger than in others. Sometimes the cup is filled with tea instead of coffee. The main functionalities of the cup, however, remain the same. It controls mental processes. It organizes time and space. It is a communication and information processing tool. It creates and maintains social interactions. It signals and institutionalizes meaning.

From this perspective, the space for designing coffee cups provides some new interesting challenges. If, for example, we could embed sensors, information processing systems and wireless communications into the structure of the cup and make it programable, how could we redesign the social and cognitive functions of the cup? Could we reconfigure the mood control functionality, for example, so that when we approach the limits of healthy consumption of caffeine, the cup starts to play Mozart instead? Could the cup know when we need to get up and walk around a little? Could the cup detect that there is hot liquid in it, and invite our co-workers for a chat, or open our e-mail for informal communication, for example?

These questions indicate that the functional character of a coffee cup is not so fixed at all. Instead, it is clear that we often take the functions of a cup too much for granted. This obviousness has made it difficult to see that the actual use of coffee cups extends far beyond its role as a container. In fact, its role as a container would not make much sense without cultural and social practices that have adopted coffee into their portfolio of social interaction tools.

4.   User as a Social Practice

In modern society, artifacts are often created as independent objects. They, however, gain their functionality only when they are plugged into an infrastructure of ongoing social relations. This means that the user also needs to be conceptualized as a relational entity; not just as an individual user, but rather as an agent of interpersonal interactions. This is a conceptually interesting move, as it implies that we have to reconstruct the "user" in a way that differs from the conventional "subject-centric" view.

Categories of use – in other words, different ways of integrating products into social interaction – do not form endless sets of idiosyncratic uses. A blacksmith uses a hammer in ways that hammers are used in blacksmiths' practices. Cooks and surgeons both use knives, but they use knives differently and their knives are designed differently. More subtly, even exactly the same object can be used in many different ways in different social practices, as, for example, a chisel can be used differently by a carpenter, a sculptor, an archeologist or a violin maker; or as a telephone can be used differently by a stock broker, a phone marketer, a taxi driver, a teenager or a parent.

Social interaction is based on shared routines and the reduction of unpredictability. As a result, socially meaningful uses are those that are recurrent uses, repeated again and again. Such "themes of use," as it were, stay relatively constant across time. Practical variations can then be created around these themes (de Certeau, 1988). To design products that can be used to orchestrate and play meaningful themes, we therefore have to redefine "use" in a way that allows us to speak about the "user" as a social practice.

Functional design has traditionally been understood as involving the creation and combination of functional capabilities. These capabilities, in turn, were understood as being objective features of the designed products, and possible to describe independently of those social practices that actually make the concept of functionality possible. For example, a refrigerator and a baking oven were understood as objects that have the capability to generate coldness or heat. More fundamentally, however, modified functionality means modifications in our social relations. The refrigerator, for example, has transformed the practices of hunting and gathering, which now occur in shopping malls, and extend across the globe.

The relationships between product functionality and social practices are complex, and in some special cases it may, indeed, be possible to describe functionality as an objective characteristic of a product. Simple "non-revolutionary" products plug into existing practices and require little reorganization of our social relationships. An electronic typewriter, for example, is socially quite close to a mechanical typewriter. Although the operational aspects of typewriting change in some relatively minor ways when we switch from mechanical to electrical typewriters, this technical change does not have a deep impact on the practice of typewriting, or, for example, clerical work in offices. More revolutionary products, however, may lead to lengthy experimentation and adjustment processes. Computer-based word processing systems already to a large extent transform the practices of writing and communication. The "usability" of a specific system, therefore, becomes a question of either matching the product to a given form of social activity or – for more radical products – a question of social learning whereby we have to discover how to use the product to develop new practices.

Mass manufactured products have typically been products for given predefined and socially stable uses, and therefore the social character of these products was not always apparent. Designers could take the social structure for granted and there was no need to explicitly design the social dimensions of the product. Cultural variations were limited and rapid social change was more of an exception than a rule. For innovative products and for societies where the timescales of social change approach product lifetimes, the social dimensions of the product and the processes of social learning that underlie product adoption become more important. If a new product has functionality that remains unused because the social activity system where it should be used does not have the capability to change, the functionality remains latent or the product dies away. Computer systems often fall into this category because software can often be created faster than the society can change. For example, many early artificial intelligence and expert systems were developed for medical diagnosis. The main reason why they remained laboratory experiments was that, in real life, medical decision-making is associated with social and legal responsibilities. The liability for erroneous computer-made diagnoses cannot easily be defined in a society where decision makers are expected to be human actors. The adoption of computer-based medical diagnosis systems could, for example, require changes in current laws and terms of insurance policies, as well as guarantees from electricity suppliers that the power does not go off in the middle of a critical diagnostic task. In practice, the successful design of a computer-based medical diagnostic system may therefore require the capability to redesign laws and other institutions that embed social relations.

Similarly, if the society has the capability to change, but its cultural and material artifacts are structurally and functionally rigid, social change may remain a theoretical possibility. In practice, for example, organizational information systems often define how organizational procedures operate. Procedures are often very difficult to change simply because such a change would require extensive changes in existing information systems. When organization developers suggest a minor new improvement in the current organizational practices, they are often told that the improvement is impossible because it would cost millions. Sometimes the cost would be associated with rewriting old software code; sometimes simply with finding out how the old system actually works and could be modified.

"Killer applications" are a special category of products that implement radical functionality. They remove critical bottlenecks and respond to underlying tectonic social tensions by releasing accumulated social power and by facilitating the reconfiguration of social relations. Cars, telephones, e-mail and peer-to-peer file sharing systems on the Internet are illustrative examples of such technologies. They have empowered the users to articulate and achieve goals that were difficult or impossible to achieve before. Often such "killer applications" also enable many different types of use and multiple interpretations of the meaning of the provided functionality. Cars, telephones and the Internet can be used in many different ways in different social practices. Their broad and rapid penetration in the society is facilitated by the fact that there are multiple social diffusion processes operating in parallel. The car, the telephone or the Internet is not a single "product," although we use a single word for each of them. In fact, they are complex material and technical artifacts that embed and enable multiple social practices.

The conceptualization of the "user," therefore, extends beyond the boundaries of a single individual. It then becomes important to understand what the proper boundaries of the design problem are. If we cannot design a product simply based on a given list of engineering specifications or by looking at the characteristics of a specific individual, where should we look? In more philosophical terms, what, exactly, is the ontological unit for design? In the next section, I will discuss one common approach, which was based on a mechanistic decomposition of human activities into tasks. Then I will look more carefully into an alternative model, where social practices emerge as expressions of activities of socially diversified "communities of practice."

5.   Task Functionality

The individualistic concept of the user has already been implicitly rejected by organization researchers for a long time. In their descriptions, the user was converted into an abstraction, in which the actor was represented as a work task. Functionality, in turn, became defined as the capability to efficiently accomplish this specific task. This view was reflected in Adam Smith's discussion of the division of labor in his famous pin factory, where workers specialize in different tasks and the tools that are needed to get the tasks done. It was also the basis for the Tayloristic system of manufacturing. A modern version of this view can be found in enterprise integration systems and information technology supported process redesign.

The problem with the task-based view is that it is built on a process abstraction that does not match well with social reality. Human interaction does not consist of tasks. Even productive social activities such as "work" can only rarely be accurately understood as sequences of tasks. Charlie Chaplin was right in his film portrayal of this fact: process abstraction forces humans to act deterministically and to imitate machines. This has become particularly visible in knowledge-based organizations, where informal communication and interaction are important (Tuomi, 1999). Although there may be "processes" in organizations and also outside them, these processes rely, in fact, upon an extensive infrastructure of social relations. Indeed, many process re-engineering projects failed in the 1990s because they took the process abstraction for reality.

A more realistic view of social activity, including productive activity, is based on studies of social learning. Here the question is how people gain the competences that are needed to participate in social activity and how they become proficient actors within given systems of activity. Whereas the "mechanistic" task abstraction leads to a concept of user and functionality that are defined within a larger fixed process that converts inputs to outputs, an abstraction that is based on social learning leads to an abstraction that is dynamic. In this view, functionality and its complement, the user, are not fixed. Instead, they evolve as two interdependent aspects of the same phenomenon – one as a social process, which at each point of time forms the social practice in question; and the other as a characteristic of an artifact that operationalizes and implements social processes in the material world.

6.   Communities of Practice as Loci of Social Learning

During the last decades researchers have proposed that the unit of social learning could be understood as a "community of practice."[2] An important contribution to this line of thinking has been Lave and Wenger's (1991) proposal. Lave and Wenger studied communities such as traditional Mayan midwives, anonymous alcoholics, US Navy quartermasters and supermarket butchers, and argued that novice practitioners become experts through a gradual socialization process. The first step in this process is that they are given the right to be "peripheral participators" in a community of practice. Each community of practice has its own stocks of practice-related knowledge, as well as tools that it uses in its practice. This model was to an important extent based on the Vygotskian cultural–historical model of learning. In the Vygotskian tradition,[3] cultural artifacts, such as technological tools, were studied in great detail, as they were understood to be important carriers of social practice. Vygotsky also emphasized the role of artifacts as extensions of human thinking and as enablers of languages and conceptual systems.

---

[2] These researchers include Ludwick Fleck, Ed Constant, Donald Schön, Mary Douglas, Julian Orr, Jean Lave and Etienne Wenger, and John Seely Brown and Paul Duguid, see Tuomi, 2002, Chapter 6.

[3] From a design perspective, a central work is Vygotsky (1987). Introductions to the Vygotskian tradition include Wertsch (1985, 1991), Kozulin (1990), and van der Veer and Valsiner (1994).

I have proposed elsewhere (Tuomi, 2002) that the adoption of new technological products often depends on the dynamic capabilities and constraints of communities of practice. When a community of practice explores the possibilities of a technological artifact, it can adopt the artifact only if the artifact facilitates existing practices, or if the community is able to change and align its practices according to the constraints of the novel artifact. The first case is generally driven by the objective of improving the efficiency of existing practices. Supermarket butchers, for example, can start to use better butcher's knives, without changing their practices or knowledge about their practice. They can, however, also adopt new automated machines that spit out sausage slices faster than the human eye can see. This may require new knowledge and, for example, new work organization. Using automatic meat cutters, it may become possible to cut meat in large factories, or to slice meat in ways that are impossible by human hand. The quartermasters on Navy ships may become able to navigate using geostationary satellites and computerized maps. This latter case underlies the creation of new innovative practices. Creation of such innovative practices, in turn, indicates that the product and material artifact in question is an innovative product. Although many innovative products exist in theory, they become real only when they are adopted in social practice. The bottleneck in this process is "downstream innovation," i.e. the innovative capability of the user community. For example, modern navigators may be perfectly able to navigate in fog and in the middle of the night, but if navigators say that ships can be moved only in clear daylight and during standard office hours, global positioning satellites would probably never have been launched.

The innovative capability of user communities depends on the institutional rigidity of the community in question. To be able to adopt new functional products, a community has to change its practices. These are embedded and grounded in existing relations of interaction, meaning, and material structures and artifacts, and cannot always be changed easily. In fact, the very concept of "community of practice" has been mainly used to describe "conservative" communities that reproduce their existing practices and which are inherently resistant to change. Social learning, in Lave and Wenger's sense, is about becoming a socialized member of an existing community of practice, and not about innovative learning that transforms the very social practices of the community. Therefore, the Lave and Wenger's conceptualization of community of practice is not necessarily, without modifications, well suited for studies on innovation and adoption of new technological products. Brown and Duguid (1991, 2000) have applied the community of practice concept in describing innovation processes; their original focus, however, was on communities as producers for others. The adoption of products, however, requires that the community itself changes. We therefore have to simultaneously describe the communities of production and the communities of use. In some special cases, these communities may collapse into one. For example, open source software developer communities can often be described as communities that simultaneously act as the producers of technical goods and as their users.[4]

Communities of practice do not exist in isolation. It is not always up to Navy navigators to decide their working hours. Social practices form complex interrelated networks and this creates constraints on social learning. When one community wants to change its practices, in general it is constrained by the practices of other communities. Any adjustment to embrace a new technological opportunity therefore typically requires mutual adjustment and co-creation of new forms of social practices within several communities. Such non-local learning may be difficult. Indeed, the observed long time lags in the introduction of many key technologies of modern society reflect this slow adjustment process.[5] Although one particular community may have capabilities to adopt a new technology, it can only do so when other communities are willing and able to make the necessary adjustments. For example, it might appear obvious for a designer that great cost savings could be achieved by building a sales system that links information technology, phone support and product management. In practice, the designer may have difficulties in implementing and deploying such a system if the phone network does not support interfaces with information systems, or if the legal validity of contracts require physical signatures. The design problem, therefore, requires also that the designer considers the interfaces between the different interacting communities that are stakeholders in the product adoption process.

The concept of community of practice is important and useful for several reasons. It allows us to see that humans use technological products, tools and material artifacts that gain their meaning in relation to social practices that are produced and reproduced in socially diversified communities of practice. The communities embed a history of accumulated social learning, and a full membership in the community requires often time-consuming internalization of the interpretations, values and practices of the community. Individuals define their identities and they interpret the meaning of their social action in relation to such communities. The communities, in turn, operate within a broader system of interrelated communities. Product functionality, therefore, can be understood in relation to this social and socially diversified context. Whereas the traditional view abstracted functionality as tasks and socially decontextualized actions, a community of practice-based view defines functionality in relation to a social

---

[4] The distinction of production for others and production for oneself, of course, has been extensively discussed in the Marxist tradition, where alienation of producers from the results of their work was a central theme. Arendt (1998) provided an influential analysis of this issue, which distinguished the categories of labor as reproduction of the conditions of life and work as the production of artifacts. In particular, Arendt analyzed the transformation of work in modern societies where it increasingly has become work for others.

[5] The literature on long waves of economic and socio-technical transformation has emphasized that new technologies require adaptation of social institutions and their related practices. See, for example, Freeman *et al.,* (1982), Mandel (1995), and Perez (2002).

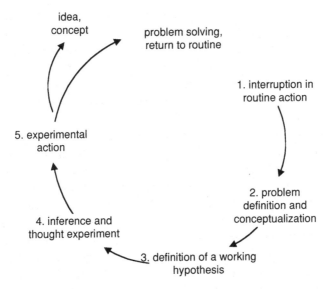

Figure 2-1. Learning cycle according to Dewey (Tuomi, 1999:309, adapted from Miettinen, 1988).

infrastructure that consists of communities that are created and maintained through continuous socialization and social learning.

7. Social Learning and Design for Technology Appropriation

The above discussion indicates how the design of functional artifacts is fundamentally a question of designing social relations. The problem of design, therefore, cannot be in any trivial way reduced to considerations of abstract functionality in the traditional engineering sense any more than it can be reduced to esthetic considerations about product color and shape. Implicitly and intuitively the social dimension has perhaps been included in traditional industrial design. Usability design, in turn, has extended that traditional engineering design toward everyday practice and real social contexts. There remains, however, a gap to be filled. This gap can be filled by refining design methodologies so that they take the very social foundations of product use into account. This requires that we define design methodologies where social learning is incorporated. For this, we need models of social learning.

One such model can be built taking Dewey's cycle of experimental learning as a starting point. The Dewey learning cycle is schematically shown in Figure 2-1. According to Dewey (1991), new forms of action emerge in a process that starts when some routine activity breaks down. This breakdown is then perceived as a problem that requires conscious attention to the causes of the breakdown. As a result, the problem becomes articulated and conceptualized. Based on the articulated conceptualization, the learner then defines a "working hypothesis" about ways to potentially repair the breakdown. The working hypothesis is tested mentally. If it seems promising, it leads to experimental action where the hypothesis is tested as a concrete solution to the problem. If the experiment is successful, the problem is solved and action can proceed. Simultaneously, a new conceptual idea is generated that can be communicated with others.

To give a very simple example, when we print a web page we may realize that the text extends beyond the page margins. We may generate various theories why this is the case, for example, that the text is formatted for a display screen and not for a printer. Looking around in the printer settings, we may then create a working hypothesis that the problem could be solved by scaling the printed page so that the text fits on the paper. If the approach looks promising, we can try and do this. If the result is satisfactory, we may generate the operational concept "adjusting the scaling for web pages that otherwise would not be completely visible on the paper." During the lunch break, when someone tells that there was a similar problem, we can then explain what the problem is and how it can be solved.

Design methodologies that incorporate the learning aspect need, then, to answer two questions. The first is about the design process itself. If social learning is important, and if many of its core parts occur in the user communities, how can these learning processes be integrated into the product development and manufacturing process? The second question is about the products themselves. If social learning and the reconfiguration of social interactions are important for the appropriation of new technological products, how can the products be specified so that their designs support problem articulation, experimentation and social learning?

The basic Deweyan learning cycle can be used to describe how new functional products and new product functionality enter into the process of human learning. Typically, new innovative products are either generators of breakdowns in social practice, elements in working hypotheses, or the means to implement new forms of routine action. Strictly speaking, Dewey's model, however, focuses only on individual learning. It can be expanded and interpreted as a schema for wider social learning by switching the unit of analysis from an individual to a group.

A well-known adaptation of Dewey's model is Kolb's (1984) "experiential learning" model, which has been used to implement team-based learning processes in organizations. Theoretically more robust models can be built using, for example, Engeström's expansive learning cycle (Engeström, 1987, 1999; Tuomi, 1999). Engeström's model has the benefit that it has strong conceptual roots in the Vygotskian tradition, which links social activity, cultural artifacts and the conceptual systems of language. This theoretical tradition makes it also possible to cross the boundaries between communication and artifacts.

Engeström's model has been extensively used in organizational development during the last two decades (e.g.,Virkkunen *et al.*, 1997a, b). It can,

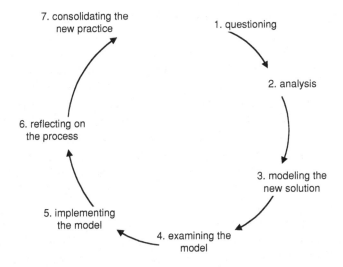

Figure 2-2. Learning cycle in Engeström's model (Tuomi, 1999:311).

however, also be deployed in a relatively straightforward way to extend product design processes so that they include the social dimension as an integral part. The model starts from the assumption that learning is inherently social and that it generates new forms of social practice. The basic learning cycle in the Engeström model is shown in Figure 2-2.

From a designer's point of view, Engeström's model is, however, a risky one. It starts from questioning the current practice, with the aim to create a model of a new possible form of practice. In this approach, learning is understood as a means for development, change and expansion of current practices, instead of transmission of existing knowledge that socializes people to prevailing knowledge and power structures (cf. Jarvis, 1992). Due to its "expansive" character, its results are unpredictable. The model is specifically a model of innovative learning, and it is "revolutionary" in the sense that it creates new forms of social practice. For commercial product developers this may be a challenge. There are no internal guarantees in the model that the generated new practice requires a specific product or technical tool, or the business firm that produces them. Instead, the learning process may as well generate a new way of doing things where the product or tool may become redundant. In fact, design that takes into account the social dimension of use often designs away artifacts or simplifies their functionality. This is partly because a redefinition of the problem may make old problems disappear, but also because artifacts often contain the historical remains of old practices that have become non-functional or dysfunctional in the course of general social development.

Technical artifacts act commonly as boundary objects (Star, 1989) that link complementary practices. For example, an architectural drawing or computer model may be used as an interface between architects, electrical engineers, interior designers, financial experts who make cost estimates, and civil engineers who calculate structural stresses and strengths. This means that such objects cannot be designed simply for a given specific community of practice. Indeed, boundary objects function from a social perspective essentially as interfaces between practices. When social interactions are mediated by technical products or artifacts, the flexibility of product functionality, therefore, to a large extent determines the possible developmental dynamics of the linked communities. Metaphorically, boundary objects can either oil the interactions between communities or nail them down in ways that make change impossible without destructively breaking the connection. The degree of social flexibility that is built into material and functional objects is, therefore, to a large extent determined by the designer.

Socially successful products have historically often resembled oil more than a nail. They have acted as social learning platforms. On such platforms, the users have been able to experiment with new forms of social practice and reconfigure existing practices in innovative and often unanticipated ways. This process has been particularly visible in information and communication technologies, and in particular in Internet-related innovations (Tuomi, 2002). However, a sociologically oriented study of most modern artifacts also shows similar characteristics in more mundane products. For example, as it has often been noted, the car created complex social transformations that refined the structures of cities and families, but at the same time produced a new conceptualization of individual freedom, as well as picnic baskets, portable plastic chairs and experimental sexual relations. The last point, in fact, probably partly explains the design of traditional post-war American cars, for example.[6]

8.   Conclusion

In this chapter I have tried to expand the user-centric view of design beyond the individual user, arguing that users and uses can only be understood against a wider social context. Material objects are used as concrete artifacts in complex

---

[6] Engineers often claim that the function of a car is to "transfer people from point A to point B." As a consequence, they easily think that transport vehicles should be optimized from this point of view. The link between the American system of values in the 1950s, sexual relations, interests of oil industry and big cars easily remains invisible in this "engineering" perspective. I am grateful to Manuel Castells for reminding me that the design of cars has also important demographic dimensions. The back seat may sometimes be as important in the car design as the driver's seat. In modern Spain also small cars apparently play an important role in mating rituals, probably partly due to a historical combination of Catholic traditions and old cities with small streets, but also because of congested houses with extended families with multiple generations under the same roof. Cars, therefore, do not only move people but they are also important social spaces.

systems of social interaction, and the functionalities of artifacts both constrain and enable that social interaction. New technological products are appropriated in social practice through a process of social learning, where, in general, social practices need to change before a new technological product can be taken into use. Social learning models, therefore, need to be integrated into product development and manufacturing processes. An improved understanding of the social character of artifacts helps us to design product functionality that facilitates this social learning and the adoption of new technological opportunities. This is becoming particularly important as everyday objects are enhanced with programable functionality and linked with their environment through sensors and communication networks.

Above I have only briefly discussed some learning models that could provide the foundation for new socially aware design methodologies. This area obviously deserves more theoretical and empirical work. I have emphasized the importance of "downstream" innovation processes in the creation of technology facilitated social practices. I have also noted that product functionality and characteristics can be explicitly designed to take social learning processes into account so that the product itself can support innovation in user communities.

The traditional approaches to design separated functional design and the more "artistic" design of external appearances. Engineers commonly believed that they were responsible for the "actual" design of the product and that industrial designers join the design process only when the product needs to be packaged and marketed. Usability design, better understanding of product life cycles, mass-customization and product individualization, emotional design, and human-centric design have considerably narrowed the gap between function and form in technological products. A more social understanding of product functionality, which sees product meaning as grounded in social interaction, has the promise of filling the gap. As products are becoming increasingly interactive and linked in complex information and communication infrastructures, it is becoming increasingly important to understand the social basis of material objects.

References

Arendt, H. The Human Condition; 1998. The University of Chicago Press, Chicago.

Bakhtin, M. Speech Genres and Other Late Essays; 1987. University of Texas Press, Austin, TX.

Brown, J.S., Duguid, P. Organizational learning and communities of practice: Toward a unified view of working, learning, and innovation. Organization Science, 1991; 2: 40–57.

Brown, J.S., Duguid, P. The Social Life of Information; 2000. Harvard Business School Press, Boston, MA.

de Certeau, M. The Practice of Everyday Life; 1988. University of California Press, Berkeley, CA.

Dewey, J. How we Think; 1991. Prometheus Books, Buffalo, NY.

Ducatel, K., Bogdanowicz, M., Scapolo, F., Leijten, J., Burgelman, J.-C. Scenarios for ambient intelligence in 2010. Luxembourg: Office for Official Publications of the European Communities. http://www.jrc.es/cfapp/reports/list.cfm; 2001.

Engeström, Y. Learning by Expanding: An Activity Theoretical Approach to Developmental Work Research; 1987. Orienta Konsultit, Helsinki.

Engeström, Y. Innovative learning in work teams: Analyzing cycles of knowledge creation in practice. In Engeström, Y., Miettinen, R., Punamäki, R.-L. (Eds.), Perspectives in Activity Theory; 1999. Cambridge University Press, Cambridge: 377–404.

Freeman, C., Clark, J., Soete, L. Unemployment and Technical Innovation: A Study of Long Waves and Economic Development; 1982. Greenwood Press, Westport, CT.

Jarvis, P. Paradoxes of Learning: On Becoming an Individual in Society; 1992. Jossey Bass, San Francisco, CA.

Kolb, D. Experiential Learning: Experience as the Source of Learning and Development; 1984. Prentice Hall, Englewood Cliffs, NJ.

Kozulin, A. Vygotsky's Psychology: A Biography of Ideas; 1990. Harvard University Press, Cambridge, MA.

Lave, J., Wenger, E. Situated Learning: Legitimate Peripheral Participation; 1991. Cambridge University Press, Cambridge.

Luhmann, N. Social Systems; 1995. Stanford University Press, Stanford, CA.

Mandel, E. Long Waves of Capitalist Development: A Marxist Interpretation, Revised edition; 1995. Verso, London.

Maturana, H.R., Varela, F.J. The Tree of Knowledge: The Biological Roots of Human Understanding; 1988. New Science Library, Boston.

Miettinen, R. Miten kokemuksesta voi oppia? Kokemus ja reflektiivinen ajattelu John Deweyn toiminnan filosofiassa (How it is possible to learn from experience? Experience and reflective thinking in John Dewey's philosophy of activity; in Finnish). Aikuiskasvatus, 1998; 2: 84–97.

Norman, D.A. The Invisible Computer; 1999. The MIT Press, Cambridge, MA.

Perez, C. Technological Revolutions and Financial Capital: The Dynamics of Bubbles and Golden Ages; 2002. Edward Elgar, Cheltenham.

Star, S.L. The structure of ill-structured solutions: heterogeneous problem-solving, boundary objects and distributed artificial intelligence. In Huhns, M., Gasser, L. (Eds.), Distributed Artificial Intelligence, 2; 1989. Morgan Kauffmann, San Mateo, CA: 37–54.

Tuomi, I. Corporate Knowledge: Theory and Practice of Intelligent Organizations; 1999. Metaxis, Helsinki.

Tuomi, I. Networks of Innovation: Change and Meaning in the Age of the Internet; 2002. Oxford University Press, Oxford.

van der Veer R., Valsiner, J. Understanding Vygotsky: A Quest for Synthesis; 1994. Blackwell Publishers, Cambridge, MA.

Virkkunen, J., Engeström, Y., Helle, M., Pihlaja, J., Poikela, R. Muutoslaboratio työn uudistamisen välineenä. In Sallila, P., Tuomisto, J. (Eds.), Työn Muutos ja Oppiminen: Aikuiskasvatuksen 38. vuosikirja; 1997a. BTJ Kirjastopalvelu Oy., Helsinki: 77–103.

Virkkunen, J., Helle, M., Poikela, R. From individual troubles to collective solutions: towards an intervention methodology of expansive learning. In Arling, H. (Ed.), Proceedings of the 1st Nordic Baltic Conference on Activity Theory; 1997b. University of Helsinki, Center for Activity Theory and Developmental Work Research, Helsinki: 66–85.

Wertsch, J.V. Vygotsky and the Social Formation of Mind; 1985. Harvard University Press, Cambridge, MA.

Wertsch, J.V. Voices of the Mind: A Sociocultural Approach to Mediated Action; 1991. Harvard University Press, Cambridge, MA.

Chapter 3

FOLLOWING THE EMERGENCE OF UNPREDICTABLE USES? NEW STAKES AND TASKS FOR A SOCIAL SCIENTIFIC UNDERSTANDING OF ICT USES

Alexandre Mallard

1.   Following Unpredictable Uses: A Paradox and a Challenge for the Social Sciences

In the field of Information and Communication Technologies (ICTs), innovation requires a relevant understanding of uses. This concern has benefited considerably from the social sciences. Specialists in sociology, psychology, marketing and ergonomics have for a long time been invited to take part in innovation projects in order to inform designers and project managers from the user's perspective concerning the particular requirements they have of products or services. Yet one of the results of the numerous studies carried out by social scientists since the beginning of the 1980s relates to the difficulty of predicting the uses of new technological devices. A general conclusion of social science research conducted in this domain seems to be that it is quite difficult to point to precise strategies for achieving success in innovation on the basis of reliable predictions concerning their future use.

Somehow, this result shows the problematic evolution of the role assigned to social sciences in innovation projects. Starting, historically, with the task of describing the practices and behaviors of people when confronted with new devices of communication, they end up with the (impossible) mission of paving a way through the territory of unpredictable uses. The hypothesis of this chapter is that this paradoxical situation teaches us more than the traditional difficulty of filling the gap between forecast and reality. The significant degree of unpredictability as regards ICT usage is the consequence of a general process of "uses drift," a process that should be scrutinized by the managers and social scientists involved in new technology projects. In this chapter, I will study this

Leslie Haddon (ed.), Everyday Innovators, 39–53.
© 2005 *Springer. Printed in The Netherlands.*

process and show that in order to propose reasonable forecasts concerning use, social scientists do not really (or do not only) have to focus on users' activity and possible creativity. More generally they have to anticipate the products' and services' trajectories of use and their associated drifts. I will also insist that this requires, in turn, crossing the boundaries between the analysis of project dynamics and the analysis of users' practices.

2.   From Unpredictable Uses to Uses Drift

2.1.   *Some Examples of Unpredictable Uses*

The notion of unpredictable use in the field of ICTs rests on a series of quite well known stories narrating both innovation failures and unexpected success, as they became apparent when the products and services began to be utilized. For instance, among French telecommunications specialists the case of the Minitel is a typical example. At the dawn of the 1980s, it was supposed to help the French society to enter the information era. Eventually, it was the (sex) chatlines, and not the information services, that proved a tremendous success with the public and that boosted the usage of so-called "telematics."

Another more recent example of the disjunction between expectations and reality was the development of SMS communication. One might think that such a medium would be used as a way of sending useful information to distant people when the phone call is not necessary or not suitable. For example, this might occur when cancelling an appointment, sending the phone number of a useful contact, reminding someone to do something important, etc. However, while usage had increased exponentially at the beginning of the 2000s in Europe, studies of the early adopters' population and practices suggest that this boom was primarily due to teenagers and young people who used SMS to send expressions of emotions. At this stage, the use of SMS is not primarily a new way of coordinating distant groups. Instead it involves the practices through which people can share emotion at a distance and manage intimacy in public places (Rivière, 2002).

The practices of peer-to-peer exchange constitute another interesting case. Neither the Internet operators nor the leading companies of the cultural industries had really anticipated that the decentralized exchange of information and content through the Internet could reach the scale that it currently does, through specific peer-to-peer software (Beuscart, 2002). This results in innumerable issues in the area of the copyright regulation, but also has implications for the smooth running of electronic networks. The development of peer-to-peer practices tends to make data exchange symmetric, whereas the broadband network infrastructure was partly designed to support asymmetric exchange. Hence, this is a problematic concern for telecommunication engineers.

2.2. The Hypothesis of Creative Users

These stories emphasize the active role of users who seize the products and services that the telecommunications industry holds out to them and creatively invent unexpected practices around these devices. Here, the particular creative potential of users is offered as an explanation of why usage defies rational forecasting. The development of online communities takes us in the same direction as particularly active users collectively elaborate new products and services (Gensollen, 2004). The case of open source programming is interesting in this respect as it is now commonly portrayed as a fight between groups of users organized in networks and the major software companies, with the former trying to develop alternative operating systems as credible competitors to the proprietary standards imposed by Microsoft or IBM.

The economist Eric Von Hippel (2002) has proposed a model that can account for this kind of innovation dynamic, whereby users originate an innovation and also carry out production and distribution. According to Von Hippel, this model can also apply to physical products. It is economically viable to manage without a manufacturer if three conditions are fulfilled: the existence of an incentive for users to innovate, the existence of incentives to reveal innovations and the possibility to distribute innovations at low cost and under competitive conditions. This model features interesting innovation patterns that have probably existed for a long time in certain domains but which had not been seen until now by innovation specialists. These patterns may become more important in the future.

2.2.1. "Users Are Wonderful! Aren't They?"

Although this diagnosis is seductive, it is probably false to set it up as the general explanatory model of unexpected uses in the field of ICTs – for many reasons. Firstly, innovation usually requires interaction between various actors – including users. The situation where users are the main creative force is only one possibility among several others. In the case of Minitel, for instance, the commercial providers that offered chatlines services were as important in the process as the users that began to chat on the network. Secondly, the emphasis on the user as innovator reactivates the old concept of a market-pull innovation pattern, as opposed to the technology-push one. Yet several decades of research into innovation processes teaches that pure market-pull schemes are quite rare, as rare as pure technology-push scenarios. Successful innovations can more realistically be explained as the interweaving of the forces of technology and of the market more than their opposition. Thirdly, experience suggests that the degree to which users are creative is subject to large variations. Users often "just" reproduce what has been thought in advance for them by the designers. On occasion they bring minor changes and improvements to a device that was in itself already a novelty. In some situations, they will totally transform the meaning and conditions of use of the original product or service. As a matter of fact, where users will behave creatively seems also to be quite . . . unpredictable!

Thus, the relation between unpredictable uses and creative users is not straightforward. Unpredictable use may be explained by various phenomena other than the sole innovative potential of users – although it is clear that this potential is an important variable to take into account.

2.3. *The Question of Uses, Seen from the Side of the Project or from the Side of the User*

Let us come back to the idea of the unpredictability of uses. It makes sense when one compares uses at two different moments in an innovation's trajectory. Usually one draws a contrast between the anticipation by the designers at an early stage of development and the final practices of "real end-users" once the product or service has been designed, made, distributed . . . and used. In practice, there is a trajectory along which the changes are usually more continuous, a trajectory that can be long and complex and involve various actors. This is especially true in the field of ICTs, which has undergone many changes in recent times, making the innovation patterns even more composite.[1] The literatures of both management and sociology have studied what happens at the stages of initial design and final use, but without really providing the analytical tools that make it possible to see it as a continuum. Roughly, this literature can be divided into two parts.

Some researchers concentrate on the dynamics of project activities (Lundin and Midler, 1998). Within this framework, the future behavior of the user in relation to the product under construction is one of the possible sources of uncertainties that has to be identified and reduced in the course of the engineering process. Uses are anticipated and depicted by project participants. They constitute one of the variables – among other innumerable technical and economic

---

[1] In the field from telecommunications, industrial strategy analysts would traditionally discern three types of actors: the equipment suppliers (providing the terminals and sometimes the network infrastructures), the operators (in charge of the transfer of information and communication flows) and the service and content providers. This pattern of innovation has been re-evaluated and made more complex in order to take into account developments since the 1990s, notably the process of convergence between computers and telecommunications, the liberalization of the telecoms sector and the "IP revolution." Strategy analysts now propose various models to describe the vast industrial and business ensemble that has emerged and initiated new mechanisms of innovation. For instance Fransman (2001) proposes to describe the field of the "infocommunications" with a model made up of six layers: equipment and software, networks, end-to-end connectivity providers, navigation and middleware, applications and users.

parameters – that have to be determined and adjusted during the progress of the project. In this context, unpredictable uses are more or less attributed to insufficient effort being made by the project to represent users' behavior or market needs and to integrate the relevant data into the product or service. Hence the importance of a user-centric approach that allows for a better understanding of users' needs and expectations (Boullier, 2002).

Many of these approaches usually admit, implicitly or explicitly (Akrich, 1992), that whatever the effort was made during the project there remains a residual uncertainty in this anticipation of uses, as the consequences of the real encounter between the users and innovations can never be fully predicted. Here, we can turn to the other trend in the social sciences literature. This focuses on the specific processes that take place when the product or service enters the universe of the final user. Studies in this field argue that uses have to be constructed including by the user him- or herself in a way that does not necessarily match designers' intentions (Jouet, 2000). Here, the gap between initial and eventual uses is not at all a residual problem. Instead, it is the very phenomenon under study, which can be explained by various factors that I will elaborate below.

Thus, both traditions of research acknowledge that the emergence of uses is the result of a process that has begun at the stage of design and that is carried over into the assimilation of the product into the users' world. Somehow, they also politely ignore each other and make difficult the task of following the continuous process through which uses undergo various transformations. Facing these conclusions, I think it is reasonable to argue that the unpredictability of uses is not the result of the particularly creative nature of users. Instead, it is the result of particular innovation trajectories leading from the original conception to the users' practices. I will employ the term "uses drift" to refer to this evolution of uses along these innovation trajectories. The idea of drift evokes the fact that an innovation's use is like a boat in the ocean: it sails in the direction in which the winds blow. And the winds can blow in many different directions. There are various factors that have conflicting influences on the future of the innovation. In other words, uses drift is not necessarily a user-centred process, but rather a multi-facetted dynamic that the social scientists involved in ICTs projects have to understand correctly if they want to produce usable knowledge for managing the innovation.

3. The Dynamics of Uses Drift

In order to describe this kind of drift, I propose here to concentrate on four different dimensions that will play a role in the process. Somehow, they feature four forces that can determine the direction in which "the wind will blow." These are: the product or service itself, the user, the collective character of users, and the environment of use. Uses emerge and evolve at the meeting point of these four dimensions. These dimensions, which I have separated for analytical purpose, are not at all independent but rather mutually interdependent.[2] For innovators, as well as for users, they provide areas where uses can be adjusted and drift in ways that are a concern but which cannot be totally controlled (Ciborra, 2001). I propose now to comment on the processes that might take place around these four poles.

3.1.   *Configuring Uses through the Product or Service*

For designers and innovators, the product or service is a main focus when considering uses. Indeed, it is sometimes the only parameter on which they can operate in order to control the appropriation process. The stage of design is an important moment for this "programming" of uses. The sociology of innovation has provided an analysis of this activity in terms of "inscription" (Akrich, 1992). Designers consider possible scenarios of use and subsequently inscribe in the product or service the elements that support the realization of that scenario. For example, a designer will have to decide about the size of the characters that will appear on the screen of a mobile phone. This decision implies that he or she needs to elaborate ideas about the situation in which it will be used. How old are the users? In what context do they look at the screen? What kind of information do they need and, subsequently, what is the length of the message that the screen will have to display? The designer implicitly or explicitly formulates hypotheses about these questions and chooses the best technical parameters to address them. In this way, the designer will *inscribe* the scenario of use in the artifact. To put this into context, it is common that many more scenarios have been inscribed than the scenarios eventually lived out when the product is actually used. Hence the product or service may have unexplored functionalities: the designer has dreamed up various situations of use that never happen in practice. The process can also provide the user with some freedom: innovators do not always want to tightly control and regulate all uses. They may prefer that the users decide or invent some practices by themselves.

Social scientists are among the actors in innovation projects who participate in the conception process at this stage. They are asked to say who the potential

---

[2] One could probably propose further levels of uses. Two other categories can be considered here: the notion of task (employed particularly in ergonomics) and the notion of process (utilized especially in studies of business and organizational uses of ICT). I do not claim that this proposition is the better one, but the hypothesis is that any issues associated with question of tasks and processes are adequately covered when considering groups and environments, in the extended sense that I use here.

public is for a given product or service, to describe current practices in the area of activity identified for it, and to anticipate users' reactions and behaviors when confronted by the product. In this situation, the social scientist somehow acts as a spokesperson for the user. His or her function is to bring into the social world of designers a bit of the social world of the users, in order to prevent a dangerous gap emerging between the two. Designing engineers are not at all stupid and innocent about uses and users: they normally have quite a relevant perception of what the users can and will do with the innovations. However, their area of expertise does not include the construction of special settings that makes the emergence of reliable information on this matter possible. The specificity of the social scientists' intervention lies in this task of mediation: they will design special experiments (surveys, laboratory tests, etc.) that will produce information in this domain. But whatever the particular status that social scientists may have in project teams, they are usually in competition with other "spokespeople for the user" who can bring in contradictory or complementary elements (Akrich *et al.*, 2002). The inscription of scenarios then depends on the arbitration between and the aggregation of several points of view that are not always compatible with each other.

The stage of design has a privileged status as far as proposing uses is concerned, but the generation of uses is not closed off after design. All the actors intervening in the chain that goes from the product conception to the market may add some elements to those planned initially by the designers (Silverstone and Haddon, 1996). Sociological studies of the activity of professionals working in the market have shown that potentially the process of inscription of new uses can continue so long as the product goes from hand to hand. Even at the stage of commercial distribution, the work of packagers and merchandisers can have consequences for use, although these operations are primarily oriented towards the point of purchase (Barrey *et al.*, 2000). Each of these operations can potentially position the product or the service in a different way and create new opportunities for use. Just think about the way in which mobile phone terminals reach the user. They are very rarely sold as autonomous devices, but rather packaged and distributed by mobile operators, who associate them with specific subscription packages and program them with certain functions – a configuration that probably has consequences for uses.

Finally, one should pay attention not to *reduce* the product or service to a mere "container for use" that would have been filled up during the journey going from conception to purchase. In a particular context objects can manifest unexpected properties or capacities. One never knows exactly what objects are made of and what they can do. Their capacity to resist or to surprise the user – and the designer – is an important feature, in the same way as the puppet resists and surprises the puppet-master as much as it is animated by her (Latour, 2000).

3.2.   The User

How can we think of the role that the user plays in the process of uses drift? Social science research on use has studied the theoretical and practical reasons that explain why users never exactly, or never always, accomplish scenarios like computer-run programs. It offers various perspectives to account for the role played by the end user in the adoption of new devices. I will examine briefly four specific conceptual approaches of this dimension of uses drift.

The first approach revolves around the notion of lead user. It is used mainly in marketing studies in order to point to the categories of users that have a distinctive innovative potential and are in advance of the rest of the market. In theory, it would be possible to learn from their behavior to anticipate the trajectory of the whole population. The underlying hypothesis is that the innovative potential is unevenly distributed – with "laggards" or other categories of people being at the other end of a scale, ones who either adopt late, who only use the products routinely or who perhaps do not use them at all. The notion of lead user is interesting, but weakly predictive. In other words, the capacity of users to innovate can be very different from one domain to another (compare for instance innovating in field of clothing compared to innovating in the area of new technology) and each innovation might generate its specific lead users.

A second approach relates to the notion of tactics, as proposed by Michel De Certeau (1990). For him, innovation in use is not restricted to a particular audience (such as lead users) but rather it refers to the very activity of the ordinary consumer. De Certeau proposed contrasting (company) strategies with (user) tactics. In the face of market promoters who use strategies to spy on the consumer and to promote certain uses, the user is not passive and mobilizes innumerable tactics to draw artifacts into his or her specific world – sometimes perverting their functions. De Certeau stresses that it is the practices and know-how embedded in various daily life activities (what he calls "arts de faire"), and not the artifacts themselves, that are at the heart of the user's concern. Using a linguistic metaphor, he considers that the user mobilizes artifacts for these activities in the same way as the speaker mobilizes syntax and grammar to compose his own sentences.

A third approach lies in more recent research on the sociology of ICT use that has extended this view and proposed various analytical concepts suggesting that users' relations to new objects is primarily based in their capacity to mobilize them as external resources in activities that pre-exist and that have their own logic (Jouet, 2000). The notion of "appropriation," for instance, describes the process that governs the integration of the product or service into the user's activity and has been invented to oppose claims about technology's "impacts" on people. Thinking in terms of impacts boils down to arguing that everything in the user's world will be transformed by the innovation. Conversely, talking about learning process (Lelong, 2002), appropriation, or even "insertion" or "domestication" (Haddon, 2003; Ling, 2002) – an expression that sounds as if users would "tame" products more than they would be tamed themselves – stresses the transformations that the innovation had already had to undergo in order to be used in the first place.

The fourth approach, the so-called "structurationist approach," developed primarily in the study of organizational uses of ICTs, offers another perspective for understanding the user's role in uses drift (Orlikowski, 2000). This approach focuses on the various kinds of structures that organize human action in general, considering the distribution of power, the enforcement of social norms and the emergence of meanings and technology. In this frame of analysis, the development of uses for a new ICT system is seen as the production/reproduction – the "enactment" – of structures of action. On the one hand, the new uses are rooted in the pre-existing structures. On the other hand, they contribute to generating new structures of action. For example, the way in which a new computer system is used in a given workplace depends on the procedures, rules and habits that governed the use of the former systems. But then, at the same time, the new system can produce new procedures, rules and habits. In this framework, the role of the user is both innovative and "reproductive" in relation to former structures of action. This approach is also particularly sensitive to the trajectory of uses and rejects the notion of the "stabilization of uses" that has been proposed elsewhere in the sociology of technology (Bijker, 1995; Akrich, 1992). Thus, uses are never definitively fixed and users can always innovate with the technologies and artifacts that they have at their disposal.

As I explained earlier, the aim of these four approaches is to stress the role played by an actor who is largely outside the production of products and services. However, it is worth noticing that the reality is more complex. Part of the process of conception, marketing and distribution aims at targeting a particular public for the product or service. Yet, most of the time no one knows who the user will be before the product or service is actually used. Furthermore, even if the user is not directly integrated into the conception process, he or she will not remain untouched by the main architects of new technologies. Telecommunications companies are quite aware of the importance of the unexpected ways in which users appropriate products and they try at the same time to control, stimulate and observe them through the channels of advertising and customer services. Advertising suggests various use situations, although it is a priori more oriented towards purchase than towards uses. Customer services also try to address the issue of use, beyond the traditional role of after-sales services and technical support (Mallard, 2004). For instance in the customer service section of some mobile phone companies, staff have to often point out the use of some functionality that is little used by or even unknown to the user: "Do you know that you can use the number XXX in order to . . . ?" Beyond the invitation to consume (and access to the corresponding services is sometimes free), this kind of stimulation is intended to stimulate the user's capacity to explore the product and to develop new uses.

3.3.   Emergent and Organized Communities of Users

The composition, size and structure of groups of users that adopt innovations is the third important factor for understanding uses drifts. We use here the notion of community in a very broad sense, which does not imply, for instance, that members know each other. In order to sketch the importance of this collective use of ICTs, it is enough to mention work on the economics of technological competition (Arthur, 1988). Of particular importance is the notion of "network externalities" that writers in this tradition have proposed to describe the fact that the utility of a technology increases with the number of its users (Katz and Shapiro, 1985). This notion conveys the intuitive idea that the interest in acquiring a communication tool (a fixed telephone, a mobile, a fax, e-mail, etc.) may be very relative: the more one interacts with people who are themselves equipped with the tool, the more attractive the tool seems.

In these economic models, network externalities affect the trajectory of the diffusion of an innovation: they are responsible for the exponential growth in the number of users once it exceeds a given threshold. From the point of view of uses drift, network externalities lead to a growth in the size of the spheres of communication.[3] Yet they also entail a transformation of use that goes beyond this quantitative jump. With the associated increase in the frequency of use, the device progressively becomes connected to a greater variety of activities and contributes to changing them. For instance, when all the members of a group of friends in a urban area are equipped with a mobile telephone, it becomes possible to change radically the way collective activities are arranged (going to the movies, meeting in a given place, etc.), a phenomenon that is much slower when only one or two members are equipped. Similarly, studies of the learning trajectories of Internet users show that if only a few people in one's relational network are connected this is more likely to lead to one terminating the subscription (Lelong and Beaudouin, 2001).

The importance of collective use also explains why the telecommunications and Internet industries pay so much attention to the topics of communities. The success of many new products or services depends on the existence of a collective dynamic in their use. Many innovation failures are explained by the difficulty of building relevant collective users. These experiences have

---

[3] Note also that beyond communication practices, every activity has a collective dimension which can be of greater or lesser importance. Thus, network externalities play a role for every product or service, but to different degrees and with different consequences for the innovation trajectory.

progressively imposed the idea, which appears today as a rule of thumb for project managers, that the developers of an innovation whose success rests on a collective dynamic should try integrate the innovation into pre-existing communities from the beginning, and not try to build the necessary communities of users from scratch.

Finally, note that this collective dimension is what explains the particular role that sociologists play in the analysis of uses at the stage of product or service conception. The role of ergonomists is often implicitly or explicitly to set up usability tests (Boullier, 2002). However, sociological expertise is particularly important in order to analyze not only the development of activities in particular contexts of action (a task that sociologists largely share with ergonomists or psychologists) but primarily how relevant communities of users will emerge and be structured. This collective dimension also explains why ICTs pose difficult questions for laboratory tests. Simulating the collective dimension is a problem, more so than the exploration of variables associated with the objects' constitution, with the environment or with the users' competence.

3.4.   The Environment

For the user, action makes sense in a space which is populated by a whole series of other entities beyond the product or service itself. Under the heading of "environment," I refer to various elements including the time and space in which use takes place as well as the surrounding social context and its equipment. These parameters can help structure the user's practices and learning. Specialists in mobile technology know how complex a task it is to integrate such changing environments of use into the design.

The environment can contribute to the use of a device and its role has been much discussed in studies of cognitive science and ergonomics. The notion of "situated action" (Suchman, 1999) has been proposed to counter the conception that reduces activity to a process that would first be planned in the mind and then physically executed. Instead, action is always inscribed – "situated" – in a particular environment made of artifacts and objects that can provide specific possibilities, supports and opportunities for the exercise of perception and movement. It can lead to "cognitive economies" (Conein and Jacopin, 1993). For instance the very organization of the environment of a library makes it possible to find a book without ever having to remember the particular location where it was placed. This kind of approach has explored the bodily as well as cognitive conditions that determine the use of products or services. Changing the environment changes the "energy" the user has to spend or the task he or she has to perform in order to manipulate the device. For example, a smaller screen makes the browsing of a web site less practical; using the mobile phone in a car without a free hand can require special abilities, etc.

A second possibility refers to the characterization of the social environment and its composition. Traditional cleavages such as the one between private and public or the one between private and professional provide significant contrasts in the environments' "contextures." "Private," "public" or "professional" environments are different contexts influencing how we use communication tools, for a number of reasons. These include the identity of co-present actors and the rules, norms and etiquettes that frame acceptable practices. They include the motivations for users' behavior (utilitarian, playful, profit-oriented, etc.) and sometimes even the range of equipment that will be available in those different settings. As soon as the use takes place in another context, things might change. Can a mobile phone ring in a public place? Will the practice of chatting be admitted in a corporate environment? Does the family computer have the correct operating system necessary for running software designed for professional information systems?

The third possibility relates to the characterization of the tools, devices, objects and facilities that can be associated with the product or service during its use. What does it mean exactly to "be associated with an object during use"? Actually, it can mean a lot of different things. Surrounding objects can play the role of a location for action (the table on which the telephone lies) or an attaching device (the system that allows one to attach the mobile phone to the belt). They may be objects jointly mobilized in a particular operation (like the paper for printing a letter word-processed on a computer) or used to support some function (the operating system for the software). They may constitute channels for bringing resource to the object (the Internet connection or power plug for the computer) or they may actually be competitors in the realization of some action (the fixed phone beside the mobile phone lying on the desk), and so on. Clearly, this list is not exhaustive, but it shows the importance for designers of new systems to have a good idea of the other equipment available to potential users – a requirement that is sometimes as important as the availability of socio-demographic information about these people.

Thus, looking at the environment means also looking at the possibility of combinations between the products and services. The idea that such a combination plays a role in innovation is quite traditional in the economics of innovation. Arthur (1988) has integrated such "system effects" in his analysis of the diffusion process for some time. The economist Hal Varian has recently proposed a generalization of this idea, arguing that new technologies have given rise to a special regime of innovation that explains the importance of standardization and of system effects. According to Varian (2003), ICTs fall within a line of technical inventions like spare parts or integrated circuits, inventions that have contributed to increasing our capacity to make modular components of products and services and then to combine them together. Historically, this process has generated a specific phenomenon of economic growth, labeled *recombining growth* by Varian.

From this view, ICTs initiate a new era in this history, extending our capacity to combine the material things with informational ones, generalizing the process and accelerating it. In the domain of ICTs, innovations can be combined as if they were spare parts by different actors and at different moments of the innovation trajectory. This also means that many combinations are possible from the viewpoint of the user. Proulx (2002) stresses that users' practices take place more and more in a space of action that is populated by a "vast constellation of technical objects" (mobile telephones, PDAs, fax, portable computers, Walkmans, etc.), which increasingly tend to be connectable to each other. Thus, the existence of innovation through combining technologies may lend more importance to the role of the environment in the process of generating of new uses.

4.   Conclusion

This chapter aims to help us understand better the processes by which uses emerge in the field of ICTs. Starting with some examples of traditional situations of unpredictable uses, I have discussed – and discarded – the interpretation that links them to the sole innovative potential of users. I have introduced the notion of uses drift and briefly examined how the phenomena that it covers have been treated in the sociological literature devoted to innovation and use. I have proposed a review of the factors and dynamics that are engaged and combined in developing uses. This approach should make more explicit the basis on which the dialogue between social scientists and designers can take place. Thus, the role for a social scientist is not (or not only) to provide some insights into the potential users' social worlds. It also involves making an inventory of and evaluating the various competing influences that might contribute to the drift of uses in the case of any given product. This requires integrating elements that are exterior to the "design-to-distribution chain" and elements that, on the contrary, influence this chain and the way it might evolve in the future.

The factors that I have examined under the four headings studied above make explicit dimensions of investigation that most social scientists usually take into account in their work. Thus, the approach proposed here can help in making the checklist of issues to investigate. It can also provide an analytical framework for a whole series of activities that they have to perform in the course of their work, for instance when they have to interact with project participants at the beginning of a survey in order to elucidate the context of the intervention. At this stage, the work consists of gathering various pieces of information that appear simply concrete and factual but which in fact play a very important role in the interpretive process. Very often for example, one of the first tasks of a sociologist working on a project is to understand what the designers expect the users to do with the product and, conversely, what lead users marketing staff intend to target in order to encourage early diffusion. Some of the network externalities and system effects that might support the diffusion process will also very often be mentioned at this stage of defining the social scientist's work. It will be important for him or her to recall that all those elements, which can appear as purely background information, have to be considered as provisory hypotheses that have been formulated at a given moment in the ongoing innovative process. They involve the inscription of the social scientist's work at a particular moment in the innovation trajectory. In this sense, the analyst should consider the relationship between a sociological analysis of the final use and a sociological analysis of the very project to which he or she is contributing. Both realities are liable to become connected to each other and need to be integrated.

References

Akrich, M. Beyond the social construction of technology: the shaping of people and things in the innovation process. In Dierkes, M., Hoffmann, U. (Eds.), New Technology at the Outset; 1992. Campus/Westview, Frankfurt/New York: 173–190.

Akrich, M., Callon, M., Latour, B. The key success to innovation (Part II). The art of choosing good spokespersons. International Journal of Innovation Management, 2002; 6: 207–225.

Arthur, B. Competing technologies: an overview. In Dosi, G., Freeman, C., Nelson, R., Silverberg, G., Soete, L. (Eds.), Technical Change and Economic Theory; 1988. Pinter Publisher, London.

Barrey, S., Cochoy, F., Dubuisson-Quellier, S. Designer, packager et merchandiser : trois professionnels pour une même scène marchande. Sociologie du Travail, 2000; 42: 457–482.

Beuscart, J.-S. Les usagers de Napster, entre communauté et clientèle. Construction et régulation d'un collectif sociotechnique. Sociologie du Travail, 2002; 44: 461–480.

Bijker, W.E. Of Bicycles, Bakelites, and Bulbs: Toward a Theory of Socio-technical Change; 1995. MIT Press, Cambridge, MA.

Boullier, D. Les études d'usages: entre normalisation et rhétorique. Annales des Telecommunications, 2002; 57 :190–210.

De Certeau, M.D. L'invention du quotidien. 1. arts de faire; 1990 Gallimard, Paris.

Ciborra, C. From control to drift. The Dynamics of Corporate Information Infrastructure; 2001. Oxford University Press, Oxford.

Conein, B., Jacopin, E. Les objets dans l'espace. In Conein, B., Dodier, N., Thévenot, L. (Eds.), Raisons pratique 4. Les objets dans l'action. Edition de l'Ecole des Hautes Etudes en Sciences Sociales; 1993 Paris: 59–84.

Fransman, M. Evolution of the telecommunications industry into the internet age. Communications and Strategies, 2001; 43: 57–113.

Gensollen, M. Économie non-rivale et communautés d'information. Réseaux, 2004; 22.

Haddon, L. Domestication and mobile telephony. In Katz J.E. (Ed.), Machines That Become Us: The Social Context of Personal Communication Technology; 2003. Transaction Publishers, New Brunswick: 43–57.

Jouet, J. Retour critique sur la sociologie des usages. Réseaux, 2000; 100: 487–522.

Katz, M., Shapiro, C. Network externalities, competition and compatibility. American Economic Review, 1985; 75: 424–440.

Latour, B. La fin des moyens. Réseaux, 2000; 100: 39–58.

Lelong, B. Savoir-faire technique et lien social. In Chauviré, C., Ogien, A. (Eds.), Raisons pratique 12-La régularité; 2002., Editions de l'EHESS, Paris: 267–292.

Lelong, B., Beaudouin, V. Usages domestiques d'internet, nouveaux terminaux et hauts débits: premier bilan après quatre années d'expérimentation. Paper for the Conference e-Usages – International Conference on Uses and Services in Telecommunications (ICUST); June 12–14, 2001, Paris.

Ling, R. The diffusion of mobile telephony among Norwegian teens: a report from after the revolution. Annales des Elecommunications, 2002; 47: 210–225.

Lundin, R.A., Midler, C. Projects as Arenas for Renewal and Learning Processes; 1998. Kluwer Academic Publishers, MA.

Mallard, A. Suivre et accompagner les usagers vers les nouvelles technologies – L'exemple des Stations Internet de France Télécom. Communication at the Conference of the Association Française de Sociologie; February, 25–27, 2004, Villetaneuse.

Orlikowski, W.J. Using technology and constituting structures: A practice lens for studying technology in organizations. Organization Science, 2000; 11: 404–428.

Proulx, S. Trajectoires d'usages des technologies de communication: les formes d'appropriation d'une culture numérique comme en jeux d'une 'société du savoir'. Annales des Télécommunications, 2002; 57: 180–190.

Rivière, A.-C. La pratique du mini-message. Une double stratégie d'extériorisation et de retrait de l'intimité dans les interactions quotidiennes. Réseaux, 2002; 20: 138–168.

Silverstone, R., Haddon, L. Design and the domestication of information and communication technologies: technical Change and everyday life. In Silverstone, R., Mansell, R. (Eds.), Communication by Design. The Politics of Information and Communication Technologies. Oxford University Press, Oxford: 44–74.

Suchman, L. Plans and situated actions: The Problem of Human-Machine Communication; 1999. Cambridge University Press, New York.

Varian, H.R. Economics of information technology. Communication at the Seminar of the GDR TICS; March, 6, 2003, Paris.

Von Hippel, E. Horizontal innovation networks - by and for users. MIT Sloan School Management Working Paper 27.

Chapter 4

THE INNOVATORY USE OF ICTs

Leslie Haddon

1. Introduction

The extent to which users can be innovative or creative when using ICTs is a key undercurrent within this book. While attempting to conceptualize the innovation process in general, Mallard draws attention to various theoretical frameworks that emphasize ways in which users are creative, but suggests there are limits to that ability. In their empirical study, Battarbee and Kurvinen explore the creative process in achieving multimedia messaging, while Sotamaa examines the various levels of user innovation within the field of computing gaming – examples of which are cited in this chapter. Clearly the "innovativeness" or "creativity" is important, but equally clearly it refers to a number of different activities. Reviewing past and current research on ICTs, the chapter aims to chart some of different ways in which users are innovators.[1]

In fact, this has a further relevance for two other main themes of the book. One theme concerns issues to be faced in ICT development when trying to imagine users and uses. By exploring what innovatory use can mean, the levels on which it can operate, we can re-consider what types of things we should be researching if we want to understand how potential users will relate to ICTs. And this might have implications for design. The second theme is how to involve users in the design process (see also Haddon, 2002; Hoogma and Schot, 2001) Once again, if we can appreciate the different ways in which users can be creative, this can have a bearing upon the types of feedback, or input, we would want from users when asking them to evaluate their experience of ICTs.

---

[1] "Users as innovators" was one strand of the COST269 Helsinki conference on which this book is based. The chapters from Tuomi, Mallard, my own, Battarbee and Kurvinen, Mahé, Rantavuo, Vehviläinen, and Joshi came from this strand. Hence, in different ways, many of the contributors comment upon these questions of innovativeness and creativity.

Leslie Haddon (ed.), Everyday Innovators, 54–66.
© 2005 *Springer. Printed in The Netherlands.*

However, first it is important to add some reservations about these key terms "innovate" and "creative." Generally, these words have positive connotations, but the outcomes of creativity need not always be so beneficial. We might consider, for example, the damage that can be caused by the creative development of computer viruses. And those hacking into computer system or into protected copyright software can have an ambivalent image, depending on exactly what they do and whose perspective one takes. Associated with images of the "innovative scientist" or "creative artist" these terms also run the danger of setting high expectations among researchers. This can lead to disappointment when they evaluate the degree of creativity involved in certain uses of ICTs. In particular, one can question the degree of novelty of certain innovations or innovatory uses if they have predecessors. However, given that new practices are usually developed out of older ones (Jouet, 2000), one also has to ask how novel does "innovatory use" have to be?

Finally, there is another key term often associated with discussions of creative use, as shown in some of Mallard's examples, and that is "unanticipated" use. Of course, we can ask who did not anticipate that use – usually this means industry. But we can also ask the question: in relation to what was it not anticipated? An example here might be when a pattern of use is at odds with certain wider societal discourses concerning how technologies should be used. This happened in the United Kingdom when some home computer producers and enthusiastic amateurs expressed disappointment in the 1980s when early computers were mainly being used for playing games (Haddon, 1988).

With these reservations, we can now return to the organization of the chapter. There are times when we see that the initiative to develop or use ICTs in a certain way is coming from users rather than involving an innovation process initiated by companies or other institutions (such as the state) or from professional designers. Hence, the first part of the chapter examines some of the different forms, large but also small, that this type of innovatory use can take and how this can contribute to the technological landscape. These are nevertheless the types of "exceptional" examples, often "unanticipated uses" and pioneered by some subset of the population, that are regularly cited in discussions of the innovation process – one of the traditions to which Mallard referred. In the second part of this chapter, we turn to the other tradition that Mallard highlights: approaches focusing on the creativity of people when dealing with ICTs in everyday life. Here, we switch the level of analysis to look at daily acts of "innovativeness," routine ways in which users actively manage their technologies.

Although the following explanation of Table 4-1 indicates some of the distinctions between these different levels of innovation, there is inevitably something of a continuum between them. In principle, there may be examples where it is difficult to decide whether a particular form of innovation belongs to one level or another.

Table 4-1. Types of innovation

Types of innovation	Examples (discussed below)
Enthusiasts designing and re-designing ICTs, improving existing or developing new applications.	Technical hobbyists and early microcomputer projects, including the role of amateur enthusiasts in writing early games.
Enthusiasts developing new practices using ICTs, creating new content or establishing new patterns of interaction.	Early radio broadcasting by radio hams; on-line communities or other grassroots initiative.
The more widespread emergence of creative design and content.	Club and personal web-pages.
The emergence of new patterns of use or new practices within the wider public or subgroups of it	Using the early telephone for social purposes; the practices emerging around SMS.

At the top of Table 4-1, we have the level of design and re-design that is usually associated with technologically skilled and often enthusiastic users who somehow transform the potential of ICTs. In his later chapter, Sotamaa exemplifies this through the case of "moders," games fans who modify existing games.

This level of innovation can be illustrated further with the example of the first microcomputers, a development largely unanticipated by industry[2] (Haddon, 1988). There were those who built their own small computers even before the first microcomputer kits appeared, before hobby computing became established. However, once computer hobbyist communities started to appear these enthusiasts were encouraged by peers, clubs, and the hobbyist press to explore the possibilities of this technology. The hobbyists developed a range of innovatory projects and ways to use the microcomputer. The legacy of this period of hobbyist inventiveness was the development of what became the PC industry. Hobbyists gave the product area early visibility that eventually helped it to become a consumer electronic, developing, in particular, the numerous computer games that helped shape the interactive games industry.

In the field of industrial innovation, the "lead users" noted in Mallard's chapter have been characterized as being competent, resourceful, and interested in innovation (Hoogma and Schot, 2001). On the whole, users of consumer products do not fit this description so well, but the type of enthusiastic amateur described above comes closest. Often they are professionals in some field (e.g., engineering, programing) related to their hobby. Sometimes it becomes hard to draw the line between characterizing them as users or designers, as in the case of the university students who were invited to experiment with the first

---

[2] The computer industry at that time could not see why developing a less powerful, initially severally limited, machine would be desirable. Meanwhile, the consumer electronics industry could not see why people would want computers in their home.

minicomputers and who developed innovative "hacks" – the origin of the term "hacker." One example of such a hack was the first action computer game discussed in Sotamaa's chapter (Levy, 1984). The thin line between user and designer was also exemplified in the later history of games, where some amateur enthusiasts developed their hobby into businesses in their own right or else became professional games designers working in this new cultural industry.

The case of the microcomputer also illustrates how the nature of the technology enables or constrains the possibility of innovation. The core of the earliest microcomputers basically consisted of an assembly of microchips. Thus, expensive tools for precision engineering were not required for the microcomputer's construction. Most of the computing principles that were involved had already been worked out in the previous decades and that information was widely available, as opposed to being the closely guarded secret of corporations. Once the microprocessor chips that constituted the building blocks of a small computer became accessible and affordable, the relative "makability" of the microcomputer enabled a hobbyist involvement. The same point had been true of early radio technology. Indeed, a number of commentators have drawn the analogy between the early history of hobby microcomputers and that of ham radio. Finally, to give a more contemporary example, the availability of freeware enables a whole community of enthusiasts to continue refining operating systems such as Linux whereas this could not happen with the guarded secrets of Microsoft software design (McKelvey, 2001).

Exploring the example of PC games enables us to think in a little more detail about the type of innovation taking place. We saw that games per se were first developed on the earliest minicomputers, long before microcomputers appeared. Indeed, by the time games were being developed for these smaller machines a games industry had appeared based on arcade machines and on dedicated home video game players (Haddon, 1999). So in this instance the innovativeness lay in converting some existing games to the new microcomputers, getting the code to fit in the small memories, sometimes developing new genres of games, or else developing new games within existing genres. This relates to an earlier observation that innovativeness is often built upon something that has gone before.

Turning to the next level in Table 4-1, innovation, even by enthusiasts, may involve not so much technical manipulation but rather new practices, doing new things with the technology. In his chapter, Sotamaa provides the example of games players producing Machnima films to illustrate this.

A more historical example would be the case of early ham radio. While the most common activity was point-to-point communication between hams, some of this community also pioneered the first radio broadcasting, playing music over the airwaves. They showed what was possible and what could be popular before radio broadcasting was taken up by commercial corporations in the United States (Douglas, 1986).

Contemporary examples would include those people setting up various forms of community on the Internet, ranging from fora that involve mainly on-line interaction, such as listservs, to arrangements that relate to some off-line community, such as the web site where local resident groups can interact as a supplement to face-to-face contact.[3] While these fora can be set up by organizations (such as local councils), there are also grassroot initiatives spear-headed by enthusiastic amateurs. Such innovations have helped to create some new forms of participation in and flow of information among "communities of interest" or locally based communities.

However, hobbyists or enthusiastic technologically oriented amateurs are not the only innovative users. If we move on to the next level in Table 4-1, we now see innovation beyond those "elites" that have relatively high levels of technical expertise. Here, we might think of the voluntary club or association web pages prepared by their members. Or we might consider personal home pages. These can still involve creativity in various senses: in terms of choices about design, about information/content, about links to other web sites, etc. In this context, Sotamaa also refers to gaming web sites and gamers distributing their own content.

In terms of their consequences, such innovations can offer new forms of visibility and facilitate new contacts (e.g. for such associations as folk dance groups, but also for individuals). Like the early hobbyist community, web site creation is also a form of creativity that is being actively encouraged, as Internet Service Providers (ISPs) invite their subscribers to consider this option. These ISPs or other companies even provide the software for creating such sites as yet one more thing that users can do on-line. If we try to think of a hardware equivalent of such creative activity that extends beyond special interest hobbyists, we might consider the people who wire up their home for distributing audiovisual signals around the house, much in the spirit of do-it-yourself home improvements.

We now turn to the last level of innovativeness in Table 4-1. Just as early radio broadcasting involved new practices when using a technology rather than doing something to it in terms of design, the same development of new patterns of use can occur outside of technical hobbyist communities. An historical example would be the way in which people started to use the early telephone for social, or to be more exact socializing, purposes. The telephone operators had not anticipated this, given that they had intended the phone to be used for more utilitarian goals (Fischer, 1992). A more recent example of the role of a particular social group in helping to create new practices would the *Kogyaru*, the Japanese street-savy high school students who pioneered and popularized early recreational uses of mobile communication, first with pagers in the early 1990s and then with mobile phones in the later half of the 1990s (Ito and Okabe, 2003). Sotamaa's chapter discusses this level of innovation in relation

---

[3] Perhaps the best example in the United Kingdom of this is Redbricks based in Manchester.

to various forms of communication between gamers that have emerged, as well as the teams and leagues that have grown up around game playing.

Finally, we can show in more detail the nature of such social innovativeness with the much-quoted example of SMS or text messaging. This function was originally added to compete with paging systems. The earliest pagers simply displayed the phone number to call back. Later, alphanumeric pagers could give short messages of 80 characters. SMS was a two-way version of this with 160 characters, offered as a function to compete with pagers.[4] But the social innovation among users, especially youth, lay in the way it was taken up and the practices that developed around it. The range of social messages, some of which would not in the past have been sent, was far greater than "call back on this number," and sometimes involved some sophistication and ingenuity (Ling, 2003; Segerstad, 2003). The area has seen the emergence of etiquettes and social expectations about replying as well as communication-related practices such as copying messages, sharing them with others, etc. (Kasesniemi and Rautianen, 2002). It was this whole set of practices that was unanticipated.

To different degrees some of the above examples might seem exceptional. We might come to regard the people taking such initiatives as being pioneers, doing things, to varying degrees visible to a wider public, which in retrospect we might see as creating something novel. In contrast, the second part of the chapter now deals with research on more common experiences of ICTs in everyday life.

2. Creativity and ICTs in Everyday Life

There are a number of different research approaches and empirical studies that cast light on this type of innovative behavior. Communication studies and media studies both show how we are, in fact, always creative in dealing with ICTs. Although not a literature in its own right, many empirical studies throw up examples of individual innovative uses of their technologies. The final examples all involve the different ways in which people deal with ICTs in daily life. Writings and studies within the domestication framework deal with how we actively manage ICTs in daily life, rather than just letting these technologies "impact" upon us. This literature, as well as that dealing with parent–children relations, also draws attention to some of the dynamics of household life that are relevant. Finally, the mobile phone literature has contributed to our understanding of what creative actions are taking place around technology over and above a narrow focus on its use.

Within communications studies, there are traditions of studying how we are always creative in the ways that we communicate, including in terms of our use

---

[4] Personal communication from Steve Hearnden, UMTS forum.

Table 4-2. ICTs in everyday life

ICTs	Examples (discussed below)
Interpreting texts and symbols; creativity in communication	Making sense of media, managing telephone conversations, multimedia messages
Discovering novel uses for ICTs	Various examples of the way individuals have found uses for camera phones
Managing ICTs	
Making ICTs aesthetically 'fit' into social spaces, displaying ICTs, personalising ICTs.	Locating of TVs and other ICTs in the home, adorning PCs, decorating mobile phone covers.
Attempting to control other people's use of ICTs; Resisting that control.	Parents controlling children's use of TV, the phone, the Internet; Children's 'parent management strategies'.
Managing communications.	Giving out mobile phone numbers; dealing with unwanted or disruptive incoming calls. Interacting with co-present others and with the caller.

of language when communicating through ICTs such as the fixed telephony and later mobiles (Schegloff, 2002). Meanwhile, in media studies there has been approaches that indicate ways in which audiences always actively interpret texts: they have to perform some cognitive work to make any sense of them at all. Admittedly, such discussions are usually arguing in terms of "active audiences" in contrast to any claims that we passively consume media. But such readings of text could still be considered to be creative, perhaps even more visibly so when people "decode" them to arrive at meanings not intended by their producers. To the extent that technologies themselves can be viewed as texts, this would also be true of how people interpret the meaning of particular ICTs, as reflected in Colombo and Scifo's chapter.

Even if these traditions ultimately indicate the manner in which people are "innovative" and "creative" all the time, these observations can neverthe-less be of relevance for ICT product development. For example, Battarbee and Kurvinen's chapter can be viewed in this context, as the authors examine how people have to work, and indeed cooperate, in order both to create and make sense of multimedia messages. Hence, this level of "innovation" on the part of the user becomes important for appreciating how we first learn to use ICTs. In this respect, we might consider the literature examining people's "apprenti-ships" in relation to learning to use ICTs, as in (the difficulties of) learning to become an Internet user (Lelong and Thomas, 2001). This is relevant for the producers of these technologies because if the apprentiship proves too demand-ing, too difficult, or too time-consuming, if the actual creativity demanded of users to make some ICT become of interest is too great, then this can in itself become a barrier to using the technology.

The first part of this chapter outlined some practices that were initially developed by some subset of the population, such as youth or certain groups of youth, but then became more widespread. Texting was an example. Yet, we need to be aware that there are many uses of ICTs that individuals or even small groups of people routinely discover but which remain fairly unique to them. They may never achieve a significant public visibility. While they often come to light in the course of empirical studies, (it is the experience of this author) they might not necessarily be reported in publications.

This level of creativity can be illustrated by examples from a small-scale British study of camera phone use conducted in 2003 (Vincent and Haddon, 2004). One household found that the small picture that could be taken by the camera phone was just the right size for *Loot*, the magazine carrying classified advertizements where individuals sell or request items. In this case, the family concerned took a picture of the car they were trying to sell and submitted it with their advert. In another case, someone with no mirror to hand, took a picture of herself to check how she looked, to check her makeup. That same person was looking at houses that she and her partner were planning to buy. She used the camera phone to take pictures of the features they liked in order to show to estate agents what they wanted when searching for their ideal home. Meanwhile, one teenager asked a friend with a camera phone to take a picture of himself and transfer it to her mobile using bluetooth. When he called her mobile, the picture would then appear.

The point is that at this time the mobile operators were advertizing ways in which the camera phone could be used, but these did not include any of the types of example listed above. These remained fairly idiosyncratic to the people concerned, and, in fact, were sometimes surprising when first described. While Columbo and Scifo in this book describe types of camera phone use at a more general level, for example, relating it to the use of photography, these examples are far more specific to very particular circumstances and goals. And yet, monitoring this more detailed form of innovation can inform product development. For example, some Finnish girls originally painted the covers of their mobile phones with nail varnish and attached stickers to them (Oksman, 2002). This later inspired the development of transferable colored covers accessories. In this case, we see that what starts out as a creative process on the part of a few users can sometimes affect the development of commercial products.

Right from its earliest formulations, the domestication framework had discussed the efforts that people go to in order to make technologies fit into their personal social spaces (Silverstone *et al.*, 1992; see also Haddon, 2004). This can include where they locate technologies in rooms either for esthetic reasons or because they are aware of the messages that such displays of ICT will give to others. For example, some people have TVs that can be shut away in a cupboard, a gesture that acts as a statement about the way they are controlling the role of television in their life. Or, in other studies, some teleworkers left their high tech paraphernalia on display to indicate the nature of their work (Haddon, 2004; Haddon and Silverstone, 1993). A related form of creativity involves efforts to personalize ICTs, for example, through the adornments people add to them, such as sticking things onto their PCs or decorating them with other objects (Lally, 2002). The earlier example of Finnish girls personalizing the outsides of their mobiles might also fit here, with the implication that product developers need to look at what people do to and with their technologies as well as how they use them.

Given its chief focus on interpersonal relations within households, domestication research has also examined the attempts by some people to control the use of ICTs by others – the most familiar of which is probably parents attempting to regulate children's use of technologies such as the TV, the phone,[5] and the Internet. Strategies may involve parents trying to negotiate rules about use, but also includes parental decisions about the location of ICTs (e.g. putting the PC with Internet access in a communal space, Livingstone and Bovill, 2001). While these may be the more common examples, qualitative research shows that more extreme measures are also possible, such as hiding the cordless phone, putting the fixed line in places where it is uncomfortable to use, and sabotaging ICTs[6] (Haddon, 2004). There are also examples of people attempting to control their partner's use of ICTs through withholding information that the technology could be used in certain ways[7] (Haddon and Silverstone, 1996).

Of course, such efforts to control the use of ICT can provoke resistance, for example, when children secretly gain access to ICTs at times when parents are not present. Research has also documented how children develop tactics to combat parents' efforts to use ICTs to monitor them. For example, when parents phone up the children's mobile to find out where their children are and what they are doing, we have cases of children claiming that the mobile signal was lost, the mobile battery was dead, or else they sent parents' calls directly to voice mail (Ling and Yttri, 2002) – all part of "parent management strategies"

---

[5] This was partly because of factors such as the cost of calls made by youth, and blocking the phone line (Haddon, 1998), but also because of time "lost" in making calls – time which could have been used for studying (from the parents' perspective) (Martin and de Singly, 2000). Some youth participating in that French study referred to this tension as "the war of the telephone."

[6] In one case, a frustrated father altered his daughter's handset extension in her room so that it would not make outside calls. She got around this problem by phoning out on the main phone and transferring the call to her room.

[7] One retired husband had always told his wife that a VCR could not be linked up to their particular TV, when in reality he knew it could be – but he did not want her to use a VCR.

to avoid surveillance and gain some privacy (Green, 2001). Once again, both the efforts to control use and resistance to that control draws attention to ICT-related behavior which could be considered to be creative, which is sometimes unanticipated by product developers and which is not simply captured by the notion of "use." Yet such background information can be relevant to design. For example, any technology sold on the basis of or otherwise offering the prospect of more parental control is effectively becoming involved in this politics of the household and should take this into account.

Turning to our relations with both our social networks and strangers, we have strategies for controlling contactability.[8] The mobile phone research has noted how users can be selective about whom they give their mobile phone number out to (Licoppe and Heurtin, 2001). But, we also see such strategies in relation to the basic phone. Examples include using the answering machine for filtering calls (a use which was never stressed in the marketing of the device), arranging for other people to answer the phone, unplugging the phone, or in some other way turning it off[9] (Haddon, 1998, 2004). Meanwhile, mobile phone researchers have charted various ways in which people have learnt to manage the experience of calls in public spaces. When receiving calls especially, mobile phone users have developed a variety of strategies for dealing with the fact that they are in the midst of co-present others. They give out signals to others through their body language (Cooper *et al.*, 2001) or they sometimes seek out spaces so as to minimize the disruptiveness of the call. Other research has examined people managing the relationship with the communicator, for example, by finding ways to speed up the call (Licoppe and Heurtin, 2001) and indicting to co-present others that they are doing this. All of these provide illustrations of strategies that go beyond use.

The above examples may all seem mundane, but they underline how much, arguably "creative," work is taking place in relation to ICTs in the course of managing them in our daily lives and in our relationships with others. Such behaviors are not always captured in user scenarios where the emphasis is on people's goals, desires, on the applications they will favor and on "user needs." And yet the innovative ways in which people cope with the issues raised by ICTs can themselves have a bearing upon the ways in which ICTs are used and experienced. One question is whether such strategies can be considered during product development.

---

[8] Various reasons for wanting to control contact have been documented in relation to the fixed phone line. For example, unwanted phone calls from acquaintances could be intrusive upon their privacy and peace. At times incoming calls could also interfere with the routines of the home, coming at unsociable or simply inconvenient moments – such as late at night or early in the morning, or when parents were getting children off to school or nursery or getting them to bed (Haddon, 1994).

[9] One interviewee described how she used to bury the telephone handset under pillows.

3.   Conclusions

This chapter has explored the notion of user innovativeness, indicating the various manifestations that this phenomenon can encompass. It has not tried to define what counts as innovation and innovative use and what does not. Rather this account has tried to show the variety of senses in which behavior related to ICTs can be innovative and creative. The first part examined some of the conditions under which certain types of more exceptional or higher visibility user innovation can occur, or indeed, be encouraged. The second part dealt with more commonplace experiences, including the various strategies that people develop when confronted by issues emerging as they manage ICTs in the course of their everyday lives.

At the start of this chapter, it was argued that an appreciation of the different forms of innovativeness was important for imagining users and uses. Like many of the other contributors to this book, this above account implies that we need to consider what the object of research should be, what types of things we should be researching, when we want to understand how potential users will relate to ICTs. Just as Tuomi's chapter asks us to re-think what is happening, what is taking place, when we have a cup of coffee; so here in this chapter we try to look beyond narrow definitions and measures of "use," as when we consider the strategies people use to manage ICTs in their everyday lives. Moreover, in both cases, we might ask about the implications for design.

Second, it was argued that understanding the manifold nature of innovativeness was important for thinking about how to involve users in the design process. Sotamaa's chapter provides an example of the games industry trying to monitor and involve its more creative games "fans." But other ICT industries, to greater and lesser extents, also try to see "what people do" with their products once the technologies are in circulation for the public to acquire. Sometimes, again to varying degrees, this feeds back into design. One contribution of this chapter is to widen the view of "what people do" with technologies, when inviting them to give feedback for design.

References

Cooper, G., Green, N., Harper, R., Murtagh, G. Mobile users – Fixed society? Paper for the Conference 'e-Usages'; June 12–14, 2001, Paris.

Douglas, S. Amateur operators and American broadcasting: shaping the future of radio. In Corn, J. (Ed.), Imagining Tomorrow: History, Technology, and the American Future; 1986. MIT Press, Cambridge, MA: 34–57.

Fischer, C. America Calling. A Social History of the Telephone to 1940; 1992. University of California Press, Berkley.

Green, N. Information ownership and control in mobile technologies. Paper for the Conference 'e-Usages'; June 12–14, 2001, Paris.

Haddon, L. The home computer: the making of a consumer electronic. Science as Culture, 1988; 2: 7–51.

Haddon, L. Il controllo della comunicazione. Imposizione di limiti all'uso del telefono. In Fortunati, L. (Ed.), Telecomunicando in Europa; 1998. Franco Angeli, Milano: 195–247. Available in English at http://members.aol.com/leshaddon/Index.html.

Haddon, L. The development of interactive games. In Mackay, H., O'Sullivan, T. (Eds.), The Media Reader: Continuity and Transformation; 1999. Sage, London: 305–327.

Haddon, L. Information and communication technologies and the role of consumers in innovation. In McMeekin, A., Green, K., Tomlinson, M., Walsh, V. (Eds.), Innovation by Demand: Interdisciplinary Approaches to the Study of Demand and its Role in Innovation; 2002. Manchester University Press, Manchester: 151–167.

Haddon, L. Information and Communication Technologies in Everyday Life: A Concise Introduction and Research Guide; 2004. Berg, Oxford.

Haddon, L., Silverstone, R. Teleworking in the 1990s: a view from the home, SPRU/CICT Report Series, No.10; 1993, University of Sussex, Falmer. Available at http://members.aol.com/leshaddon/Index.html.

Haddon, L., Silverstone, R. Information and communication technologies and the young elderly, SPRU/CICT Report Series; 1996, University of Sussex, Falmer. Available at http://members.aol.com/leshaddon/Index.html.

Hoogma, R., Schot, J. How innovative are users? A critique of learning-by-doing-and-using. In Coombs, R., Green, K., Richards, A., Walsh, V. (Eds.), Technology and the Market: Demand, Users and Innovation; 2001. Edward Elgar Publishing, Cheltenham: 216–233.

Ito, M., Okabe, D. Mobile phones, Japanese youth and the replacement of social contact. In Ling, R., Pedersen, P. (Eds.), Front Stage/Back Stage: Mobile Communication and the Renegotiation of the Social Sphere, Conference Proceedings; June 22–24, 2003, Grimstad, Norway.

Jouet, J. Retour critique sur la Sociologie des Usage. Réseaux, 2000; 100: 486–521.

Kasesniemi, E., Rautianen, P. Mobile culture of children and teenagers in Finland. In Katz, J., Aakhus, R. (Eds.), Perpetual Contact: Mobile Communication, Private Talk, Public Performance; 2002. Cambridge University Press, Cambridge: 170–192.

Lally, E. At Home with Computers; 2002. Berg, Oxford.

Lelong, B., Thomas, F. L'apprentissage de l'internaute: socialisation et autonomisation. Paper for the Conference 'e-Usages'; June 12–14, 2001, Paris.

Levy, S. Hackers: Heros of the Revolution; 1984. Doubleday, Garden City.

Licoppe, C., Heurtin, J.-P. Managing one's availability to telephone communication through mobile phones: a French case study of the development dynamics of mobile phone use. Personal and Ubiquitous Computing, 2001; 5(2): 99–108.

Ling, R. The socio-linguistics of SMS: an analysis of SMS use by a random sample of Norwegians. In Ling, R., Pedersen, P. (Eds.), Front Stage/Back Stage: Mobile Communication and the Renegotiation of the Social Sphere, Conference Proceedings; June 22–23, 2003, Grimstad, Norway.

Ling, R., Yttri, B. Hyper-coordination via mobile phones in Norway. In Katz, J., Aakhus, R. (Eds.), Perpetual Contact: Mobile Communication, Private Talk, Public Performance; 2002. Cambridge University Press, Cambridge: 139–169.

Livingstone, S., Bovill, M. Families and the internet: an observational study of children and young people's internet use. London School of Economics and Political Science. Confidential Report to BTexact Technologies; 2001.

Martin, O., de Singly, F. L'évasion amicable. L'usage du téléphone familial par les adolescents. Réseaux, 2000; 18(103): 91–118.

McKelvey, M. Internet entrepreneurship: why Linux might beat Microsoft. In Coombs, R., Green, K., Richards, A., Walsh, V. (Eds.), Technology and the Market: Demand, Users and Innovation; 2001. Edward Elgar Publishing, Cheltenham: 177–200.

Oksman, V. Wireless kids – mobile communication cultures of teenagers. Paper given at the EMTEL Conference New Media and Everyday Life in Europe; April 23–26, 2002, London.

Schegloff, E. Beginning in the telephone. In Katz, J., Aakhus, R. (Eds.), Perpetual Contact: Mobile Communication, Private Talk, Public Performance; 2002. Cambridge University Press, Cambridge: 284–300.

Segerstad, Y. Language use and adaptation in Swedish mobile text messaging. In Ling, R., Pedersen, P. (Eds.), Front Stage/Back Stage: Mobile Communication and the Renegotiation of the Social Sphere, Conference Proceedings; June 22–24, 2003, Grimstad, Norway.

Silverstone, R., Hirsch, E., Morley, D. Information and communication technologies and the moral economy of the household. In Silverstone, R., Hirsch, E. (Eds.), Consuming Technologies; 1992. Routledge, London: 15–33.

Vincent, J., Haddon, L. Informing Suppliers about User Behaviours to better prepare them for their 3G/UMTS Customers, Report 34 for UMTS Forum www.umts-forum.org; 2004.

EMPIRICAL STUDIES: USERS AS INNOVATORS AND CRITICS

The chapter by Katja Battarbee and Esko Kurvinen in particular enables us to explore some of the themes of social use and creativity from the previous section. Both it and the chapter by Fausto Colombo and Barbara Scifo are very topical given the recent appearance of camera phone technology and its uncertain prognosis at the time of writing. More generally, they underline the merits of diversity in research, showing the insights to be gained from two very different methodological approaches with different foci. Meanwhile, Olli Sotamaa explores the case of computer gaming fans to provide examples of different ways in which these particular users can be creative and how this can feed back into industry.

Battarbee and Kurvinen outline a Finnish experimental project exploring what happens when people try to work out how to use camera phones and send picture messages. The authors start by stressing that while public discussions of innovation, including MMS, often ask what benefits they offer in utilitarian terms, what goals they help to achieve, sometimes we should pay attention to the pleasures involved, including pleasures inherent in communication itself. This is taken into account in the design literature that stresses "experience" rather than the narrower focus on "use," and the authors show how various methodologies utilized in product development attempt to capture this dimension. More specifically, they introduce the concept of "co-experience" to characterize how people collectively interpret experience through interaction. They later use this notion to question those methodologies that assume user needs are fixed, in contrast to studies that explore the ways in which uses are discovered and emerge through a process of interaction.

Setting the scene for the analysis of MMS, the authors discuss the focus within design on routine user creativity when encountering technology in everyday life, echoing some of the earlier discussions in the chapters by Mallard and Haddon. The authors illustrate different ways in which users of MMS are innovative when communicating, especially when having to respond to other people and their interpretations as an ongoing social process. This involves

different forms of creativity when initially composing MMS messages as opposed to interpreting them, paralleling discussions of the processes of encoding and decoding texts in media studies. The detailed examination of case
studies of MMS messages going back and forth itself indicates a methodology for analyzing this combination of text and image. Here Battarbee and
Kurvinen, plausibly, suggest the understandings and expectations of the participants, showing how one message influences the next, providing feedback
about what image to send, how to frame it, and what styles of text to use.

Technology, then, provides a new channel for collective creativity. But
features of the design also shape what can and cannot be done, both
in terms of initially creating messages and responding to them. The authors
argue that one important factor for the success of such MMS services is a
low-cost threshold to encourage interaction. This may be more important than
ease of use. Turning to the particularities of images, the authors argue that
these provide more scope for creativity (than when working with text) because
they are open to more interpretations. Images also facilitate collective memory,
capturing past interactions. Collections of saved images, both ones saved on
the off chance that they might be used later as well as those from past interactions, can provide a resource for future communications. Finally, Battarbee
and Kurvinen note one particular line of product development suggested by
this study. This would allow multiple participation in creative interaction, as
already experienced in some forms of gaming, and would perhaps encourage
sharing and collaboration using other image technologies.

Colombo and Scifo examine the diverse reactions of some Italian youth and
young adults to camera phones. They look mainly at representations of the new
devices – i.e. how their interviewees perceived and talked about them – as part
of the early process by which technology is socially shaped. After providing
background details about the early launch of these phones in Italy and why they
characterize this as supply-driven, the authors note how the fall in prices and
improvement to the phones helped overcome an initial widespread wariness.
However, before that point, it is revealing to contrast the perceptions of adopters
and non-adopters.

Given little experience of camera phones, both adopters and non-adopters
may have been in part dependent on information from the supply companies.
Nevertheless, they could evaluate the technology through the different ways in
which they interpreted the history of ICTs in general and of the mobile telephony
in particular. The adopters of this new technology saw the camera phone as
being part of a linear progression whereby it was an automatic successor to
the mobile phone. In fact, it was part of the longer evolution towards video
communication. The camera phone was exciting, offering both challenges and
learning opportunities. In stark contrast, non-adopters saw this new product
as an innovation that had been thrust upon them by the industry and they did
not feel as involved in the development process as they had done with SMS,

where they felt that users had actually contributed to the development. Hence, the non-adopters had a more critical evaluation, seeing the camera phones as a retrograde step in terms of lightness, battery-duration and esthetics. And they foresaw the new technology as potentially introducing new digital divisions, threatening to make the mobiles to which they felt attached obsolete. What both groups shared was an understanding of the diffusion of ICTs in general that suggested these phones would inevitably become widespread.

Some felt the camera phone would completely replace the camera, while others – some adopters as well as non-adopters – felt it would do so only for particular purposes on particular occasions. Its principle appeal was that it was carried with you all the time allowing the immediate exchange or showing of photos after they were taken to enhance relationships with others. In addition, when the images were sent, this occurred within two different paradigms, both building on practices that had gone before. One model was where MMS was like using "traditional" SMS text messages but simply with the addition of pictures – these were interactive with messages going back and forth. The other model was the electronic postcard, sent one-way to others, without expecting a response.

Colombo and Scifo conclude by reflecting on how to think about users as innovators from this study. Generally, this generation had experienced constant innovation in ICTs as the norm and had had to navigate through this dynamic experience. Both adopters and non-adopters certainly shared a feeling that they had some kind of active role to play in this process. However, different understandings of that active role could be captured in some new metaphors. One was that of the stock exchange player deciding when to jump on the bandwagon. Another was that of the IKEA customer, with some, but limited, options to be creative, given that the technology's design has already been fixed in many ways. Both have more limited creative options compared to the early pioneers of some technologies, such as early radio hams.

Sotamaa's chapter starts by identifying recent challenges to human–computer interface (HCI) researchers in usability. These challenges come from those arguing that designers need to consider emotional engagement with products, taking pleasures and satisfaction from use into account. Meanwhile, user-centred and participatory design have stressed the importance of user involvement in design. On both counts, Sotamaa argues, academic research on interactive electronic gaming, especially the role of gamers in product development, can provide some insights for designers in general.

Sotamaa draws attention to the movements in media studies that have questioned ideas of the passive audience for media texts, showing ways in which readers and viewers are creative, making meanings out of texts. When we turn to games, the user is firstly creative in the sense that games have actually to be played. But, in keeping with this emphasis of users as producers, gamers have been creative in terms of modifying the very games themselves. Sotamaa provides examples to show how this is true of all games, not just contemporary interactive ones. However, in the case of digital games, as with other digital media objects, the ability to manipulate software and reprogram provides extra scope for user customization.

After showing how the practice of modifying computer systems and later games dates back to the early days of computer gaming, Sotamaa provides details of a more contemporary example of this process as well as noting other levels of gamer creativity. Applying Haddon's typology from an earlier chapter, Sotamaa considers different forms of innovation, ranging from the personalizing of games to creating new forms of social interaction around the games-playing activity. More broadly, games can be seen as a form of fandom that has been discussed within the media studies literature. Sotamaa considers examples of the way fans can both exert pressure on the games industry but also provide a significant source of and testbed for new game ideas. In fact, a dialogue has long existed between the games players and the games industry, involving an element of ambivalence as industry tries both to encourage game innovation but also to control and regulate the fan base.

Chapter 5

SUPPORTING CREATIVITY – CO-EXPERIENCE IN MOBILE MULTIMEDIA MESSAGING

Katja Battarbee and Esko Kurvinen

1.   Introduction

This chapter looks at creativity as a form of user innovation from a user experience point of view. Often user innovation and user creativity are seen as connected to utility – consumers design things for themselves that they need and find useful. However, a key point explored in this chapter is that utility does not explain all kinds of user creativity.

The ways in which information and communication technologies (ICTs) have migrated from military or governmental research into the everyday uses of ordinary people have involved a more or less complete re-invention of the purpose of the technology. While social processes and social interaction have often been the driving force behind the appropriation and innovation of these new ICTs, companies, and indeed the people themselves, tend to emphasize the practical utilitarian uses of technology, such as organising appointments, emergency use, asking for or sending information, and managing responsibilities. In fact, in the autumn of 2002, during the launch of the multimedia messaging services in Finland, there was a public debate as to whether there was any use for such services. This depends on whether "use" is seen only as utilitarian or instrumental. In the case of a pilot study of mobile multimedia messaging service (MMS) discussed in this chapter, utility does not adequately explain what the participants in the field study described below actually did. Messaging is often about connection for connection's sake and the analyst can study them as such, without speculating about any other goals in addition to this activity (Koskinen *et al.*, 2002). Such self-sufficient actions include, for example, emotive communication, humor and fun.

The term "experience" has become widespread in the field of design and marketing because it takes into account a broader context for design, including

Leslie Haddon (ed.), Everyday Innovators, 71–85.
© 2005 *Springer. Printed in The Netherlands.*

the emotions users have in relation to products. In this chapter, the term "user experience" is used to describe the experiential aspects involved in user–product relationships and interaction. This includes, but is not limited to, utility and use. The study of user experiences often focuses on individuals because of the subjective nature of experience. "Co-experience" is a relatively new term that accounts for user experiences in the course of social interaction: namely, what happens to user experiences when people begin to make sense of their experiences with and for each other in the course of social interaction (Battarbee and Koskinen, forthcoming).

This chapter looks at creativity in the context of such social interaction and the role of technology in supporting and shaping the interaction. The findings suggest that, especially in the case of multimedia messaging but also as regards the adoption of other technology, the creativity that users exhibit when searching for the appropriate use for technology is tied to their social interactions and how the technology supports these interactions. Creativity, then, does not only describe the emergence of inventions and innovations but is found in everyday activities as well. Sanders (2003) defines four levels of everyday creativity that people engage in: doing, adapting, making, and creating. Meanwhile, the level of interest and expertize in different domains vary from being minimal to the kinds that are expected from professional artists. In this chapter we will look at several examples of MMS and discuss, on the one hand, how the social interactions and, on the other hand, how the technology of MMS itself supported end user creativity, mainly at the level of "doing."

2.   Mobile Multimedia Messaging Data and Method

These data result from Mobile Multimedia, a multimedia messaging service (MMS) pilot study organized by the telecom operator Radiolinja in the summer of 2002. Multimedia messages are messages created and composed on an MMS capable mobile phone and sent to other such phones or to a website for retrieval. The messages can contain any combination of text, image and audio. The qualitative study focused on 25 users belonging to three groups and over 4000 messages that they sent to each other. The participants were groups of friends who differed in terms of age from late teens to mid-30s and who lived in the Helsinki metropolitan area as well as other towns. Of the 4000 messages sent by the three groups, almost half of the messages were duplicates, where the same message had been sent to multiple recipients. The identifying details of the messages used in this chapter have been changed and the messages are published with permission.

The data were analyzed from two perspectives: a content perspective an-alyzed the content of the messages and the interaction perspective studied how messages were oriented to the themes and topics contained in previous messages. The situations in which the messages were received and created were not observed, but they can often be inferred both from the message and from the previous and following messages. Often the messages include a clue as to what the situation is. In particular, the photographs, but also the audio components, also contain implicit information about the situation. Background sounds can suggest a summer cottage or a rock festival, a photo can show a place in a generic sense (such as a shop or park or archipelago) or a particular place (the amusement park, the cottage). Photos also often included the food and drink being consumed by people and gave suggestions as to locations, weather, and other aspects of the situation. These can be further interpreted by the receiver (Koskinen *et al.*, 2002; Kurvinen, 2002, 2003).

Each message provides an instance of experiences being interpreted and offered for others and the content of the message reveals the kinds of experiences that the participants find relevant for themselves and each other. Interpretations of one message have been checked against evidence from preceding messages, subsequent messages and similar messages. However, in interpreting these messages it is important not only to look at the individual messages but also to see how they contribute to emerging themes and practices, producing a cumulative effect through small instances of creativity. In the MMS data, this can be seen as continuing threads with several replies, gradually developed shared themes and messaging styles as well a jokes or insults constructed in the form of replies. The messaging contains many instances where participants explore the possibilities of the communication medium. But apart from individual messages, what is being created is the very meaning and purpose of the technology of MMS itself.

3.   User Experiences in Social Interaction

As noted earlier, user experience is a term that has become increasingly popular in design. Utility and usability have been found to be insufficient for describing people's relationships with products (Hassenzahl, 2003; Jordan, 2000; Norman, 2004; Rhea, 1992) and this has an impact on the business and practice of product development (Pine and Gilmore, 1998). The term "user experience" includes the needs, emotions, values, expectations and other such experiences that are relevant to the design context and that will affect the evaluation of future products. User experience research methods are focused on two main aspects. On the one hand, designers need to observe people's behavior in the course of user–product interaction. This is common practice in, for example, "contextual inquiry" (Beyer and Holtzblatt, 1997), shadowing and other types of observations, including in the trials of prototypes (Buchenau and Fulton, 2000). Empathic observations draw special attention not only to observable behaviors but also to what emotions and experiences relate to the observed situations (Dandavate *et al.*, 1996; Leonard and Rayport, 1997). The empathic aspect also emphasizes the need for designers to seek out similar experiences for themselves (Fulton, 2003). However, learning about the meanings of experiences – the way experiences connect to values, attitudes, and desires – will not surface in observations. Instead, a range of approaches is needed as each method or tool can only capture one aspect of experience (Sanders, 1999). The meaning of experience can only be accessed through the interpretations that users make themselves. Therefore, other methodological tools are used to support the interaction between designer and user in order to find the best ways to learn about the user's experiences. These include, for example, interviews about the wider context of people's lives, allowing them to self-document their lives using cameras (even digital ones, as in Masten and Plowman, 2003), diaries, experience sampling, and collections of specifically designed sets of tools, such as probes (Gaver *et al.*, 1999; Mattelmäki and Battarbee, 2002; Wensveen, 1999).

User research methods vary in terms of how much intervention is introduced into the situation. Ethnographic observations aim to be as quiet, and to disturb the situation as little, as possible. In fieldwork, in general, effort is put into establishing a rapport with informants so that they will not feel the need to employ too much self-censorship (Schatzman and Strauss, 1973). At the other end of the spectrum, we find participatory design sessions where participants are invited to join in and contribute in a design event where new things are being created and tried out (e.g., Bødker and Buur, 2002). Somewhere in the middle are those situations that mix real contexts with new prototypes or other design artifacts as part of a process of exploring and evaluating the latter – these can range from focus groups to small-scale testing. Designers and researchers do try to be aware of the special communication conditions that they create and the kinds of effects these may have on what people say and do. For example, people may be polite and say what they think others want to hear. From a participant's point of view, a professional seeking their opinion and collaboration can be either extremely flattering or a highly intimidating situation, causing participants to see themselves and their experiences in a way that has hardly ever happened before. This can be both good and bad. It can be good because people normally do not analyze their everyday life even if they could. And it can be bad because it is sometimes difficult to determine how much the meanings are invented on the spot as a result of the research situation. In social interaction, the relationship to the recipient is used as a resource in communication and it is used to decide what is said and how. Showing flattery, authority, respect, humor, and familiarity are all strategies for influencing how the message and the person behind it are perceived.

Goffman describes messages as consisting of five different elements: a ritual respect to the other, regard for self, communicative restraints, a frame of interpretation and the content of the message itself (Manning, 1992). Favorable interpretations usually aim to continue the interaction, because it generally is in the interest of the participants to be able to continue interacting with each other. However, this kind of selflessness needs to be balanced with a sense of self and more selfish needs as well (Goffman, 1959). In their everyday interactions, people tell stories both to report the unusual and to maintain normality (Sacks and Jefferson, 1990). They exchange gossip and share experiences with each other, talking even when there is nothing particular to say (Goffman, 1959). The process of communicating experiences and interpreting them is inherently social. In being social, it is also creative. This is because people are constantly having to respond to suddenly emerging situations that may threaten their "face," the way they are portraying themselves, and hence the success of the whole interaction situation. Each action, in this case each multimedia message, is potentially evaluated for what kind of a response it is calling for and how its content might be interpreted or appreciated by others (Sacks and Jefferson, 1990). Therefore, the meaning of an experience, a word or a picture or even a product is never final, but subject to a social process that can take new situations into account in maintaining or reinterpreting meaning.

User experiences, then, are not only something drawn directly from interacting with a product but rather they are contingent upon social interactions and the collective evaluation processes therein. What happens in this co-experiencing is that people "lift up" or offer an interpretation of their experiences to others (Battarbee and Koskinen, forthcoming). Any emotions discussed are those considered relevant and worth reporting to others, but people also use the situation and their communication partners as resources in creating a suitable interpretation. For example, a teenager's narrow escape from a skiing accident is high in emotion at the moment it happens as well as afterwards. The emotions make this particular ride worth reporting compared to the other, less eventful rides. However, the event, and the fear and relief, will most likely not be reported the same way to parents as to friends, because these recipients have different expectations and desired interpretations of the teenager. The way other people respond to the experiences offered can be positive in that they can reciprocate, or agree, or merely acknowledge the experience. Reciprocation, i.e. responding with the same, is a strong form of affirmation and signals an alignment with the sender. The response can also be negative if the experience is ignored, made fun of or rejected. Humor and subtle hints are often used in these rejection processes to cushion the rejection and indicate that what is being rejected is the importance or interpretation of the experience, not the person. In some less formal relationships, such as some of the ones present in the MMS data, teasing and making fun of each other can be the norm rather than the exception (a detailed description of an example is found in Kurvinen, 2003). In these interactions, what they are reciprocating is the teasing and what they are affirming is that they accept this teasing from each other.

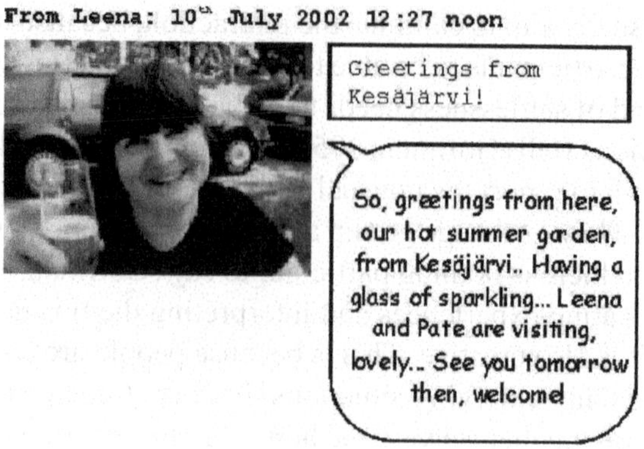

Figure 5-1. Summer greetings.

4.   MMS, Co-Experience, and Creativity

Two kinds of creative orientation can be identified in MMS. One happens in the "here and now" and relates to creativity and resourcefulness at the time of creating the message content, the audio, photo and text. The second relates to the meaning of the message, which is partially defined in that moment, but which is also open for interpretation "there and later" by the recipients. In analyzing MMS both must be interpreted from the messages themselves. The messages, especially the images in them, document the situation where the picture for the message was taken and the role of the text and the audio is to describe, name and support the description of the situation or message.

The example of the message (Figure 5-1) from the Mobile Multimedia data describes a situation where users collaborate in the creation of a message. It shows that the kind of technology and media used in the messaging can encourage and enable collaboration and involve others in the messaging. Short text messages (SMS) are already very common in Finland. Shared use of the mobile or composing text messages together is difficult because of the size of the phone and keypad, although there are reports of teenagers consulting each other when writing SMS text messages to, for example, someone they would like to start dating (Kasesniemi and Rautiainen, 2002). However, this process of getting advice on the wording of a message is invisible to the recipient, whereas seeing an image of people posing together and singing in chorus make the social context evident and shared.

The example in Figure 5-1 is a message sent from the phone of Leena to her sister. The message, only facilitated by Leena, is from the woman in the picture, probably a family friend or a relative, to the sister. We can say with confidence that the woman in the photo has never used an MMS phone before because the products were only just emerging on the market and no services had been launched at that time. Regardless of this, she is able to deliver a charming, touching invitation to share the experiences of the summer garden, and Leena, the owner of the MMS phone, facilitates this process. The message is somewhat posed with the woman holding the glass up to the camera but it is not overdone. Instead of the hot summer garden there are parked cars in the background, a familiar sight to anyone who has attended a family gathering at a summer place. The spontaneity of the framing is further enhanced by slight hesitations in the spoken message (as indicated with three dots). The mood of the message is made perfect with the direct eye contact and warm smile. The message suggests that the woman does not expect to send or receive any more messages by referring to the face-to-face meeting the next day.

In the example in Figure 5-2, the meaning or the possibilities opened by a message are not defined by the sender, or even by the intended recipient, but

From Anna-Maija: 6th July 2002 4:26 p.m.

> I just got back
> from sauna, all pink
> and flushed.. hugs
> to all!

From Kira: 6th July 2002 4:33 p.m.

> Hi this is Emma.
> Could you take a
> pic of the sauna
> cabin AND LAKE.
> PIITU WANTS TO SEE
> THE PLACE

From Anna-Maija: 6th July 2002 4:36 p.m.

> That's the sauna
> hut..

Figure 5-2. Sauna greetings and cabin photo request.

by a third party. A greeting is always open to a counter greeting, or in fact any number of possible directions. The message follows several messages earlier in the day that have shared details or aspects of summer cottage life, such as pets, food, food preparation and people, with some exchanges with others about the differences between, for example, food preparation in the city and at the cottage. The general theme of sharing the moment is continued in the message of the sauna greetings.

This example consists of three messages. The first message is from Anna-Maija to the whole group, following many such group messages sent earlier in the day. The second is a reply from Kira's phone, which includes and introduces two other people as well: Emma and Piitu. The third message is Anna-Maija's reply sent to Kira, but intended for Emma and Piitu as well. In the first message, the photo is taken at arm's length and Anna-Maija presents herself in a smiling salute. Although the message was sent to one person, the recipients turn out to be three young women. They do not comment on Anna-Maija's post-sauna appearance or use that as a resource directly, although they do reciprocate with smiling faces in their own reply photo. Instead, they ask Anna-Maija to focus on her background and request her to return to her documentary style of reporting. They specifically ask to see the cabin and lake, and finish with a more general request to "see the place," which also informs Anna-Maija how to frame the pictures: i.e. a general picture instead of details. After only three minutes she sends her first reply message showing the sauna cabin and the dots after the last word indicate there is more on the way. In fact, eight more messages follow with short textual descriptions. In our mind's eye we can picture her walking a few steps away from the sauna porch, still in a bathrobe and a towel turban and pointing the MMS phone towards the cabin. We can also imagine how the three girls sitting somewhere indoors are waiting for each new message as it arrives, heads together to see the picture, or possibly passing it around. As Piitu is named as the one who wants to see the place, the other two have maybe seen it already, and explain to her what may be lacking in the descriptions, or talk about the place more, maybe sharing a memory of the time they visited it.

The interaction in Figure 5-3 consists of four messages. The first two are part of an ongoing discussion and commentary between Risto and Liisa. The third message is from Risto to a group of young men, in which he reuses a photo he used before to reply to Liisa. The fourth message is one of the replies of the group, generally representative of the replies of the other group members as well.

It seems that Liisa and Risto expect the messages between them should be reciprocated. The person in Liisa's message is wearing large glasses typical of the 1970s, slightly askew. She is smiling and the photo is taken close to the face, which further distorts the face slightly. It would seem to be a purposefully funny photo. The message uses formal, slightly old-fashioned expressions: "spiritual values" and "work and leisure". These are at odds with the grinning funny photo.

From Liisa: 11ᵗʰ July 2002 6:35 p.m.

Listen Risto, we
have our spiritual
values, evident in
our work and
leisure!

From Risto: 11ᵗʰ July 2002 7:03 p.m.

Yeah… The photo (an
excellent one, I
laughed for several
minutes :)) said
more than a
thousand words…
A victory of spirit
over matter… I must
try to fill my
spiritual void in
this fashion…

From Risto: 11ᵗʰ July 2002 9:54 p.m.

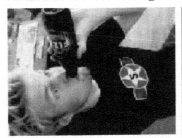

Vacation starts
tomorrow!

From Tero: 12ᵗʰ July 2002 1:07 a.m.

Been on holiday for
a week and still
going strong!

Figure 5-3. A funny photograph gets used twice.

Risto's reply arrives half an hour later, with compliments on the amusingness of the photo and a reference to his own "spiritual void." Although the message seems to be full of excuses as to why he has not been able to match the funniness of the previous message, in doing so he may have in fact succeeded. The photo suggests he is desperate to finish the bottle (of alcoholic beverage) as fast as he can, which is also purposefully funny.

The messages between Liisa and Risto play with several different elements: with styles of text, with visual language and with the tension created between mismatching interpretations to create messages that are funny and entertaining. Both are making fun of themselves in rather complicated ways. Such jokes and quips would be hard to sustain for long in face-to-face interactions, but in the more limited but controllable messaging, the content can be designed, enabling them to act out roles and be as witty as characters in a comedy. This aspect can also motivate creativity and push participants to top the previous message or come up with the next clever idea.

The re-use of images in the study was not a very common occurrence. Instead, there seemed to be high value placed on a new and fresh photograph to go with each reply. The same message might be sent to several recipients – and not all at the same time, but media elements from within messages were rarely recycled. However, in the third message (Figure 5-3) Risto re-uses the picture he obviously deems funny enough to be re-sent, but he also types a much more straightforward text to go along with it. He still makes fun of himself and the role he is playing seems to be similar, but the style of the text is different because of a different audience. This message is sent to a group of young men, each of whom reply with a similarly overdone message with the sender drinking beer. This is one of the best examples of recomposing messages to send the same picture to different recipients. This group consisted of people or smaller groups of people who connect only through Risto, thus there was more need to personalize the messages as well. The message from the sauna greetings sequence (Figure 5-1) was originally sent to the whole group, who all seemed to know each other. Anna-Maija often sent her messages by default to the whole group.

5.   Supporting Creativity with Technology

Sanders points out that the collective creativity of the users and consumers of products is where product and technology developers should be focusing their attention, because people acting alone do not accomplish things that are as interesting as when people act together (Sanders, 2002). Technology enables these experiences, it provides a framework shaping what can and cannot be done. These constraints can be described in terms of the number of steps to complete a message, the size of the message, the size of display, the quality of the colors in display, the speed of transmission, the maximum size of message, the size of memory in the device, and so forth. In the "here and now," the nature of the technology affects how simple and easy it is for people who are co-present to collaborate in its use, and it affects how, in new situations, users can negotiate new uses and meanings. In the case of multiple co-present users and multiple products, the compatibility of technologies and networks is crucial. In the "there and later," technology affects what can be shared and viewed as well as what sort of responsive actions can be taken. It can be presumed that the more the technology enables effortless and low cost responses the more interactions will follow and thus more user innovation will take place. In addition, a technology is more likely to be commercially successful if it engages users in social processes that then continue through and with aid of this technology or product.

In this case of multimedia messaging, instead of merely remembering past content, participants were able to interpret and re-interpret the themes and content of previous messages and messaging threads. When users become content authors, access to a common history enriches the storytelling (Kurvinen, 2002). The common history of a group contains many possible themes for taking up within multimedia messages, while personal collections of received messages and previously recorded media elements contain material that allows people to be prepared for good messaging opportunities. In this process, images, especially, have the potential to keep themes and conversations alive, partly because images allow multiple interpretations of the content and because no interpretation is exhaustive. In some cases this re-interpretation could be textual (as in Figure 5-3), but it is also visual: new images (or new versions of images, as in the case of the pictures of faces in Figure 5-2) respond visually and thematically to previous ones and comment upon them.

Messages are not just things created in the moment: a picture might have been taken earlier but be used in messaging later once the opportunity presented itself. This has been reported also in a previous study (Koskinen *et al.*, 2002; Kurvinen, 2002.). Colombo and Scifo, elsewhere in the book, cite users first taking pictures and only later determining how they are used in messaging. The term "planned opportunism" has been previously used to describe how mobile workers prepare for the unexpected by taking potentially useful things with them on the road (Perry *et al.*, 2001). This could easily be used to describe the process of collecting themes and content in multimedia messaging. If the main purpose of communication is just social, mutual entertainment (as described by Koskinen, 2003), content that is potentially fun or interesting can be captured in advance and kept back until a timely moment occurred when it could be used, or until such a moment could be easily created.

In sum, the role of communication technology in supporting the creativity of users is to provide the channel for maintaining social interaction. Users may then use the technology to interact, to create content and to re-interpret it through social interaction, for example, in replies, jokes, requests and emotional, intimate responses. It is obvious that if the participants of the MMS pilot study had been charged, say, one euro per sent message, they would hardly have started experimenting with messaging in the way they did. The very fact that it was a free channel encouraged use. The creative effort that helps people take up a form of communication as part of their lifestyle is weighed against its cost – "creativity in doing" only requires minimal investment in skill and effort. Also, what fun is messaging if others cannot afford to reply? Senders are motivated by tokens of appreciation, and if such are never received, messaging will fade away. Technical limitations in what can be sent are less problematic than having to think of the cost of each message – this partly helps to explain why cheap but limited SMS is so popular while in many places MMS took a while to get going at all. Even if price is not the only reason for this, it raises a significant barrier to usage.

6.   Future Directions

Current mobile phones and MMS services are mainly designed for single person use and one-to-one communication. They are built on an assumption that once the user has something significant to show, she will send that in an MMS. However, as these MMS examples indicate, people are not so much driven by their internal motivation but rather they are engaged in the collaborative processes at the sending and receiving ends. This means that individual messages are linked to each other in multiple ways, but also that people compose and interpret messages together with other people. Currently, there are products that support multi-player gaming but multi-participant communication and experiencing is not yet here.

In fact, we already have research that reveals these practices of collaborative creation and the sharing of photographs (Frohlich *et al.*, 2002, Koskinen *et al.*, 2002). Product developers should consider ways in which to support this type of activity both in connection with MMS and also when people share personal media in a broader sense.

Academics and technology developers often speak of "user needs" (Patnaik and Becker, 1999; Sanders, 1992). The concept of needs usually presupposes that users have human and personal, pre-existing and somewhat fixed needs that future technology either succeeds or fails to meet. In the light of these data, the process through which the user needs are discovered is both social and emergent. Instead of aiming at established needs or waiting for the technological breakthrough to happen, we see it more useful to study the small-scale micro-processes through which users co-operatively discover uses for the technology. For example, the existing practices or ethnomethods (Garfinkel, 1967) that people have already developed for dealing with images provide the base from which new imaging technologies can grow. These practices also provide a starting point as people begin, in co-operation with others, to develop their personal and group-specific styles. The relevance of the experiences that the technology offers is greatly dependent upon the social interactions that exist before it and that grow around it. For example, in an early study of youth gaming culture boys, unlike the majority of girls, also talked about games and exchanges tips and tricks, building a social gaming network around game-play and computer use (Haddon, 2004). Individual and gender differences may influence what kinds of social interactions and activities people like, but once a technology becomes part of social interaction, its relevance is less tied to the moment of use, and it becomes also tied to the social relationships with others, which last longer than a moment of play.

To find out what people might do with a new product or technology in an ideal setting, the first step is to find an appropriate social interaction environment for it and allow enough time for people to use it. Second, various barriers that might inhibit interaction need to be removed: people should be given open and natural means to organize their communication with other people. Monetary cost or the equivalent must be set at a level that does not discourage experimentation – in studies it is common to have the piloted service free of charge and sometimes new services are initially free or only carry a nominal fee. In addition, the necessary work and effort required in any interaction should be minimized. However, this aspect is probably the least important, because even if it is relatively high the study may still yield results. There are relatively successful examples where the prototype was cumbersome to use and slow (Koskinen *et al.*, 2002) or where prototypes were bulky (Mäkelä *et al.*, 2000). With the aid of such prototypes or field trials, one cannot be absolutely sure about the commercial success of the technology. However, what one has access to are the social processes on which commercial success can be built.

Acknowledgments

We wish to thank professor Ilpo Koskinen for continuous support and shared interests. Also, Seppo Väkevä and Pasi Nuppunen at Radiolinja for collaboration on the pilot and the anonymous participants of the pilot study for letting us use their messages. Thank you to the editors for helpful comments in restructuring a previous paper into this chapter. To our co-workers and fellow researchers: we wish we could send you a multimedia message.

References

Battarbee, K., Koskinen, I. Co-experience – user experience as interaction. CoDesign Journal, forthcoming; 1(1).

Beyer, H., Holtzblatt, K. Contextual Design: A Customer-Centered Approach to Systems Design; 1997. Academic Press, Elsevier.

Buchenau, M., Fulton S.J. Experience prototyping. In Proceedings of DIS 2000; 2000, ACM Press, New York: 424–433.

Bødker, S., Buur, J. The design collaboratorium: a place for usability design. In ACM Transactions on Computer-Human Interaction; 2002, 9(2): 152–169.

Dandavate, U., Sanders, E.B.-N., Stuart, S. Emotions matter: User empathy in the product development process. In Proceedings of the Human Factors and Ergonomics Society 40th Annual Meeting; 1996, 415–418.

Frohlich, D., Kuchinsky, A., Pering, C., Don, A., Ariss, S. Requirements for photoware. In Proceedings of CSCW'02; 2002, ACM Press, New York.

Fulton S.J. Empathic design: informed and inspired by other people's experience. In Koskinen, I., Battarbee, K., Mattelmäki, T. (Eds.), Empathic Design – User Experience in Product Design; 2003, IT Press/Edita Publishing, Helsinki: 51–57. Garfinkel, H. Studies in Ethnomethodology; 1967. Prentice-Hall, Englewood Cliffs.

Gaver, B., Dunne, T., Pacenti, E. Cultural probes. Interactions, 1999; 6(1): 21–29.

Goffman, E. Presentation of Self in Everyday Life; 1959. Doubleday, New York.

Haddon, L. Information and Communication Technologies in Everyday Life: A Concise Introduction And Research Guide; 2004. Berg, Oxford.

Hassenzahl, M. The thing and I: understanding the relationship between user and product. In Blythe, M.A., Overbeeke, K., Monk, A.F., Wright, P.C. (Eds.), Funology: From Usability to Enjoyment; 2003. Kluwer Academic Publishers, Dordrecht: 31–42.

Jordan, P.W. Designing Pleasurable Products: An Introduction to the New Human Factors; 2000. Taylor & Francis, London.

Kasesniemi, E., Rautiainen, P. Mobile culture of children and teenagers in Finland. In Katz, J.E., Aakhus, M.A. (Eds.), Perpetual Contact: Mobile Communication, Private Talk, Public Performance; 2002. Cambridge University Press, Cambridge: 170–192.

Koskinen, I. User-generated content in mobile multimedia: empirical evidence from user studies. In Proceedings of ICME03, 2003 IEEE International Conference on Multimedia, July 6–9, 2003, Baltimore, USA: 645–648.

Koskinen, I., Kurvinen, E., Lehtonen, T.-K. Mobile Image; 2002. IT Press, Helsinki.

Kurvinen, E. Emotions in action: a case in mobile visual communication. In McDonagh, D., Hekkert, P., Erp J. van, Gyi, D. (Eds.), Design and Emotion; 2002, Taylor & Francis, London: 211–215.

Kurvinen, E. Only when Miss Universe snatches me: teasing in MMS messaging. In Proceedings of Conference on Designing Pleasurable Products and Interfaces; June 23–26, 2003, Pittsburgh. ACM Press, NY: 98–102.

Leonard, D., Rayport, J.E. Spark innovation through empathic design. Harvard Business Review, November–December 1997; 75(6): 102–113.

Manning, P. Erving Goffman and MSodern Sociology; 1992. Stanford University Press, Palo Alto.

Masten, D.L., Plowman, T.M.P. Digital ethnography: the next wave in understanding the consumer experience. Design Management Journal, Spring 2003; 14(2): 74–81.

Mattelmäki, T., Battarbee, K. Empathy probes. In Proceedings of the Participatory Design Conference 2002, Malmö Sweden; 2002, Computer Professionals for Social Responsibility, Palo Alto: 266–271.

Mäkelä, A., Giller, V., Tscheligi, M., Sefelin, R. Joking, storytelling, artsharing, expressing affection: a field trial of how children and their social network communicate with digital images in leisure time. In Proceedings of CHI 2000; 2000. ACM Press, New York: 548–555.

Norman, D.A. Emotional Design. Why We Love (or Hate) Everyday Things; 2004. Basic Books, New York.

Patnaik, D., Becker, R. Needfinding: the why and how of uncovering people's needs. Design Management Journal, 1999; 10(2): 37–43.

Perry, M., O'Hara, K., Sellen, A., Brown, B., Harper, R. Dealing with mobility: understanding access anytime, anywhere. In ACM Transactions on Computer-Human Interaction, 2001; 8(4): 323–347.

Pine, B.J. II, Gilmore, J.H. Welcome to the experience economy. Harvard Business Review, July–August 1998; 76(4): 97–105.

Rhea, D.K. A new perspective on design: focusing on customer experience. Design Management Journal, Fall 1992; 3(4): 40–48.

Sacks, H., Jefferson, G. Harvey Sacks: Lectures, 1964–1965; 1990. Kluwer Academic Publishers, Amsterdam.

Sanders, E.B.-N. Converging perspectives: product development research for the 1990s. Design Management Journal, Fall 1992; 3(4): 48–54.

Sanders, E.B.-N., Dandavate, U. Design for experiencing: new tools. In Overbeeke, C.J., Hekkert, P. (Eds.), Proceedings of The First International Conference on Design and Emotion; 1999, Delft, the Netherlands; TU Delft: 87–92.

Sanders, L. Collective Creativity. LOOP: The AIGA Journal of Interaction Design Education, 3rd edition; 2002. Accessed 15.7.2003 at http://loop.aiga.org/content.cfm?Alias=sandersucd.

Sanders, L. Scaffolds for building everyday creativity. In Creating Communicational Spaces Conference, 1–4 May 2003, Edmonton, Canada. http://www.ualberta.ca/COMSPACE/ accessed 23.11.2004.

Schatzman, L., Strauss, A.L. Field Research: Strategies for a Natural Sociology; 1973. Prentice-Hall, Englewood Cliffs.

Wensveen, S.A.G. Probing experiences. In Proceedings of the Conference 'Design and Emotion'; November 3–5, 1999, Delft University of Technology, Delft: 23–29.

Chapter 6

THE SOCIAL SHAPING OF NEW MOBILE DEVICES AMONG ITALIAN YOUTH

Fausto Colombo and Barbara Scifo

1. Theoretical Framework and Research Design

This chapter aims to illustrate briefly the initial results of a sociological research project[1] into the processes involved in the social shaping of the new multimedia and multifunctional mobile phone, with special attention to the use of the camera phone by young Italian users.

The research design for the project grew out of the tradition of research looking into the non-technological dimensions of information and communication technologies (ICTs). This tradition has its origins in both a socio-constructivist approach to technology (Bijker, 1995; Edge, 1995; Mackenzie and Wajcman, 1999; Williams, 1999) and an approach to the consumption of ICTs that focuses on symbolic and cultural practices (Mackay, 1997; Silverstone and Haddon, 1996; Silverstone *et al.*, 1992). These paradigms have resulted – as also noted by Woolgar (2002) – in a series of progressive shifts in the study of technology and socio-historical change over the last two decades: from production to consumption, from innovation to use, from large-scale or long-term processes to everyday contexts.[2]

In this context, this study explores the relationship between mobile phones and social actors from a user-oriented perspective. This means putting the processes by which the mobile phone is appropriated into the everyday lives of the users at the center of our understanding of several elements. These processes included the social dynamics of technological innovation and resistance to it, the processes socially shaping mobile technology and the social consequences of its

---

[1] The research, begun in May and finished in October 2003, was financed by Motorola, directed by Fausto Colombo and Barbara Scifo and carried out by a workgroup of the Osservatorio sulla Comunicazione, the media research center at the Università Cattolica in Milano.
[2] For a synthesis of this approach, see Oudshoorn and Pinch (2003).

spread. Such themes have been clearly documented within recent literature and an ongoing scientific debate [see, for example, in addition to the growing body of conference proceedings, the collected volumes edited by Haddon (1997), Brown *et al.* (2001), Katz and Aakhus (2002), Katz (2003), Nyìri (2003), and the monograph of Ling (2004)]. This kind of approach proves most interesting in the initial phase of a technology, where it is possible to explore the various potential paths of development on an equal footing, before any definitive directions are taken that establish the frameworks of use. Mobile telephony is now going through a phase of this kind, characterized by the redefinition of both its functioning and use (Flichy, 1995).

We have decided to focus on young consumers (from adolescents to young adults) and chosen to consider business users only as a comparative sample. This choice is not intended to take for granted the widespread view that young people are the principal protagonists in the processes of any technological innovation. This view is a typical myth conveyed in social discourses about the use of new media by the young generations and exemplified by expressions such as the web generation, net generation, and cyber-generation (for a critique of these discourses, see Hartmann, 2003; Livingstone, 2002). Instead, it is intended to take stock of the effective, historical relationship between young people and mobile telephones as a particular technology, as the now-rich body of empirical research into the uses and social meanings of mobile phones by adolescents and young people in the different countries clearly shows.[3]

Given the explorative nature of the project and the theoretical framework adopted, the research is based on a qualitative approach that integrates different methods: focus groups,[4] individual in-depth and non-directional interviews, diaries and socio-linguistic analysis of multimedia (MMS) messages. The fieldwork involved 70 males and females from Milan and the surrounding area. With regard to the sampling, two different criteria were combined. The first was age, distinguishing between teenagers (between 14 and 17 years old), youth (between 18 and 24 years old), and young adults (between 25 and 34 years old).[5] The second criterion was purchasing behavior, namely distinguishing between current owners of the new devices and non-owners, either because they are

---

[3] This is not the place to quote the numerous contributions on this theme, but by way of example we would like to point to the monographic by Lorente (2002) published in the Spanish review translated as "Journal of Studies on Youth" and entitled (in translation) "Youth and the Mobile Phone." This brings together a number of studies of different national experiences.

[4] This technique has been used to run group interviews both with people belonging to the same natural social network, i.e. groups of friends or classmates, and people who do not know each other.

[5] The division by age groups put forward here is based on the social divisions used by the IARD Research Institute, which publishes an annual report on the condition of youngsters in Italy.

actively opposed to MMS mobiles or merely potential consumers of the new devices and services who have not yet acquired them.[6] The sample subjects had to have terminals with color displays and icon interfaces, with MMS protocols and a camera incorporated or as an option, since these features are held by the manufacturers to be driving the new purchase market.[7]

Here, we shall point out some precautions taken in interpreting the results presented below:

a) The difference between owners and non-owners does not necessarily coincide with that between users and non-users. Think, for example, of the spread of the use of the Internet and of computer-literacy regardless of whether people themselves have personal subscriptions and computers, because this sometimes takes place through the devices of their parents or of children of the same age who possess the technology. Moreover, owning a device does not necessarily mean that people use all the new functions incorporated within it (think for instance of the VCR or other more sophisticated electronic devices).

b) We chose – due to the time and financial constraints on the research – not to consider as a discriminating variable the different attitudes toward technological innovation. Such attitudes naturally differentiate the sample subjects (for instance, so-called techno-fans from techno-phobes). Hence, this choice prevents us assessing the weight of this variable, which naturally acts on the processes of consumption of this specific new technological artifact.

The research was conducted in two different phases. The first lasted from May to July 2003, one year after MMS services were offered by the main Italian providers, just as a new summer campaign was being launched. Here, the main focus of the enquiry was upon the representations of the new devices, to be elaborated below, and more generally on how the interviewees viewed technological change in mobile telephony. The second phase lasted from September to October 2003 following the increase in sales of camera phones and in the use of the new devices, spurred on by the providers' promotional campaigns. During this phase, we investigated people's early experiences of appropriating the new devices and the social uses and meanings of MMS messages. The relatively long time span of the research made it possible to observe people's

---

[6] This applied to the 8 focus groups as well as the 15 individual in-depth and non-directional interviews. As concerns the natural groups, three different networks of friends, camera phone adopters, have been chosen.

[7] Our interviewees own the following phones: Nokia 7650; Nokia 3650; Nokia 6610; Nokia 3510i; Motorola T720i; Siemens M55; Siemens SL55; Sony P800; SonyEriccson T68i; Sagem X5; and Sharp GX10.

progressive familiarization with the new devices and to note the rapid reduction in the resistance initially put up by young users. This resistance gave way to a shared acceptance of the future role of "universal technology" amongst these young users.

This chapter will illustrate some of the results that emerged from the first phase of the research that was conducted with the focus groups from May to June 2003, following the launch of the devices. A more general discussion of the practices emerging during the establishment of this new medium is reported elsewhere (Scifo, 2005). In this chapter, we have decided to deal specifically with the key data coming from the four focus groups conducted with youths and young adults (ranging from 18 to 35 years), considered by the suppliers to be the principal drivers developing the consumption of new devices among consumers.[8]

From amongst the manifold socio-communicative dimensions that emerged, we shall here stress only some points considered crucial for understanding how this new phase in the technological evolution of mobile phones was socially shaped. These related to the forms of social representation of the new medium, i.e. the set of common meanings related to the new medium and shared by the mobile telephony users. In media research, analysis of such representations is often conducted in order to comprehend how people use the emerging media. In contrast, our research starts from the conviction that – as pointed out by Alasuutari (1999, p. 88) – "repertoires or discourses that people invoke when they discuss media on a meta-level" represent *per se* legitimate and independent themes to be analyzed. In other words, we assume that these cultural images of new media are fundamental in shaping the processes of innovation. In this context, we shall refer to the cultural images of the new mobile telephones as they are discussed by subjects in the process of socially constructing the meaning of these technologies. These images may be in tune with or contradict the public images presented by the media, in particular by advertising. Yet, these images have a bearing upon either people's creative responses to the technology on offer or their simple acceptance of the innovation.[9] And they are all the more significant given the substantial financial investment made by the manufacturers of mobile phones and by the operators.

Compared with this level of analysis, the results we present here will concentrate on two aspects in particular, though they are naturally closely connected:

a) the identity (communicative, functional, esthetic, etc.) of the new mobile devices in their dual nature as objects that are material, social and

---

[8] Hence, this chapter will forgo the presentation of the results – in themselves highly interesting – relating to adolescents. Few of these possessed these new devices, largely due to their cost.

[9] On this subject, as applied to the Internet in Italy, see the essay by Pasquali (2004).

symbolic and as technologies handling information and communication;

b) the new form of visual communication mediated by the telephone, MMS, where photography is fundamental (held to be the new "killer" application in mobile telephony) and related to social connectivity (person-to-person communication) rather than to flows of information (person-to-information communication – e.g. where the user pays the operator for standard contents, such as jokes, news, cartoons, etc., that have been prepared by different content providers).

Moreover, the comprehension of these objects of study has been contextualized:

a) By considering how the interviewees themselves understood and reconstructed the social history of mobile telephony in Italy. This means looking at the relationship between the current images and uses of mobile telephony in relation to past and future ones and showing where the continuities and discontinuities lie between what is taken for granted and what is new.

b) Within the broader communicative and technological environment in which the sample subjects operated. This means looking at the relationship between the images and uses of mobile telephony compared to other ICTs and showing the analogies and differences. We do this because these other devices and related communication practices represent a decisive factor for comprehending how people represent and adopt the new mobile telephony.

2.   Background: The Early Diffusion of the Camera Phone

The initial phase of the spread of the camera phone in Italy merits some preliminary consideration. In the first place, we should recall the period in which our study began: this was the launch phase of the product and was motivated by two needs. The first was a commercial one: in a mature market new features are sought by suppliers in order to promote new purchases. The second need was a competitive one, given that in Italy the two major service providers of mobile telephony (TIM and Vodafone) decided to postpone their launch of the UMTS standard. They did this by strongly promoting the Wap–GPRS standard and services based on devices with color screens, such as the ability to take photos with integrated digital cameras and exchange MMS messages. On the other hand, the UMTS has been launched by H3G with an intensive advertising campaign based solely on video communication.

A phase of this kind – in which the supply drives the change rather than a grassroots demand (as was the case, for instance, with SMS, otherwise known as text messaging) – is characterized by extremely low network externalities. This fact that there were few users overall meant that these initial users and first potential buyers, as early adopters, had only a limited number of other people with whom to exchange informal information about the product. This made them extremely dependent upon institutional information about MMS (e.g. from advertising, offers from the producers and service providers, articles in the press), which often, in practice, proved to be over-optimistic if not, indeed, illusory.

In effect, during the course of our entire research from May to October we were able to observe a fairly rapid shift. In the initial period (before the summer), aspirant buyers seemed unsure and full of doubts, adopting a defensive strategy of the wait-and-see type. In the later period (after the summer holidays), many of these doubts appeared to have been resolved and the camera phone began to be adopted in a more extensive and, above all, "creative" manner.

We suggest that an extremely important factor in this rapid change was that of money. In particular, the prices of the devices progressively approached those of traditional phones, thereby transforming the presence of the photo cameras into a cheap convenience. To this must be added the rapid evolution of the devices themselves. This occurred both in esthetic terms through miniaturization and design improvements and in terms of technological performance, given the considerable improvement in the quality of the images recorded. Finally, the promotional campaigns launched by the operators for the MMS services also proved decisive.

These were the supply-side factors that stimulated the progressive adoption of the camera phone. However, there were also social factors at work. The intense, and sometimes original, usage that began to take shape occurred in those places boasting a strong sense of community (e.g. among peer groups or professional groups), in which the expressive aspect of visual communication combined with the more functional reasons for making contact. For example, when friends needed to co-ordinate where to meet this might involve sending one another a picture of the meeting place. Between the two periods under consideration, however, and faced with the doubts and perplexities either preceding a decision to buy or following an evaluation of purchase, our users found themselves able to formulate forecasts concerning the future of these new types of mobile devices. And as we will see, most users seem to have chosen to formulate a veritable theory of the technological spread of innovations. This is based, on the one hand, upon the pressure of the launch campaigns, and, on the other, upon their own past experience as protagonists involved in the spread of traditional mobile telephony. These embryonic theories of innovation, very close to Rogers' classic theory of diffusion, constitute the crux of our discussion.

3.   Findings

3.1.   *Owners, Non-owners and Representations of Innovation*

The subjects interviewed project their definition of the devices onto what we could call a popular historiography of the telephony and of ICTs in general. They do so at two levels. The first is by constructing a perspective of the early phase of the diffusion of the new mobile devices, i.e. they seek to define it on the basis of the innovations that characterize it and oppose it to other phases. Second, they re-define the whole history of the development of mobile telephony in the light of the latest novelties and by foreseeing future developments. In doing so, they spontaneously offer implicit paradigms for interpreting the social history of mobile telephony and ICTs, as if constructing embryonic theories of technological innovation and development.

3.1.1.   *The early diffusion phase of the new mobile devices*

The defining characteristic of this phase was the new iconic dimension, understood as:

> the interface consisting of a color display, with the presence of the icons menu and the possibility to personalize the device; an instrument of visual communication produced and mediated by the camera phone, where photographs taken with the camera are destined to be stored for person-to-person communication.[10]

For the owners, in particular, this image signals a gradual transition to video communication. The superimposition – in the market and in advertising – of the MMS service (enabled by the GSM standard) upon the new video communication (based on the UMTS standard) is in practice interpreted in a particular way. The former is seen as "the present," and the latter is seen as an embryonic form of "the future."

For non-owners the distinction is more problematic. They do not have a very clear idea of the differences between the possibilities offered by GSM and the ones offered by UMTS. This is because non-owners lack the personal experience of camera phones that can trigger this understanding. However, even non-owners interpret this phase as being a dynamic one, speaking of a transition and referring to examples of other ICTs such as the transition

---

[10] In actual fact, the interviewees in this definition phase also do other things with their phones, such as seeking better ringing options (from polyphonic tones to the possibility of music via radio or MP3) or moving toward using them with computers (via gateway functions for computers and PDA). The representation we are confronted with involves a hybridization of the phone with these other ICTs – as well as revealing their rivalry.

from ISDN to broadband or, even earlier, the changeover from mainframes to personal computers.

What they all agree on is that this phase will lead irreversibly to a universal, or almost universal, spread of the new devices, in line with a basic diffusionist theory (Rogers, 1995; to which we shall return later). However, the non-owners do not feel that they are the protagonists in this phase, but more like "pioneers" or "guinea-pigs." This phase seems to be driven by the market. Users will just have to wait for demand to stabilize in order to be able to make informed choices and adopt styles of use compatible with their communicative styles.

3.1.2.   *Historical phases of development: Paradigms of interpretation*

All the interviewees reveal certain shared convictions about the mechanisms by which communication technologies evolve. These mechanisms entail:

- the transformation of the object (as both hardware and software);
- its social meanings and spread; and
- the role of the ordinary people in influencing the direction of development.

As regards the first point, there is common belief that a technological object evolves in a linear or multilinear way. For the traditional mobile phone, this has mainly involved miniaturization, an increase in battery duration and a reduction in costs. Furthermore, we can include certain new functions that came as a surprise but revealed the device's enormous potential (for example text messages, which according to the interviewees represented "the real revolution" of mobile phones).

Regarding the second point, the interviewees describe the linear evolution of this technological novelty from being a niche product with the significance of a status symbol to a universally diffused device gradually adopted by everyone, regardless of economic status, gender, or age (although the precocious use on the part of children is shunned).

Moving on to the third point, the GSM mobile phone experience exemplifies a pact between operators and manufacturers on the one hand and the users on the other. The latter are implicitly seen as contributing to the development of mobiles, both in terms of the evolution of the object itself (the writing systems developed to facilitate SMS are a response to the unexpected social success of text messages) as well as its increasing diffusion.

However, certain significant differences arise here. This understanding is not shared between the camera phone owners and non-owners. The former seem to apply this same model to camera phones while the latter consider that this innovation is being guided from the outside and hence they do not feel so involved. In a certain sense, this last consideration interrupts the virtuous circuit

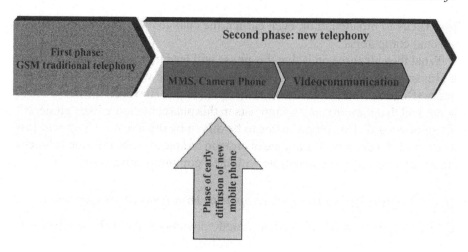

Figure 6-1. Owners' representations.

that makes the development of this new generation of devices an extension of the GSM mobile phone success story. And it provides the basis for a more critical evaluation, similar to that of many other technological innovations, based on a certain wariness and a strong sense of detachment.

Taking this as a starting point, we can try to represent the different interpretations that were arrived at by owners and non-owners as regards how the new-generation mobile phone fitted into a longer historical trend (Figure 6-1).

Owners simply consider new devices to be the natural successors to the traditional GSM: therefore, they see an evolution even if there are discontinuities. In fact, the advent of these devices signifies the conclusion of a phase when GSM was dominant. It is true that this phase is also only at an initial stage: it is part of a natural evolution toward video communications. Furthermore, this evolution is part of the more complex trend in ICTs toward convergence and interoperability.

The owners see themselves as being completely integrated into this phase, which they describe as an exciting challenge, offering continuous surprises (although some are not up to the standard presented in advertising). On personal level, it provides learning opportunities that are part of their relation with technology in general. On the whole, these subjects represent technological development as being one of constant progress. Although there are some turning points, this evolution always leads to technologies that are superior to the previous ones (Figure 6-2).

For non-owners the situation is more complex. They do not perceive the new phase as a natural evolution but instead as a choice imposed by manufacturers and operators that are motivated by market needs. This means that they do not consider the traditional GSM cycle as being complete and they would have

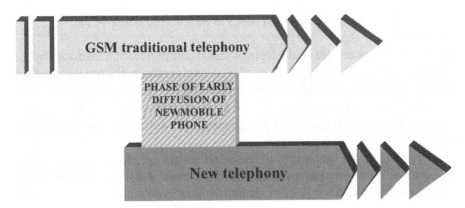

Figure 6-2. Non-owners' representations.

preferred innovations more in line with the tendencies still underway in terms of miniaturization, lightness, design, autonomy, etc.

In many ways, the new camera telephony therefore comes across as having taken a step backward (in terms of its large dimensions, weight, fragility, a design which is not always attractive, low battery life, reduced memory, etc.). What is claimed to be a step forward (in terms of photography, MMS) is actually considered to be useless rather than being appreciated,[11] and non-owners do not feel involved in this. Thus, this phase of innovation is described as a sort of no man's land into which they are absorbed against their will: "their" technology (the universally diffused GSM, easy to use like a technological Esperanto) suddenly appears obsolete. Meanwhile, the "new" technology re-introduces divisions between early adopters and later adopters. This trend creates amongst non-owners a critical wariness of the new devices and of their possible use in the future (when costs will decrease and they will function more efficiently). This leads them to foresee a future phase in which there will be only a partial use of all the functions offered, where personalizing the device simply means not using certain services. This appears very different from that of owners, who simply consider any development as a challenge and an opportunity to learn.[12]

---

[11] This sense of being useless is also connected to the idea that such new objects represent a type of consumerism that some people felt to be immoral (as they talked using words like *exaggeration, superfluous needs, ridiculous functions, unjustified prices, toyland,* etc.).

[12] In the case of users, another important factor is the idea that possessing these camera phones is a resource for building one's social identity in a number of ways. It allows people to feel ahead of their time, associating themselves with technological advancement. However, it also allows them to feel part of youth peer groups, given that the new camera phones are typically a phenomenon of this age group. Above all, it allows people to feel trendy, in the double sense that it is a trendy object (i.e. the latest trend, a status symbol) and a fashion object that can be personalized (i.e. a fashion accessory).

3.2.   The Camera Phone and MMS in Relation to Other ICTs

We shall now concentrate on the form of visual communication mediated by the new telephone devices, the MMS service, to explore the initial processes of appropriation by young Italian users. In this section we shall focus on the analysis of MMS practices directed at social contacts (person-to-person information), given the limited experiences of using person-to-information multimedia services in Italy.

In particular, the comments of the interviewees enable us to reconstruct, at the level of representations, an idea of which ICTs and related socio-communicative practices help to shape this new communicative technology. In this regard, we can speak about processes of "hybridization" and "remediation" (Bolter and Grusin, 2000).[13] When making comparisons to the camera phone and MMS, the ICTs to which the interviewees refer are the camera and the traditional cell phone. And the communicative practices to which they refer are photography, sending postcards, SMS, e-mail and video communications.

3.2.1.   The representation of the object

As we might expect, the camera is the dominant technology in defining the identity of this new technological hybrid, the camera phone. The relationship between these "old" and "new" technologies is defined in terms of whether the latter inevitably replaces the former, or whether the camera is irreplaceable, or whether the two technologies are complementary and can be integrated. As we will see below, these different relationships depend upon the social situations in which they are used and on the photographic performance of the devices.

Replacement

For some owners of the new devices, the camera phone has in practice already replaced the camera (especially in its compact version). Hence, in their image of the future, a complete and universal replacement of the camera is envisaged, partly by virtue of the certainty that the camera phone will improve in performance. Once again we are faced with a viewpoint assuming the linearity of technological progress.

Complementarity

Other camera owners, however, who are in agreement with certain non-owners, adopt or envisage using the camera phone only in certain social circumstances. They see it being used when there are unexpected occurrences, of

---

[13] We use these terms to indicate the typical trend for new media to be contaminated by, but at the same time to assimilate, the techniques, the forms and the social meanings of previous media that had a similar function – instead of, or before, substituting for them. By this process, the introduction of any new technology also leads to a re-shaping of the whole media system.

the kind that happen all the time even though they are exceptional. Or else they see it being used at special events such going out to dinner, on holidays, etc. However, they do not see the camera phone being used at other times, such as predictable, important and festive occasions, like a trip, a ceremony, etc., in which the quality of the traditional camera's photographs are not in competition with those of the new camera phone.

In both cases, whether respondents envisage the replacement of the camera or its complementarity with the camera phone, they appeal to pragmatic or instrumental arguments (invoking convenience and utility): it is the immediate and constant availability of the cell phone, accessible to its owner any time, anywhere, which represents the principal appeal of this new technological hybrid. So, it seems that – compared with the camera – the camera phone asserts its value as a personal medium (almost like an extension of the body) and one closely bound up with the legacy of the traditional cell phone. This personal significance surpasses – in certain circumstances – its value as mobile technology, which is shared by the camera. This defining feature of the object enables users to excuse the poor picture quality of the camera phone that all interviewees recognize when comparing its pictures to pictures taken with a regular camera.

Integration

Another outstanding view about the relationship between the two devices that the interviewees – especially non-owners – hold is related to the respective functions that they believe are appropriate and pertinent to the two "original" devices. They see the digital camera as being a production terminal, the telephone as being a transmission one. This distinction makes it possible to avoid losing the telephone's original identity as a medium of communication, so dear to non-users of the new devices. From this point of view, the only form of relationship recognized between the two objects is that of integration, through their interaction: I take photos with the digital camera and then transfer them to the cell phone in order to transmit them to someone.

Irreplaceability

Finally, there is the position taken by some non-owners who resist the idea that the two technological objects should become a hybrid. They want the phone to keep its original identity – i.e., they want the phone to be just a phone and nothing else. And they think that the camera phone does not produce good enough quality images to replace existing cameras. Such users have a more "authorial" conception of what it means to construct photographs, where the person taking the picture carefully composes the shot taking many considerations into account. This is far removed from the taking instant snapshots with a camera phone.

3.2.2.   The representation of the communicative practice

The new socio-technological hybrid of the camera phone re-mediates or re-shapes both photography and phone communication, enhancing a potential that is already present in the original practices. Or at least this is what has emerged from these early experiences of use. In terms of photographic practice, the connection with telephony accentuates the role of photos as a resource for exchanging, a practice that can enhance relationships between people. In the case of traditional photography, this involves passing round pictures that have been taken. With digital photographs on the PC, it entails sending them by e-mail. The novelty of the camera phone seems to consist in the immediacy of the exchange after taking the snapshot.

In the rare cases when the images are sent by phone, the accent is placed on the practice of saving the photo. This practice of saving messages already exists in the case of SMS, and here this telecoms-related behavior is reconfigured so that it now involves storing images and multimedia messages. However, the similarity of this practice to that of the photo album also means that one is also, in effect, storing signs of relationships with other people (also true of SMS) and documenting and collecting visual keepsakes. This is shown by the practice of storing – both on the cell phone and on the PC – photos taken with one's own camera phone, even if they are then never used in communicational exchanges.

Within this relationship between telephony and photography, other forms of communication seem to define both people's images and use of the new camera phone. One, often taken for granted, draws on the established use of the mobile for sending SMS messages. The other, perhaps regarded as less obvious, draws on another fully pre-digital form of remote visual communication, namely the postcard.

MMS, in part because of the similarity of the acronym that defines it, is naturally identified as the successor to the SMS (but forerunner of video com-munications). It is interpreted as a natural linguistic-expressive enhancement of SMS (we now have not only text, but also text and image). It is motivated by the same desire to conserve (and construct) one's own social memory. Moreover, the strong social entrenchment of the practice of sending SMS, the "mythical" appeal based on the fact that the messages are experienced as absolute and unrepeatable, their emotional force and the specificity of their expressive form (i.e. the way they are composed) makes SMS a fundamental touchstone for MMS.

As for the postcard, the parallel with MMS is that we have service that enables a photo taken by a camera phone and accompanied by a text to be transformed into a postcard that the operator undertakes to send to an address specified by the user. The respondents referred to this explicitly and found it pleasurable. It anchored MMS within another well-established social practice, renewed through the even greater potential for personalizing the image. Moreover, the use of e-mail to send "postcard" photos taken by the camera phone provided another interesting way of circumventing the fact that the initial spread of the devices was limited.

So, what we can observe is that the new device does not assume a single stable configuration, it does not have one single use and meaning. Instead, it tends to oscillate between different representations and uses, essentially constituted in relation to the existing and widespread practices and rituals associated with photography and the cell phone. Which representations and use will prevail in the future is still uncertain.

4.   Conclusions

On the basis of the results illustrated earlier, we shall now seek to derive some hypotheses about the relations between users and innovation. First, we would like to recall what we set out to explore. Through looking at the spread of the new generation of cell phones, we considered the representations that owners and non-owners of the new multimedia devices express as they define the new technological artifact and the new communicative practices they make possible. This choice is based on recognizing the centrality of such representations in the early social shaping of a technology on the road to the domestication of an innovation.

The particular feature of our case study should also be borne in mind. The new camera mobile telephones were located in between two types of innovation. The first is a radical innovation, opening up new photographic possibilities or replacing, to a substantial degree, earlier camera technology. The second involves the transformation of an existing technology, the mobile. However, in addition, we can also say that these new-generation telephones are an almost unique case involving the transformation of an established technology that is nevertheless relatively young and widespread with a high degree of satisfaction on the part of users. These distinctive features make the question of how camera phones are represented in people's minds and through what they say even more significant. They appear to be the result of negotiations between two things. The first consists of the widespread images presented by the mass media. The second involves the knowledge the competencies that either people already possess (shaped by the way they had appropriated a preceding technology, in this case GSM) or which is currently being formed (by the first users of the new devices).

These are, therefore, the findings that seem most significant.

1.   In drawing an analogy with and differentiating camera phones from other ICTs, as well as in noting the continuities and discontinuities with the

past, our interviewees express a sort of theory of technological evolution based on their own experience (of the historia magistra vitae kind). In this "theory," a diffusionist model prevails that is widely accepted as being universal. Our interviewees express no doubt about the final success of the new devices, even though some of them do not feel involved in the early phase of their innovation. Meanwhile, while others criticize its technical imperfections, all are convinced that the replacement will gradually take place and that the defects will be corrected in the process. To back up this conviction, the interviewees refer to their recent experience as observers of, and protagonists in, the spread of GSM in particular, and the whole universe of ICTs more generally. This leads to our hypothesis that they feel immersed in a socio-technical context in which innovation and dynamism are the norm. The age variable is naturally relevant: the subjects of the research all fall into the generations for whom the development of the ICTs was taken as being a natural experience.

2.   A second important point that can be gleaned from our analysis concerns the evaluation of the role of the users as innovators. In particular, it seems to us that the results of our work call into question the typical metaphor of the bricoleur (De Certeau, 1980)[14] from two points of view, suggesting two alternative metaphors. In the first place, we may observe that a representation such as the diffusionist paradigm varied depending on the role of different mobile phone users in the process of change. Here, the interpretations are highly articulated. The role of the supply side in driving the innovation is well recognized, understood in a techno-economic sense (a mix of technical innovation and the law of the market are at work). This role, as usual, is understood in relation to the recent development of mobile phones. However, these consumers do not see this supply-push as diminishing their role as users and their capacity to resist or shape the new technology. This is because they attribute to the supply side a complexity that is bound up with constraints imposed by the laws of the market. These involve mechanisms of competition, which mean that companies ultimately need to find a point of contact with, and collaborate with, users.

---

[14] The French word "bricoleur" literally refers to the sort of worker who is capable of mending or maintaining any machinery or installation by re-using items from elsewhere. This typically involves improvising new uses for these items. So, in cultural theory, and especially the analysis of subcultures, the term refers to "*the process by which elements are appropriated from the dominant culture and then their meanings are transformed* [. . .]" (from Edgar and Sedgwick, 1999, p. 48). In the context of this chapter, the metaphor of the bricoleur alludes to the behavior of users when they adopt the technological resources that the industry offers to them but at the same time uses tactics that somehow deform these goods, giving them more personal and symbolic meanings.

Against this backdrop, the knowledge and the competencies mobilized by their own popular theories guide users toward making choices that provide a fruitful integration with the push coming from the supply-side. For example, one path involves deciding if and when to jump on this innovation bandwagon, while waiting for devices and services to be perfected, costs to fall and a sufficient spread of the devices to make their benefits worthwhile. This kind of user resembles a gambler on the stock exchange rather than a bricoleur.

The earlier appearance of the camera phone felt as if it were a terrain for the "pioneering" efforts of the early adopters has been replaced by a sense of "consensual colonization." The supply of this new technology means that it no longer seems to resemble a wilderness but rather it is as if there was a railway that permits more convenient expansion in an area that has already started to be colonized. This reminds us how unusual it is to speak of users as innovators in a society where continuous innovation is now experienced as part of the landscape, in which, to use the metaphor of a ship at sea, people navigate sensing the wind and the waves instead of keeping their gaze fixed firmly on the front of the boat.

The idea that new technologies are shaped by a process of bricolage (a view that seems to be devalued by the way our interviewees characterize systematic change) re-appears in the concrete practices when using camera phones and MMS. Here, users exploit the ambiguities and gray areas of the technologies supplied, a technology that oscillates between the evolution of the camera and that of the mobile phone. The emerging use reveals users' ability, based on experience, to adapt and personalize established practices and uses, re-shaping both of the earlier media into a new set of functions that are not yet completely assimilated into their lives.

However, here too we find ourselves facing some important variations. The case of the mobile phone may ultimately be ascribed to the second of two models of how a new technological apparatus diffuses. The first is shown by the case of the earliest radios as well as the first embryonic networks before the Internet. Initial buyers of radio kits, which had to be constructed, or the implementers of the first BBS systems acted both as early adopters and, in various senses, as early producers. Both users behaved like radio hams, dedicated not only to getting the devices to work at all, but also to encouraging the spread of these innovations. The early users of these technologies were veritable builder-bricoleurs. The second type of model concerns those technologies offered in a form that is already complete. The owner is far less free to shape uses, but rather uses are suggested and inspired in an initial phase of diffusion via social discussions "from above." Such is the case of television and mobile phones (and hence camera phones too). In these cases, the user behaves not so much as a bricoleur but rather as a customer at IKEA, the Swedish self-assembly furniture retailer. He or she can add to and personalize the object bought but only within the series of options set out. Hence, the stock exchange player and the IKEA customer provide two metaphors that describe the form of bricolage of these early users of technological novelties and suggest further aspects to be researched.

References

Alasuutari, P. Rethinking the Media Audience: The New Agenda; 1999. Sage, London.

Bijker, W. Of Bicycles, Bakelites, and Bulbs: Toward a Theory of Sociotechnical Change; 1995. MIT Press, Cambridge, MA.

Bolter, J.D., Grusin, R. Remediation: Understanding New Media; 2000. MIT Press, Cambridge, MA.

Brown, B., Green, N., Harper, R. (Eds.) Wireless World: Social and Interactional Aspects of the Mobile Age; 2001. Springer, London.

De Certeau, M. L'invention du Quotidien. I Arts de Faire; 1980. UGE, Paris.

Edgar, A., Sedgwick, P. (Eds.) Key Concepts in Cultural Theory; 1999. Routledge, London.

Edge, D. The social shaping of technology. In Heap, N., Thomas, R., Einon, G., Mason, R., Mackay, H. (Eds.), Information Technology and Society: A Reader; 1995. Sage, London: 14–32.

Flichy, P. L'innovation Technique; 1995. La Découverte, Paris.

Haddon, L. (Ed.) Communication on the move: The experience of mobile telephony in the 1990s. Report for COST 248; 1997, Telia, Farsta.

Hartmann, M. The web generation: The (de)construction of users, morals and consumption. EMTEL 2 Report; 2003.

Katz, J.E. (Ed.) Machines that Become Us. The Social Context of Personal Communication Technology; 2003. Transaction Publishers, New Brunswick.

Katz, J.E., Aakhus, M. (Eds.) Perpetual Contact. Mobile Communication, Private Talk and Public Performance; 2002. Cambridge University Press, Cambridge.

Ling, R. The Mobile Connection. The Cell Phone's Impact on Society; 2004. Elsevier, San Francisco, CA.

Livingstone, S. Young People and New Media; 2002. Sage, London.

Lorente, S. (Ed.) Juventud y teléfonos móviles, Revista de Estudios de Juventud 57; June 2002.

Mackay, H. Consuming communication technologies at home. In Mackay, H. (Ed.), Consumption and Everyday Life; 1997. Sage in Association with the Open University, London: 259–308.

MacKenzie, D., Wajcman, J. The Social Shaping of Technology; 1999. Open University Press, Buckingham, Philadelphia.

Nyíri, K. (Ed.) Mobile Democracy: Essays on Society, Self and Politics; 2003. Passagen Verlag, Vienna.

Pasquali, F. Metafore e immagini culturali di Internet. In Pasquali, F., Scifo, B. (Eds.), Consumare la Rete. Un'indagine Sulla Fruizione e la Navigazione del Web; 2004. Vita e Pensiero, Milan: 97–118.

Oudshoorn, N., Pinch, T. How Users Matter. The Co-construction of Users and Technology; 2003. The MIT Press, Cambridge, MA.

Rogers, E. Diffusion of Innovation, 4th edition; 1995. Free Press, New York.

Scifo, B. Domestication of camera phone and MMS communications: The early experiences of young Italians. In Nyíri, K. (Ed.), A Sense of Place; 2005. Passagen Verlag, Vienna.

Silverstone, R., Haddon, L. Design and the domestication of information and communication technologies: Technical change and everyday life. In Silverstone, R., Mansell, R. (Eds.), Communication by Design. The Politics of Information and Communication Technologies; 1996. Oxford University Press, Oxford: 44–74.

Silverstone, R., Hirsch, E., Morley, D. Information and communication technologies and the moral economy of the household. In Silverstone, R., Hirsch, E. (Eds.), Consuming Technologies: Media and Information in Domestic Spaces; 1992. Routledge, London, New York, NY: 15–33.

Williams, R. The social shaping of technology. In Dutton, W.H. (Ed.), Society on the Line: Information Politics in the Digital Age; 1999. Oxford University Press, New York: 41–43.

Woolgar, S. (Ed.) Virtual Society? Technology, Cyberbole, Reality; 2002. Oxford University Press, Oxford.

Chapter 7

CREATIVE USER-CENTERED DESIGN PRACTICES: LESSONS FROM GAME CULTURES

Olli Sotamaa

1.   Introduction

The field of Human Computer Interaction (HCI) studies has lately undergone some significant transitions. The focus of research has shifted from tasks to actions, from offices to the streets and the home, from laboratories to settings where people actually spend their time and from simple "ease of use" to evaluating the suitable level at which an activity should be challenging. Traditional design ideals have been confronted by visions of "affective computing" and HCI research has identified the central position of emotions in designing user experiences. Alongside the standard usability concerns there is an increasing interest in questions concerning enjoyment, fun and pleasure (cf. Blythe *et al.*, 2003; Jordan, 2002). Meanwhile, and elsewhere, academic game research has challenged the traditional usability methodologies by analyzing the components of pleasure in gaming. The concept of "social usability" has been introduced to acquire "a broader understanding of the ways and needs to use and consume media products, and the habits and practices associated with them" (Järvinen *et al.*, 2002, pp. 10–11). In search for criteria for evaluating "playability," Järvinen *et al.* suggest that alongside functional and structural factors one should study the audiovisual and social dimensions of games and gaming. In other words, current research in both fields is expanding our ideas about different types of emotion and pleasure to be experienced in relation to information and communication technologies (ICTs).

Widely adopted principles of user-centered and participatory design raise the perspectives of user and context of use to the center of the design process. Not only academic design studies but also business oriented analyses of innovation highlight the importance of observing real people in real life

Leslie Haddon (ed.), Everyday Innovators, 104–116.
© 2005 *Springer. Printed in The Netherlands.*

situations and encourage approaches that make user participation an insep- arable part of production (Kelley, 2002). Similarly, the games industry has rapidly learned to appreciate active and constant dialog between developers and gaming community. Gamers are allowed to alter the source code of games and create imaginative modifications of original games. A popular "mod" can significantly extend the life span of a game title. Furthermore, the global gam- ing community can also serve as an inexpensive research and development team.

Thereby, it seems obvious that game design and research on gaming culture can inform the design of emotionally satisfying and challenging ICT products in numerous ways. Still, as Clanton (2000) has pointed out, HCI designers and game developers have complementary skills but so far have few contacts and little awareness of one another. The objective of this chapter is to introduce games research to a wider design audience. I hope the examples encourage designers from various fields to think about the different types of active roles that users can play.

In this phase, we must pose the question: why is it important to take a look at computer games. I suggest, we can find more than one answer to this. First of all, from their origins and over the course of many years, computer games have always been in the front line in developing new means of interaction. Games from the 1970s text-based MUDs (Multi-User Dungeons) to the 21st century MMORPGs (Massively Multiplayer Online Role-Playing Games) have introduced forms of human–machine interaction and computer-mediated com- munication that are also widely used today outside gamer communities. Com- puter games are also pushing the development of new technologies through demanding superior graphic cards, graphic processing units, advanced gaming peripherals and so on. Furthermore, in pointing out the profound blurring of such categories as production and consumption, professionalism and passion, and work and leisure I suggest that game cultural activities already indicate the future relationship between people and new digital technologies.

Although games studies as an academic discipline is still in the making, the different approaches applied can provide interesting insights for people designing and researching satisfying user experiences more generally. Game studies examine why particular games inspire and excite and are fun to play. Other approaches focus on the meaning and significance of the games to the player looking at how games contribute to an understanding of oneself and other people and what the potential effects of games on social behavior are. The manifold dimensions of contemporary games require methodological diversity. First of all, games exist as products consisting of code and different features. Second, games can be approached by examining the experiences of particular gamers. Third, we can look at the larger cultural and social framework and the different interpretations and discourses that give significance to games (Mäyrä, 2002, pp. 5–6).

The emphasis of my approach is on studying players and game cultures. Players actively construct meanings and new ways of using games. They also create content for other gamers to consume. Simultaneously, particular industrial mechanisms attempt both to encourage and to control and regulate player innovation. Therefore, by analyzing what the players can and cannot do we have potential indicators of how the nature of new media user experience is changing and of what the wider scale transitions in the relationship between people and new digital technologies might be.

2.   Gaming and Culture

The particularity of games in general is based on the fact that they cannot simply be read or watched: they must be played. The creative involvement of the player is a fundamental feature of any game. In other words, the result of the game is highly dependant on the skills and creativity of the player (cf. Aarseth, 2001). Thus, the gaming experience is always constructed in a dialog between the player and the rules of the game. Yet, the general history of gaming includes a variety of interesting examples where existing rule systems and appearances of boards or cards have been modified in order to produce new games. Many traditional board games like backgammon or chess have appeared in several significantly different versions throughout the centuries. Also such an everyday example as a game of soccer played in the backyard shows that play as an activity seems to be open to various kinds of alterations: the soccer game can be played with a varied number of players, the duration of the game can be very flexible, almost any object at hand – be it a tree or a bag – can serve as a goal post, and so on. At the level of rules, games are made of more or less fixed structures. Still, playing them often consists of bending and reworking these rules. As Salen and Zimmerman (2003) point out:

> *Because a game by its very nature has room for the movement of free play, it is always possible for players to drive a wedge into the system, bending and transforming it into a new shape* (Salen and Zimmerman, 2003, p. 565).

In this connection, it is useful to recall that in recent decades several theoretical movements have been eager to highlight the fact that all media audiences are active and therefore they should be understood in terms of production, not of reception. Following this argument, it can be claimed that gamer-made designs can empower gamers and communities and help them to become active participants rather than passive consumers. On the other hand, the industrial context and practical developer choices can limit and regulate gamer activities. What we need here – as a growing literature has lately identified – is a closer integration of studies of media production and consumption. The meanings that new media technologies acquire are not fixed but are continuously nego-tiated through their life cycle. To arrive at a profound picture of the meanings attached to artifacts and media texts neither processes of production nor forms of consumption should be privileged (Deacon, 2003; du Gay *et. al.*,1997).

Furthermore, I suggest that to understand contemporary games requires examining them in relation to the qualities of new media more broadly. As Manovich (2001) points out, digital media objects are open for algorithmic manipulation and therefore media have become programmable. In the con-text of computer games, this leads us in two different directions. First of all, programmability brings us back to the issue already emphasized by Aarseth, namely the nature of computer games as simulations. In brief, "the story" or "the result" of a game is not determined beforehand but has to be understood as a process. The idea of programmability is also tied to the processes of decentralization and personalization that make the daily media environment more fragmented. According to Lister *et al.* (2003) until the 1990s there was a rigid separation between what was acceptable for public distribution and what was acceptable for personal, domestic exhibition (e.g. to friends). Lately, the so-called "prosumer technologies," aimed not only at professionals but also hobbyists, have made the production accessible to a wider range of people. Powerful and inexpensive machines are today available to the hobbyists so that they can easily experiment with editing and mixing media contents.

As Kamppuri and Tukiainen (2004) point out in their study, "culture" is a relatively recent concept in the field of HCI research. HCI was originally heavily built on cognitive science and therefore cultural, social and historical contexts were mostly excluded from its research agenda. The cultural perspective has risen in significance during the past decade but the uses of the concept have still been varied. Often culture is still taken for granted, or else it is limited to national cultures and seen as coherent wholes (Kamppuri and Tukiainen, 2004, pp. 43–44, 53). In order to produce an alternative perspective I suggest we take a look at how game researchers have approached culture.

On a general level "culture" can be defined as social and symbolic meaning-making. From this perspective game cultures are not restricted to interactions with technological systems but encompasses all the player activities and deal-ings connected to gaming. Often new game cultures and cultural qualities arise in relation to particular games and game genres. Therefore, rather than speak-ing of a single coherent computer game culture, different game cultures can be interpreted as "subcultures." The cultural studies tradition defines subcultures as groups of people who share interests, values and practices. Important mark-ers include a particular language, shared rituals and interests in collecting and producing artifacts that promote one's belonging to a group. This understanding of subculture comes very close to fandom and fan activities – but we will come back to this connection in a moment (cf. Mäyrä, 2004, pp. 4–7). Furthermore, Salen and Zimmerman (2003) introduce two ways of understanding games as culture: in terms of reflection and transformation. As any system of representation, computer and video games reflect existing values and ideologies: games oversimplify and construct biased views but they can also be used to educate and introduce ethical dilemmas (see for example, newsgaming.com). On the other hand, by introducing new forms of expression games have a potential to transform their surrounding contexts. From the player perspective this implies that player activities are not restricted to creative in-game play. In the words of Salen and Zimmerman, *games offer players forms of participation that extend the boundaries of play beyond the edges of a magic circle* (Salen and Zimmerman, 2003, p. 507).

Gamer-made contents and designs can play a significant role in the gamer's life-world, but at least according to the game press they also have a potential to change the whole composition of the game industry (cf. Edge, 2003). In fact, as Haddon points out in Chapter 4, in the case of computer games there is a rather thin line between user and designer. In the following, I introduce a couple of telling examples from the history of computer games. These examples attempt to demonstrate the significance of hobbyist activities in particular cases. After that I take a closer look at the different manifestations of player innovation.

3.   Player Innovation

The urge to modify existing computer systems can be tracked at least back to the first generation of hackers. According to journalist Steven Levy, who has studied the early hackers of the 1960s and 1970s, a hack is *a project undertaken or a product built not solely to fulfil some constructive goal, but with some wild pleasure taken in mere involvement* (Levy, 1984/1994, p. 23). Thus, the hacker approach to computers was right from the beginning very different from the official one: instead of seeing computers as tools, the hackers treated the early machines as if they were toys. Hacking is often understood as an action involving a high level of enthusiasm and enjoyment but the resulting "hacks" can also be entertaining. In the context of this article, it is noteworthy that Levy sees the first modern computer game *Spacewar!* (1962) as being one of the most significant early hacks. *Spacewar!*, built on the minicomputer PDP-1 by MIT students, was partly based on the innovative use of earlier program code. Even the controls for the game were hacked from push-buttons used for 1940s telephones. Typical of the exploratory projects of the time, *Spacewar!* was freely distributed to other PDP-1 owners to play and to rewrite (Haddon, 1988, pp. 55–57; Levy, 1984/1994, pp. 50–69). As *Spacewar!* shows, early computer games were important vehicles for learning about computers and programming. Exploring games helped to understand the potential of the machines. Tinkering with computers and improving the existing algorithms went hand in hand with playing games. Games posed challenges and puzzles that were somewhat like programming itself (Haddon, 1988, pp. 58–59). In other words, in the early days of computer gaming – as they moved from mainframes and from minicomputers to microcomputers – modifying games was an organic part of the gamer life-world. The arrival of the first microcomputers (mid-1970s to early 1980s) introduced programming manuals that widely used games as a vehicle to explain the structure of computer languages. At the same time, computer magazines presented games as a suitable activity for relaxing in the midst of programming. Early magazines not only reviewed games but they also offered tips on how to break into the programming structure and make the games operate differently. At first, games were mainly both produced and consumed by early microcomputer hobbyists. The introduction of cassette technology made it possible to save and distribute the gamer-made alterations. This had not been possible in the case of earlier home video game machines. At least in the UK the cheap cassette technology also encouraged the hobbyists to found the first mail order ventures selling entertainment software (ibid., pp. 59, 69–70).

For a slightly more recent example, we can look at Id Software's Doom (1993). Already Id's earlier first-person shooter *Wolfenstein 3-D* (1992) had inspired modified gamer-made versions, which according to David Kushner's *Masters of Doom*, were in turn a source of inspiration for the developers at Id software. To give one example, there was a version where the game music had been replaced by a theme song from the children's show Barney and instead of the SS boss character, players encountered a smiling purple dinosaur (Kushner, 2003, pp. 115–116). In *Wolfenstein* this kind of replacement always required erasing parts of the original code. Once a picture was changed, there was no easy way to bring the original back. In the case of *Doom*, the media files were intentionally separated from the main program and located in an accessible directory. This reorganizing of game data made it possible to replace sounds and graphics in a non-destructive manner. Id programmer John Carmack also facilitated the amateur designers by making available the source code for the level-editing and utilities program. In only a matter of weeks gamers began swapping *Doom* modifications or "mods" and "homebrew" or amateur editing tools on Bulletin Boards and across the Internet. (Ibid., pp. 165–169.)

These examples show that enthusiastic users can have a significant role in the development of new technologies. Users appropriate technologies in various ways other than the designers originally intended. In Chapter 4 of this book, Leslie Haddon explores innovative use of ICTs and produces a tentative grouping of the different ways in which users can be creative or innovative. I suggest Haddon's four-level categorization can be used as a starting point in introducing and evaluating different types of innovation taking place among gamers.

The first level includes designing and re-designing ICTs and applications. Haddon associates this level with technologically skilled and often enthusiastic users. A telling example from games culture is the phenomenon noted above called "modding." "Mods" and "modders" come in many forms. Console gamers install "mod chips" to their systems. These programmed microcontrollers bypass the region code system that the game industry has created to control the international markets. In addition, hardware modding is not limited to allowing gamers to play imported games but in the hands of a creative hobbyist the games console can become a versatile video player, mp3 jukebox, or a personal game archive. Some gamers also use significant amounts of time and energy on "case modding": decorating and altering the semblance of their gaming devices. While hardware modding has so far been limited to fairly small groups of enthusiasts, game content modifications have been a great success all over the world. The digital nature of games allows them to be manipulated and reprogrammed – even by individual consumers. Players personalize the appearance of their in-game characters by creating models and skins and create new maps and adventures based on existing game titles. For example, sports game fans create detailed copies of national and local leagues including player statistics, uniforms, and stadiums. Moreover, modders also develop and share new tools and editors that enable production of more sophisticated modifications.

Turning to the next level in Haddon's categorization, innovation need not be merely technological, but it can also consist of introducing new practices and doing new things with technology. "Machinima" films are a fairly recent example of this from games culture. These computer-generated animations utilize game engines to create virtual 3-D environments. Machinima films come in several genres: some films follow a narrative plot while others are mostly experimenting with the modified engine features. Similarly games like *The Sims* (Maxis, 2000, PC) are no longer used merely for playing but gamers also use them as a medium for producing and distributing contents of their own.

The various ways in which online games are making use of the Internet provide a good example of practices that exceed the objectives that global information networks were originally intended to fulfil. No longer are people playing alone but they connect with other gamers via the Internet to compete and share experiences. Text-based adventure games called MUDs, short for Multi-User Dungeons, originated in the late 1970s and introduced communication patterns that today are widely used in chats and other real-time online environments. Furthermore, networked multi-player games are very social in nature and inspire gamers to unite. While role-playing games and shooter games give birth to clans, tribes and guilds, sports games are played in local and global teams and leagues. Here, we move towards the next level. Gaming as a hobby often finds its expression in online forums and personal websites. Gamer groups and individual gamers regularly update thousands of websites to promote the achievements of a particular clan, to share the significant pieces of information (patch updates, walkthroughs, strategy guides, etc.) and to keep in contact with other gamers.

Finally, some innovations reside not in improving the performance of technology or in creating new forms of gaming, but in groups of gamers creating complex sets of practices and negotiating the meanings around gaming technologies. Sometimes finding a time and a place to play can itself require some creativity in everyday life. It is important to bear in mind that these categories of user innovation obviously overlap. In the following we move on to examine how innovative gamers both follow and challenge the theories of media fandom.

4.   Fans and Modders

Fandom and fan cultural formations are traditionally associated with "cultural forms that the dominant value system denigrates" (Fiske, 1992, p. 30). Therefore, it is no surprise that such typical objects of fandom as pop music, television series, movies and cartoons have recently been accompanied by modern computer games, all being the ideal commodities of digital popular culture. Fans draw their resources from commercial media culture while also reworking them to serve alternative purposes. In his influential study, Henry Jenkins borrows de Certeau's term "poaching" to characterize the relationship between fans and corporate producers of media texts as "an ongoing struggle for possession of the text and for control over its meanings" (Jenkins, 1992, p. 24). Later on, Jenkins suggests that "[f]andom originates, at least in part, as a response to the relative powerlessness of the consumer in relation to powerful institutions of cultural production and circulation" (ibid., p. 278).

The history of media fandom can at least partly be seen as the history of a series of efforts to influence programming decisions (ibid., p. 28). In this connection, in order to examine the collective power of the gaming community, we can look at the case of the *Babylon 5* computer game. On September 1999, Sierra studios cancelled the production of the long-awaited computer game, *Babylon 5: Into The Fire. Babylon 5* fans organized a worldwide boycott of Sierra titles and gave all their support to the game development team. With the encouragement of this large community, the developers of the game formed their own company to continue the project. Eventually it proved impossible to get the rights to the original material but several fan-created freeware games and B5-themed game modifications have later seen the light. When pressuring industry proved to be difficult, gamers themselves took on the role of programmers and producers. My point here is that innovative gamers, who rework and develop further the products of the games industry, share characteristics with fans of other media texts and therefore earlier fan ethnographies can assist in understanding the motivations and strategies behind gamer actions. At the same time, other forms of fandom offer a useful point of comparison that can highlight important differences and clarify the particularities of game cultures.

As mentioned earlier, the theory of "active audiences" has emphasized the productive nature of all media use. Still, fans hold a particular position in relation to media texts since their productivity often takes a textual and material form: they create things. The commitment of fans is manifested in various ways. Fans write stories, "fanfiction," using characters and settings of some original media presentation (film, television series, computer game, etc.). Similarly fan paintings, songs, and videos comment on the original industry produced texts and add new meanings and points of view on them. Today, the forms of fan creativity often have counterparts in games culture ranging from themed websites to image manipulations, collages and Machinima films. Abercrombie and Longhurst have studied television audiences and produced a five-class classification (Abercrombie and Longhurst, 1998). If we apply this schema to the context of gaming culture *consumers* are the ones who occasionally play games and see them as one leisure time activity among others. In case of the *fan*, gaming becomes an inseparable part of everyday life. *Cultists* see gaming and being part of gaming community as a central element of identity while for an *enthusiast* gaming and talking about games becomes subordinated to producing them. To clarify what this means in context we can turn to my interviews among computer game mod makers. When asked about the influences of modding they often highlighted the fact that the time spent on playing had significantly diminished and launching the game mostly meant that some new component had to be tested. (Sotamaa, 2004). In the case of *petty producers*, cultural production is no longer random but the skills are marketed to an imagined community – the members of particular gaming culture (cf. Järvinen, 2003). Applying this classification helps us to see that players hold very different positions and sets of skills in relation to games. Therefore, instead of seeing gamer communities as coherent and homogenous groups, game cultures seem to consist of different subgroups with complementary roles.

Just over 10 years ago, Henry Jenkins noted that *fans lack direct access to the means of commercial cultural production and have only the most limited resources with which to influence the entertainment industry's decisions* (Jenkins, 1992, p. 26). In the same manner John Fiske wrote:

(F)ans do not write or produce their texts for money; indeed, their productivity typically costs them money. Economics, too, limits the equipment to which fans have access for the production of their texts, which may therefore often lack the technical smoothness of professionally-produced ones. There is also a difference in circulation; because fan texts are not produced for profit, they do not need to be mass-marketed, so unlike official culture, fan culture makes no attempt to circulate its texts outside its own community (Fiske, 1992, p. 39).

Investigating the contemporary game scene immediately indicates that the landscape of fan culture has developed during the past decade. The networked

PC has opened a variety of new possibilities and caused visible changes in everyday fan activities. One of the traditional claims of the fan critics is that fan cultural texts are not produced to make profit. Indeed, earlier fan activities were mainly discussed in fan conventions and copies of texts were circulated in the fan community. This system with its own rules for production and distribution is called a "shadow cultural economy" by Fiske. Today the Internet is extensively used both for distribution of materials and as a platform for discussion. Furthermore, industrial media companies have been eager to bring the petty productions of fan culture from the "subcultural shadows" into the "mainstream light."

A well-known example of the development described above is the Star Wars Fan Movie Awards, a yearly competition organized by Atomfilms in partnership with Lucasfilms – the producer of the official Star Wars movies. Those fan filmmakers who win an award receive a commercial distribution contract that guarantees them legitimate royalty payments. In addition, from the production company's point of view the awards offer an important opportunity to control and regulate fan production. Epic Games and Atari Inc. jointly announced a big modding competition in the summer of 2003. *"Make Something Unreal"* was organized together with Nvidia to generate modifications to Epic's popular first person shooters Unreal Tournament 2003 and UT 2004. While offering considerable prizes and significant publicity opportunities for the winning mod groups the companies also obviously expect to increase the sales of the games and the latest Nvidia graphic processors.

The game development kits that modders use are often released with commercial PC games. Tools are often available for free downloading via the official game websites. It is also quite common for modders to create tools of their own. This is not something entirely new, since games from the early 1980s like *Lode Runner* (Broderbund, 1983, C-64) already included editors that allowed players to create additional levels. The Commodore 64 scene also witnessed such titles as *Boulder Dash Construction Kit* (First Star Software, 1986), a tool set inspired by the popular *Boulder Dash* game series and a generic shooter editor *Shoot-Em-Up Construction Kit* (Sensible Software, 1987). Mods are typically downloaded from the Internet for free but they do not normally work without the retail version of the original game. Therefore a popular mod can significantly extend the life span and the sales of a game title and assist in developing a devoted fan base. The games industry has so far been mostly unwilling to estimate the commercial significance of an enthusiastic mod community but the various ways in which modding is encouraged and supported suggests that companies see some value in modder activities (Postigo, 2003,p. 596, 603). Particularly successful works of the mod community can make the jump from being a mod to a retail title. Probably the most well known example of this is *Counterstrike* (2000), a team play modification of *Half-Life* (Valve Software,

1999). Furthermore, from the games industry point of view the mod community can serve as an inexpensive research and development team. During the year 2002 members of top mod teams all over the world were flown to Electronic Arts' Westwood Studio*s* for a full day Mod College aimed at informing the mod community about the new game engine.

5.   Discussion

The very well-known quotation from usability guru Jakob Nielsen says that *"users are not designers"* (Nielsen, 1993, p. 12). In brief, this means that one should not expect users to be able to design things and therefore the input they give should not be regarded as an unquestionable truth. I suggest that computer game mods reflect a very different design policy. At least some game developers and producers regard game development as an iterative process in which modders' observations, suggestions, and designs are used as an invaluable resource. Instead of analyzing user needs and validating user requirements, which is typical of traditional user-centered design approaches, the tools are given to the users and fiddling and experimenting with them is encouraged.

Similar approaches have also emerged lately in other high-tech fields. In academic terms, this phenomenon has been discussed under the title "Toolkits for user innovation" (see Thomke and von Hippel, 2002; von Hippel and Katz, 2002). The pioneers of this approach emphasize the point that toolkits for innovation have existed for a long time since developers and designers are normally equipped with suitable tools. Many users also have personal toolsets that can be applied to modify and repair existing products and to create new ones. What is new and unique in the toolkits for user innovation is the integration of user toolsets that can customize products and enable users to produce the designs "as is" by manufacturers (von Hippel and Katz, 2002, p. 825). In connection to mods, this means that the user-driven content generated following the rules embedded in a tool kit will be compatible with original code and immediately available for sharing.

I suggest that from the industry point of view, this invitation to experiment arises not only from an interest in learning what gamers want or learning to recognize and exploit the groups whose work has proven popular among this community. Developers also want to learn that their work is appreciated and that there is a worldwide community developing their project further. I hope this can also produce a wider understanding of the games industry as a field that consists not only of manufacturers, game development studios and distribution companies but also of an enthusiastic crowd of skilled hobbyists (Postigo 2003, pp. 595–596). Enabling users to develop new features for games can have a significant effect on the tasks of game industry professionals. Instead of developing new variations and combinations of existing game types in order to satisfy the needs of the increasing variety of specified target groups, developers can leave at least a part of that job to mod developers. Mods can experiment with ideas that are too "obscure" or "far out" for mainstream productions and the ones that prove to be popular in the market can be picked for official release. On the other hand, the increase of detail in contemporary games has already caused a huge increase in the workload of mod developers. Instead of single virtuosos we already witness the rise of large global development teams. Coordinating and facilitating such teams places new challenges both on mod community members and on the game development professionals. It seems likely that even more complex symbioses between media companies and individual media (prod)users will arise.

From the player perspective the maturing of the games industry has produced new and interesting possibilities. In some cases gaming can shift from being a hobby to a full-time job. Video game tournaments with considerable prizes and sports-like national teams training several hours per day can transform gaming into a serious business. Some game developers have openly admitted that today mod projects are often used as a portfolio when applying for a job in the games industry. I would like to end this chapter with a quotation from an interview I conducted during the summer of 2004. In my opinion, this excerpt shows clearly that through designing their own projects young gamers can learn not only particular skills but also a more mature attitude towards games and the game industry.

> It [modding] has made me more aware of the little details in a game. Also instead of being interested in whether an item could be killed I am now more interested in how it's made. [—] OFP [computer game Operation Flashpoint] has made me realize that it is not so great as it first seamed, there's a lot of hard work involved, and you have good days and you have bad days. I would have to say that OFP has given me the lust to try and get a job within the game industry, but it has also in a strange way showed me that it is a serious commitment and you have to be incredibly dedicated.... so in that way it has also scared me away from a job within the gaming industry in that aspect (Modder, aged 15).

References

Aarseth, E. Computer game studies, year one. Game Studies, 1(1) (July 2001). Available at http://www.gamestudies.org/0101/editorial.html; 2001.

Abercrombie, N., Longhurst, B. Audiences: A Sociological Theory of Performance and Imagination; 1998 Sage, London, Thousand Oaks and New Delhi.

Blythe, M.A., et al. (Eds.) Funology: from usability to enjoyment, 2003. Kluwer Academic Publishers, Dordrecht and Boston.

Clanton, C. Lessons from game design. In Bergman, E.(Ed.) Information Appliances and Beyond: Interaction Design for Consumer Product; (2000) Morgan Kaufmann Publishers, San Fransisco: 299–334.

Deacon, D. "Holism, communion and conversion: integrating media consumption and production research". Media, Culture and Society, 2003; 25: 209–231.

du Gay, P., et al. Doing Cultural Studies: The Story of Sony Walkman; 1997. Sage, London, Thousand Oaks and New Delhi.

Edge The future of electronic entertainment, 126 (8/2003), 2003.

Fiske, J. The cultural economy of fandom. In Lewis, L.A. (Ed.) The Adoring Audience: Fan Culture and Popular Media. Routledge, London and New York: 30–49.

Haddon, L. Electronic and computer games: the history of an interactive medium. Screen, 1988; 29(2): 52–73.

Järvinen, A., Heliö, S., Mäyrä, F. Community and communication in digital entertainment services. Hypermedia Laboratory Net Series 2, University of Tampere. Available at http://tampub.uta.fi/teos.phtml?7310; 2002.

Järvinen, A Verkkopelien ABC – Doomista MMORPGiin, Quakesta roolipeleihin, mediumi 2.1. Available at http://www.m-cult.net/mediumi/article.html?id=231andlang=fiandissue_nr=2.2 andissueId=15; 2003.

Jenkins, H. Textual Poachers: Television Fans and Participatory Culture; 1992. Routledge, New York and London.

Jordan, P.W. Human factors for pleasure seekers. In Frascara, J. (Ed.) Design and the Social Sciences: Making Connections; 2002 Taylor and Francis, London and New York: 9–23.

Kamppuri, M., Tukiainen, M. Culture in human–computer interaction studies. In Sudweeks , Ess (Eds.) Proceedings cultural attitudes towards communication and technology, Murdoch University, Australia: 43–57.

Kelley, T. The Art of Innovation: Lessons in Creativity from IDEO, America's Leading Design Firm; 2002. Harper Collins Business, London.

Kushner, D. Masters of Doom: How Two Guys Created an Empire and Transformed Pop Culture; 2003. Random House, New York.

Levy, S. Hackers: Heroes of the Computer Revolution; 1984/1994. Delta, New York.

Lister, M., et al. New media: a critical introduction; 2003. Routledge, London and New York.

Manovich, L. Language of New Media; 2001. MIT Press, Cambridge, Mass. and London.

Mäyrä, F. Introduction: all your base are belong to us. In Mäyrä, F. (Ed.) Computer Games and Digital Cultures Conference Proceedings. Studies in Information Sciences; 2002, Tampere University Press, Tampere: 5–8

Mäyrä, F. Introduction and prehistory of digital games. Unpublished course material for Master's Course in Digital Games Research and Design. University of Tampere, Hypermedia Laboratory, 2004.

Nielsen, J. Usability Engineering; 1993 Academic Press, Boston.

Postigo, H. From Pong to Planet Quake: post industrial transitions from leisure to work. Information, Communication and Society, 2003; 6(4): 593–607.

Salen, K., Zimmerman, E. Rules of Play: Game Design Fundamentals; 2003. MIT Press, Cambridge, Mass. and London.

Sotamaa, O. Playing it My Way? Mapping The Agency of Modders. Presentation at Internet Research 5.0 Conference, University of Sussex, UK, September, 19–22, 2004.

Thomke, S., von Hippel, E. Customers as innovators: a new way to create value. Harward Business Review, 2002; 80(2): 5–11.

von Hippel, E., Katz, R. Shifting innovation to users via toolkits. Management Science, 2002; 48(7): 821–833.

INNOVATION AND ARTISTIC USERS

Artists provide a strategic case for thinking about the active role of users since their identity and daily artistic practices require them to explore what it means to be creative. They form a community that is arguably even more likely than many other users to explore the potential uses of ICTs, ones that may be neither intended nor realized in a mass market. Emmanuel Mahé constructs this argument, and details the specificity of the artist's experience, illustrating this with past and contemporary examples. Heli Rantavuo address related issues through considering the choices that student artists made when contributing to a particular exhibition. However, while artist's innovative horizons may be wider than many of the general public, both chapters illustrate various ways in which that vision and the direction of any creative use is also itself socially shaped.

Mahé examines the role of the artist as innovator, someone who acts as a deviant user of artifacts while at the same time operating within strong artistic norms. This enables the artist to imagine future, potential technical configurations and uses of technology. Mahé starts by looking at the field of technological artistic practices, outlining what is specific about this field. He illustrates what variation it contains and ultimately why these practices collectively should be characterized by the broad term "tekhne-logical arts" rather than just referring to them as video art, computer art, etc. These arts are always testing and reflecting upon the use of techniques and technology. While "use" is a very flexible word, "artistic use" is often associated with the process of using familiar objects in novel ways, "appropriating" them, or "diverting" them from their original intended purpose. So while non-artist users can use technologies in unintended ways, the difference is the case of art is that the artist sets out to do so, subverting the intended use in an act that can be described as "poaching."

Mahé examines the example of artists appropriating a technology, a particular type of camcorder – *Pixelvision* – that had been originally aimed at children but had failed in the commercial market. Part of the reason for this may well have been the poor picture and sound quality of this rather low-tech innovation, but it was precisely these qualities that appealed to artists because they enabled certain forms of artistic expression. In particular, Mahé details its innovative use by the artist Sadie Benning and the particular way that the device fitted into her life, before these practices became a mainstream artistic current. Since then the technology has itself been further transformed. The chapter then provides other examples of this type of poaching of technologies by artists – with concepts such as "pick-ups" and "traced uses." It specifies in what ways poaching does and does not follow from a longer artistic lineage – i.e. what is different about this modern poaching even within artistic conventions. After reviewing a history of how craftsman evolved into modern liberal artists, Mahé argues that the modern teckne artist has recaptured some of the old craft elements, as a digital age craftsperson. In the on-going artistic process, the artist creates unforeseen techniques – hence the appeal to ICT R&D departments. Both the departments and the artists then have to justify this collaboration, which can be best characterized as a being form of bricolage, a wandering, looking at things here and there, as when people "surf" the Internet. Here the role of the artist is often no just to develop particular uses for ICTs but rather to help explore whole new fields.

Rantavuo looks at the different ways in which, and the extent to which, art student and design students with an interest in photographic art were innovative in their use of camera phones when preparing for an exhibition in Helsinki. The point is, the students were explicitly given the task of exploring the new medium and so Rantavuo was interested in how they viewed these technologies and why their degree of innovation was, in practice, limited.

More generally in their everyday lives, the students in this study saw the camera phone as being first and foremost just another type of mobile phone, rather than being a more radical innovation that would change the nature of communication. This reflected one of the representations discussed in an earlier chapter by Colombo and Scifo. The camera function could be useful for enabling more spontaneous pictures.

But when the students turned their attention to the task at hand, preparing for the exhibition, they ignored the telephony dimension and focused on using the camera function for photography. The main emphasis was on producing photographic art. Operating within this frame of reference, the phone camera was seen to have limitations compared to other cameras. Sending multimedia messages was, for the most part, not considered as being interesting or serious from an artist's perspective. Instead, it was a mundane, albeit fun, light-hearted activity that they and others occasionally engaged in during their free time. Moreover, Rantavuo suggests, it was not that they had not thought about multimedia messaging's potential as an art form – they made the decision to dismiss MMS as such, given the wider connotations of messaging as being ephemeral and trivial.

There was one exception, an exhibit that did involve multimedia messaging. Although some students took the initiative, this was the exhibit in which the whole team participated. So the question arises as to why this particular initiative involved a willingness to make use of messaging. Rantavuo notes that part of the answer may lie in the fact that many of the students had already produced their main exhibit – in a sense they had passed a test – and they could feel a little more relaxed over this second project. In fact, the students experienced the most technical difficulties in this project due to the telephony dimension, especially the processing capacity of the network.

But in addition, to make a connection with the findings of other researchers including Battarbee and Kurvinen in this volume, this particular project was more of a group product, which could itself stimulate interest and creativity. Conversely, although the students occasionally used picture messaging in their everyday lives, it was never an established practice since they did not use it when contacting others in the group, not did the move in wider social circles of people who regularly sent such messages.

Lastly, Rantavuo, like Mahé, discusses how artists are innovative on many levels. This means not only exploring the technical nature of devices, but also exploring how the artist can experiment with the wider meanings of these ICTs. This mode of innovation can complement more traditional design work or user research in the field of innovation, and it can be potentially fruitful for companies. But it is also specific, requiring open-mindedness and dedication when exploring the possibilities of ICTs. That said, Rantavuo demonstrated that while artists, in this case artistic students, may be innovative users, they too innovate within certain artistic frameworks – as noted by Mahé. In this case, the students were influenced by certain notions about what counts as art. And perhaps their willingness to innovate is also constrained during the earlier stages of their careers, when they were still trying to prove themselves.

Chapter 8

ARTISTIC DEVIANCE AND INNOVATION IN USE

Emmanuel Mahé

1.   Introduction

1.1.   *Technologized Artistic Practices*

Technological artistic practices have become more widespread over the past few years, especially in the domain of "web art" and digital art. An ever-increasing number of artists, from well-known artists such as Nam June Paik or Jeffery Shaw to lesser known artists such as Magali Desbazeille, are using new technology and putting it to the test, sometimes creating new technologies themselves. These practices constitute, in our eyes, a specific and interesting field of study for at least two reasons. It is interdisciplinary, ranging from choreography, to music, to visual arts, to sociology, to engineering and marketing. Yet it is also specific: specialized networks have been developing for more than 30 years in the field of video art, Web art and multimedia art.

The paradox arising from the fact that it is both heterogeneous and specific creates a critical space in all senses of the word. Firstly, it is critical because of the very difficulties of constituting itself as a field in its own right. Secondly, it involves a form of art criticism (entailing reflexivity, autonomy and specificity). Thirdly, it provides a critical testing ground, which may be either positive or negative (thinking of the critical postures of artists or theorists).

The objective of this chapter is not to create a general typology of innovating artistic uses, but rather to show how artistic practices are perceived as being "deviant" or in "shift" with respect to non-artistic social standards. This makes it possible to establish (or demolish) a history of the social uses of techniques and to create the necessary preconditions of new ones. In other words, artists anticipate future social uses by overturning traditional user manuals or by

Leslie Haddon (ed.), Everyday Innovators, 121–135.
© 2005 *Springer. Printed in The Netherlands.*

creating new technical solutions. They prefigure tomorrow's uses, which do not exist today, by imagining new technical configurations.

In the rest of the chapter, the artistic works chosen as examples, taken from 1980 to 2000, are heterogeneous in terms of both form and the techniques used by the artists. Two types of analyses are proposed here. The first, more traditional, analysis examines works that have already been completed. The other emphasizes the need to observe the process of artistic creation. This is structured around two principal concepts, those of "poaching" and "bricolage." As a theoretical background, we explore the idea of "tekhne-logical" esthetics, a concept which needs to be further constructed and enriched.

1.2.   Tekhne-logical Art

Before developing our central assumption, we need to specify the underlying idea behind the classification "tekhne-logical arts." Some contemporary artistic practices make both technology and technique components of the creation process. Artists from different backgrounds such as Kasper Toepliz, Atau Tanaka, Sadie Benning, Magali Desbazeille, Siegfried Canto, Marnix de Nijs, Edwin van der Heide, and others, work both with and on the technologies that they use.

The word "technology" comes from "tekhne" (*art* in Greek) and from "logos" (*thought*). "Technique" means a practical method, skill or art applied to a particular task. It includes working methods, some of which are well specified or "codified," such as a mountaineer's technique or a violinist's technique, for example. But it also implies associated tools and technical devices. Engineers, for example, establish a "state of the art" in order to become acquainted with recent developments of a particular technique. Meanwhile, the word "technology" encompasses associated texts and their underlying theoretical bases.

In fact, we do not adopt a rigid distinction between technique and technology because this either implies social determinisms or technical determinisms. To avoid this rigid division, we note that some artistic practices are either "tekhne-logical" but not particularly technical (e.g. electronic, videographic, numerical, etc.) or alternatively they can be specifically technological (e.g. pure texts on technique). They thus involve technical uses (e.g. using a computer, a video camera, etc.) as much as social uses. And they involve texts as well as their accompanying imagery or structure. Tekhne-logical art produces *technical machines* ("installations" and "devices" are terms frequently used in the field of contemporary art) which are at the same time *social machines* (Deleuze and Parnet, 1996).

"Tekhne-logical" art is unlike other, more homogeneous, artistic fields. It is characterized by a wide variety of practical as well as theoretical approaches. But it is also unusual in that it specifies not only one social space (with its own symbolic systems) but also the places, *the topos*, where we can examine artistic practices of "diversion" (to be elaborated below) and the appropriation of contemporary technological devices. We thus prefer to use this broad definition of tekhne-logical art instead of the stricter definitions commonly used by some critics and artists (e.g., "Video art," "Numerical art," "Computer art," "Net art," "Interactive art," etc).

This art is not defined so much by the techniques used, which are countless, but rather by *its propensity to consider the technique, to test it, and, we could say, 'to feel it.'* Using technical devices or technical communication objects, or creating them, is part of the process of artistic thought in action. Tekhne-logical art is creating a theoretical and a practical field, one that is critical of contemporary techniques and technologies.

2.   Poached Uses

How do artists use technical devices? And what uses are we speaking about? The term "use" has many meanings. It simultaneously indicates both uses where there are conventions, social codes, instructions, etc. and also those uses where individuals or groups appropriate a tool, a technical device or any other technical fitting in novel ways. This "plastic function" (Souchier and Jeanneret, 2001) of the term "use" is an asset but it is also a limitation. It is an asset because it does not limit use to one single category, it means the term is flexible. But it is a limitation in the sense that it may lead to misunderstandings due to a lack of clarity as regards its exact meaning.

Art is, in fact, subject to very strong normalization. This means that there are many conventions surrounding the ways in which artists explore tools and devices (even for avant-gardist artists). We therefore need to avoid the trap of assuming total artistic freedom cut off from all standards, be they artistic or technological. It appears that the concept of "artistic use" is often associated with that of "appropriation" and, more precisely, "appropriation by diversion." The idea that an artist diverts tools from their original intended use (i.e. the use as illustrated by the user manual) is a direct result of 20th century artistic practices. Artists such as Marcel Duchamp or Rauschenberg took manufactured objects and diverted them from their "normal" social function. A urinal or a bed – or any other object for that matter – could become a work of art. What are today's diversions? How do they take place and how do they come to materially modify the technologies used (e.g. by "tampering" with them, making technical changes, creating new layouts, devising new technical solutions, creating new tools, or new elements for the device, etc.)?

In everyday life, there is often a difference between what was envisaged by the creator and how end users make use of the device, which is a central theme of this book and a point raised, in different contexts, by many of the other contributors. The difference in the case of art is intentionality: the artist often intentionally circumvents the product instructions in order to "extract" effects or results that are very different to those envisaged by the producers. Technologies that are marketed are often assigned a precise function and, very often, their intended social use is illustrated. For example, Fisher Price camcorders were initially intended for children. New visualization technologies (e.g., C.A.V.E., magnetic resonance imagery, "force feedback" interfaces, etc.) are usually intended for industrial, military, or medical applications. And yet, in each of these cases, artists seized upon these techniques and made unforeseen use of the apparatus. A significant example of this technical and social "deviance" – a form of "poaching" of uses as defined by Michel De Certeau (1980) – is the early videographic work of Sadie Benning at the end of the 1980s.

2.1.   Benning: Technical and Social Deviance

The videographic work of Sadie Benning tells the history of what was initially an intimate and private appropriation of technology that has since become largely public: that of the camcorder. The first transportable video camera with a separate video tape recorder that was aimed at the general public was the *Portapack*. Marketed in Japan in 1965 and in the United States and Europe in 1966, the *Portapack* was a technical innovation targeted at the general public both as a "technological advance" but also as a potential political and artistic source of counter power[1] and of social advance – or, at least, that was how it was perceived at the time. There was a correlation between the technical innovation (a transportable video equipment at a reduced price) and the innovation in use (through artistic research, political struggles, and struggles for identity).

Twenty years later, video cameras and then the camcorder became widespread once there were stable standards (mainly VHS and Hi8) and cheaper selling prices. In the mid-1980s, a toy manufacturer, Fisher Price, decided to sell a camcorder intended for children called the *Pxl-2000*. The recording system was clever: the camcorder was reduced in size and running costs were also lowered by replacing the bulky VHS cassette with an audiocassette. The major disadvantage, underestimated by the manufacturer, was the bad picture and sound quality. The magnetic tape in the audio cassette had initially been intended for audio recording only and so passed at a much greater speed in front of the recording head in order to be able to record sufficient audio and video signals. The result was a small, very pixellized black and white video image

---

[1] In particular Jean-Luc Gordard who gave video cameras to French factory workmen to create "video flyers." Many other militant artists or activists seized hold of this tool to create a form of anti-television (for example, the video called the "100 flowers" collective in France, the Wnet-TV "New Television Laboratory" in New York City, etc.).

located in the center of the screen in the shape of a small rectangle surrounded by a broad black frame. The sound included the noise of the cassette's motor drive since the tape speed was much higher than usual. The extremely poor picture and sound are now famous in the artistic community.

In this case, this technical innovation was, in fact, a return to older, low tech techniques associated with the audiocassette that dated from the 1960s and were invented by Philips. The innovative aspect of this device was that it was a "camera toy," rather than lying in the technical elements that made it up. The principal innovation, in line with people's contemporary wishes, was an innovation in terms of use. It allowed young children to have their own video camera, i.e. to gain an independent point of view from traditional family representations in photographs or videos. These had always been taken from an adult perspective in the past. Because of low sales, the manufacturer withdrew the *Pxl-2000* rather quickly from the market. The reason for this commercial failure is generally attributed solely to the prohibitive selling price (approximately $100 at the time) for a children's toy. However, this cannot be the sole reason because if we take average earnings of $1500 into account, this toy was actually accessible to a broad spectrum of American society, and therefore had market potential. In our opinion, two other factors were underestimated. The bad picture quality in an object intended for children was certainly a bad calculation because children often have higher expectations and technological competences than their parents. Secondly, anticipating emergent uses (allowing children an autonomous viewpoint) does not guarantee the sales necessary to make a profit.

Despite this wider commercial failure, the camera became a cult object for hundreds of collectors. These still continue to drive a micro-market of buying, selling and exchange with the whole array of associated services (e.g. usage instructions, spare parts, breakdown service, improvements to the camera, etc.). However, the most unexpected development was that this camera had a true durable success as a recognized current within present-day video art. The camera's defects were transformed into esthetic qualities: the pixelization, sound effects, interference and snow, became like 1960s artistic conventions. In particular, Vostell's electronic work and the video art experiments in the 1970s used these type of defects to deconstruct video as a medium conceptually as well as perceptually (Nauman, Sonnier, Campus, Imura, Vasulka, Viola, Acconci, etc.). If the failure of this Fisher Price product can be explained by it being premature (i.e. its social uses did not exist) its artistic success, on the other hand, may be explained by the way it fitted into 20th century modern art and earlier video art in particular. The Fisher Price camera gives the electronic image a quasi-tangible esthetic – a form of "electronic matter" – that corresponded to the wishes of most young artists in the 1980s and 1990s. There was therefore a type of artistic deviance that diverted the camera from the primary function as imagined by its creators.

Sadie Benning, a pioneer and figurehead of what is today called *Pixelvision*, is an extremely interesting case in this history. Her personal and artistic journey shows us how an emergent social use preceded an artistic social use. Benning's use of the camera corresponded first of all to a social use without any artistic pretensions. It was only later that Benning and other artists used the camera for creating artworks. Here is her biography as seen on many specialized Web sites (this text is from the *Video Data Bank* website):[2]

Sadie Benning is a lesbian videomaker who has been creating videos since she was 15 years old using a Pixelvision Fisher-Price toy camera. Benning often works in the privacy of her own room, using scrawled and handwritten notes from diary entries to record the thoughts and images that reveal the long-ings and complexities of a developing lesbian identity. Evoking in turn playful seduction and painful honesty, Benning's floating, close-up camera functions as an audience for her intimate diary revelations and as an accomplice in defining her evocative experimental form. Her work emerges from a place half-innocent and half-adult, with all the honesty, humour, and real desperation of a personality trapped and uncomfortable, just coming to self-awareness.

Sadie Benning thus created her own private diary of a teenager discovering her homosexuality. Her very particular sociocultural context (her father was a film director) undoubtedly explains why a young teenager adopted this tool so naturally. But it is not the only reason. The *Pxl-2000* camera – used to explore her room, her body, the street – is also self-reflexive: the pixellized picture and the sound produced by the cassette's motor drive bestowed a unique quality, easily recognizable, like a trademark. This very tool, a "commercial failure,"[3] can be likened to the image of the young lesbian living on the margins, rejected by dominant social standards. The toy aspect undoubtedly lowered barriers to use and the apparent brittleness of the picture, its instability, gave the recordings an impression of *tracing*, of *printed matter*, allowing large close-ups and unusual perspectives. Here the image is not calculated, as we would calculate a 3-D image. Rather, it is literally a true analogical image: an image that is a direct trace of a reality. There is truly a *Pixelvision* esthetic: a singular significant experience of reality, i.e. what has been called a "percept" (Deleuze and Parnet, 1996). This percept is not the only result of the *Pxl-2000*'s technical system, but it is the use that this girl made of it. The appropriation of the camera by this teenager was thus not only a technical use, but also it was a psychosocial use, involving the construction of the image of herself as a young lesbian.

The artistic legitimation of Sadie Benning's videos came after her first tapes. This recognition was due to at least two fundamental elements. The first was

---

[2] http://www.vdb.org. This specialized organization has one of the largest collections of Western activist and Japanese video art in the world, one of whose principal themes is that of minority identity or communities (blacks, feminists, gays, and lesbians, etc.).

[3] This analogy is often used on the many personal websites presenting *'the Sadie Benning story.'*

the video's subject matter, which initially entailed the discovery of the artist's homosexual identity and then her activist agenda (coming-out). Secondly, we have the tool and method used to create this private diary that was quickly noticed in the world of art for its esthetic qualities. The diversion of use here had two facets: the departure from social conventions (the assertion of one's homosexuality was and still is considered a form of social deviance) and the departure from the purpose of this camera (it was a toy whose role of being purely for fun was overturned). These "private" videos then became "artistic" videos and subsequently they became public videos, dating from when the Chicago *Video Data Bank* first showed and then distributed them.

The convergence of determining factors (the parents' socio-professional status, the cultural context, her growing sexual identity), contributed to the blossoming of a legitimized artistic practice. This then became a separate current within alternative video art with its schools, its purists, its reformers, its networks and its places of exhibition. With *Pixelvision*, the border between instituted artistic practice and esthetized personal life became indistinct. This is currently true of some contemporary Webcam productions[4] that look as much like "reality TV" as radical artistic performances (Thely, 2002). The American artist John Manoogian III's personal website[5] is a quite representative example of the use of *Pxl-2000* from an esthetic but also from a functional point of view. He offers Net surfers technical hints for "retouching" their camera. On the site, there are, amongst other texts, two paragraphs entitled "Tech" and "Art:"

TECH

I have two pxl's, both of which I obtained free. (yes!) One is rigged to accept ac/dc via a curly ¹/₄ inch audio string; the skinny adaptor cable that came with it was garbage. I stripped the tape roller and spindles, etc. to lighten it. I bypass the CrO2 audio format in favor of conventional videotape. I send the signal to an outboard source (currently my roommate glorybox's). If you look at my camera you can see the jack I installed at the bottom of the handle. The setup works really well, because I love the thick quarter inch jack that snaps in with a resounding CLICK. It wasn't designed to carry dc power, but I haven't had a problem. If you have a pxl you want to modify, send mail to the list. I'm also looking into an infra-red modification. Stay tuned...

ART

Pixelvision is intoxicating. The way a hand blurs across the screen. A face exploding in a blossom of light and then sinking back into a puddle of shadow.

---

[4] Thely (2002) speaks about Webcams' "malfunctioning images" (pixellized, "poor").
[5] http://jm3.net/pxl/, copyright © jm3/John Manoogian III. Much invaluable information is available on this site as well as specialized newsgroups.

The bizarre motion that is unique to the pxl brings me back again and again.
The picture is dreamy, ethereal . . . ghostly. I love it.

This site, like others, has links to other sites, forums, online chat and mailing
lists that all deal with *Pixelvision*. The artistic use of this camera even becomes
a way of life and a way of seeing things with the feeling of belonging to a
community, even if this one is subdivided into a myriad of sub-groups. New
practices are still emergent. Recently, a festival of pornographic videos made
only with the *Pxl-2000* launched a call for exhibitors. The tool, thus poached,
was literally diverted from the uses originally imagined by its industrial creators. This process transforms uses, but it also transforms the very technical
equipment itself: it is disassembled, reassembled and improved.[6]

2.2.   From Cut-up to Pick-up

The transformation of technical "defects" into artistic qualities, apparent in
Benning's work, also appears in a certain type of contemporary creation: video
art. Dara Birnbaum's video *Wonder Woman* (1979), which repeats a looped
sequence of the television show *Wonder Woman* until it becomes absurd, questions the dominant representations of women in American television series.
This deconstruction of television conventions is also a criticism of the sexist
and commercial ideology behind the image of women. The process of repetition, of looping a short television video sequence, is shared by artists such as
Klaus vom Bruch with his obsessional repetition of an advertising image (*Das
Duracell Band* in 1979–1980).

This type of poaching of images is also practiced by many contemporary
artists. The French artist *Hetzel and Gretel*, working through the night in post-
production studios, pirated images of militant, and artistic television to create
video works. The American artist Tom Kalin is a practitioner of a kind of video
sampling, and has produced gay activist works. Peter Greenaway imagined
a contemporary transposition of Dante's Inferno by adapting contemporary
imagery (e.g., radar, ultrasound, MRI, etc.). This is part of the technique of
"joining" in modern art (of which one of the latest and radical examples is the
"found footage" practiced in experimental cinema). There is also a substantial
use of hacking, diversion and recycling suitable for today's post-Modern art.

We may think that the post-Modern practice of sampling is the direct heir of
the formal poaching and symbolic system inherited from 20th century modern
art with its joining (and unsticking) of texts, images or sound. However, this
lineage is not so clear because, unlike these old collages, current practices
involving poaching are sufficient in themselves. Because the practice of joining

---

[6] A DVD exclusively devoted to Pixelvision with a large selection of artistic works and two
documentaries on the subject has recently been published at: http://www.precious-realm.com/.

has become more widespread and banal, it is no longer a marginal and protest form of poaching. Instead, it has become a form of "integrated poaching," the practice of copy–pasting in computing being a banal example. The Avant-gardist, Modernistic form of poaching was partly automated and standardized. It has therefore changed. But artistic work resists the process by which previously deviant uses become the new standard. It does so by simply creating new deviant uses that once again separate them from current norms. Contemporary artistic practices function as a form of "pick-up" (Deleuze and Parnet, 1996), following on from William Burroughs' idea of "cut-up."

The idea of pick-up or 'double theft' is not something that takes place between people. Rather, it occurs between ideas. Each one is fed into the other, following some line or lines that are neither in one nor in the other, and that carry a 'block' (Deleuze and Parnet, 1996).

Many young artists practice various forms of pick-up. They can do this by creating, for example, collectives (working together). But they can also do it while working alone with their computer connected to the Web, using the latter as a tool for research, for acquiring images, sounds and texts. They can use the Internet connected computer as a production tool for creating sites and interfaces and as a tool for broadcasting these unceasingly renewed flows. For example, in *Sampling Stories* by Anthnony Rousseau,[7] the web surfer plays with images poached from the Web, handling them and mixing them with others via an interface.

2.3.   Traced Uses

Copying, recording and collecting are examples of artistic practice that have also become artistic subjects in their own right. These, what may be called, practices of traceability also provide observation aids for the ethnologist and the sociologist. Within the framework of my doctoral research, a French artist, Magali Desbazeille, gave me access to the totality of her files recalling the history of the creation and of the production of *You Think, Therefore I Am* ('*TPJS*'), an interactive video installation which she co-created with Siegfried Canto over the course of 2 years. These files consist of an heterogeneous collection of about 400 documents. This corpus of "traces" of various forms (letters, e-mail, videos, photocopies, articles, charts, budgets, test results, etc.) informs us about the genesis of the work through various partnerships and through the way in which the artists forged and rehabilitated their initial concept according to budgetary, technical or time constraints. It allows us to tell the story of a tekhne-logical creation. There are many conjectures, but also hesitations and, finally, solutions. Here are some examples:

---

[7] Visit http://www.samplingstories.fr.st/ and http://www.silenceisnotsexy.fr.st/.

Concerning the anonymity of public transport and the circulation of interior thoughts in the promiscuity of a crowd.

The audience walks upon a video image projected on the ground in the exhibition room. The image represents pedestrians filmed beforehand from below, through a transparent ground. When they make contact with the image of a filmed pedestrian, the sound starts and the audience hears the interior thoughts of this person (...)

You Think, Therefore I am is a technological innovation and research project. Audience movements start the sound events corresponding to zones of the projected video image, zones which themselves move. The audience is surprised by the interactivity. This installation can address several persons simultaneously and is not limited to only one person.[8]

This type of ethnomethodological approach, involving the collection of interviews and observations at different stages in the evolution of the project, enables us to include and understand the genesis of the installation. The rearrangement of the techniques and software leads to innovative technical "bricolage" and "poaching" that is present whenever technical devices invented for industrial use are channeled away from their initial social function toward that of an artistic goal. All these elements lead to an original and technical symbolic system, that is to say, a novel technical device that gives rise to a new way of thinking about interpersonal communication. These constant comings and goings involved in rearranging various techniques and the invention of a particular device contribute, once these technical and symbolic systems are stabilized in the shape of *TPJS*, to a tekhne-logical esthetic such as was defined here.

TPJS can then be regarded as revealing a symbolic use of technology that may be applied in the field of telecommunications. This explains, amongst other things, why France Telecom R&D is interested in this type of installation. From this point of view, we can imagine new social conditions of communication, arising from elements of this work. Thus Desbazeille and Canto do not precede a use in particular but create deviated uses, out of step with normalized contemporary uses.

3.   Bricolage Uses

What has been called the "technician ideology" is a reference to the way in which technical innovation is seen as being more important than social innovation in research and development centers, most notably in the field of

---

[8] The complete text (with visuals) can be consulted online at http://www.desbazeille. nom.fr.

telecommunications.[9] If this ideology exists, it may encounter all those uses not envisaged which can modify the intended function of technical equipment.

As we have shown, it is not appropriate to see the artist as an individual released from all technical or social constraints. Our objective is, on the contrary, to observe and analyze these types of constraints and how the relations between the various actors are established in the course of social interaction. One first step is to distinguish between uses that have emerged in relation to established technologies and uses relating to new and changing technologies. Here, we are most interested in the former: we will be able to verify that innovation results in part from "circumventing" practices that are already common and standardized.

Among the many and various levels on which to analyze uses (ideological, methodological, institutional, political, etc.), the management perspective is particularly interesting because it "dreams of a methodical anticipation of the market for communication artifacts, set against the imperceptible and perilous character of public success" (Souchier and Jeanneret, 2001). The management perspective seeks to create models of innovation by trying to rationalize emergent uses on the part of the end users and then to develop new commercial services from these observations. Here, we have to understand the motivations behind industry's interest in artistic practices as an anticipation of possible future uses and technical innovation. This has been true in the United States since the 1960s within organizations such as the Rockfeller Foundation and the R&D departments of large companies such as Xerox, and more recently, in Europe, of companies like France Telecom R&D, Thomson, Philips, Siemens, etc.

Industrial research based on this type of "methodological anticipation" often has trouble innovating because its methods are being constantly called into question. But this approach does not exclude dead ends, uncertainties, retreats, or failures that require many adaptations or what has been called *bricolé* solutions to find answers to a given problem. "Bricole" can take on different meanings, thus defining various types of uses: it can mean to skew, to divert, to arrange, to rearrange, to re-use, to transform, to deviate, etc. This is the activity of the handyman as defined by Claude Lévi-Strauss (1962).[10] "*Nowadays, the handyman remains one who works with his hands, by using different means in comparison to those of the expert.*" The Mechanical Arts Craftsman (so called because artists were perceived as being craftsmen in the Middle Ages)

---

[9] This is from the paper by Souchier and Jeanneret (2001). In this framework, the question of what devices will be used for is posed after the technical innovation is itself produced (i.e. the 'techno-push' model). But today this question is increasingly posed before (the 'techno-pull' model).

[10] Levi-Strauss, 1962, quoted by Isabelle Chol, Université Blaise-Pascal, in 'Du'bricolage 'poétique dans quelques œuvres de la première motié du XXe siècle', http://www.france.sk/culturel/pedagbricolage.htm.

becomes the 15th century Liberal Artist (a definition which remains the same today). Until the Renaissance, artists' technical know-how was seen as being more important than their personality and their uniqueness. In contrast, what we might call subjective artists, with both technical competences and also their viewpoints, produced a new category of activity in the 15th century called "Art." This new social and symbolic group of artists was based both on the possession a technical know-how and, equally, on scientific and intellectual foundations. Art was no longer to be simply a technical and manual pursuit. It had also become an intellectual pursuit, thought in action. The mechanical artists (craftsmen) became liberal artists (artists). Art-tekhne became art-logos.

With today's tekhne-logical art, the artist becomes a craftsman again – and also a liberal artist. He or she revives the old figure of the craftsman (with technical skills), while at the same time personifying a contemporary liberal economic and social model of behavior characterized by flexibility and an atomization of their production time (e.g. artists under specific contracts). An artist working on new technologies in a systematic and in-depth manner must have real technical know-how and be a type of "digital age" craftsperson. At the same time, artists must be able to think abstractly about their work. On the one hand, they are re-defining mechanical arts and, on the other hand, they are liberal artists in two distinct ways: in an old sense (from the renaissance) and in a contemporary economic sense. On this last point, new sociological studies show us that a number of contemporary artists, notably those working within technological industries, start up their own businesses working on the same free-market business model. The tekne-logical artist creates. The contemporary tekhne-logical artist crystallizes all of these historical and current trends: he or she is a craftsperson, a businessperson and an inventor.

S/He *works* (assisted or not, alone or with others) to develop the devices and tools which s/he then uses to create open, processual work, i.e. work which is constantly in flux. It changes according to technical innovations and new ideas. The notion of a finished work (such as a painting or a sculpture) is thus called into question. The process becomes as important as the result. Artistic work is a process of construction. It is an action that develops over time, one which is evolutionary but which also involves comings and goings. It is not necessarily a finished object in itself, such as a table, a sculpture, a film or a play. To circumvent an obstacle, to find alternative solutions using elements that already exist, craftsman-artists generally do not innovate in terms of creating a particular technique. On the other hand, they generate, often in spite of themselves, what Lévi-Strauss describes as an "incidental movement:" a method that was unforeseen beforehand. The "diversion" of uses and techniques, the term generally used to indicate artistic specificity, is in fact more like an "evasion" specific to this incidental movement. It involves a self-conscious strategy seeking to create a "counter user manual."

This diversion of uses at first appears to be something noble and courageous, corresponding better to Modern Avant-garde ideology. Being active, voluntary and deviant, it indicates a transgression of established standards. It is a centrifugal movement that wishes to throw out reigning social standards (be they technical, political, cultural, etc.). Conversely, the term "evasion" would seem to indicate something less glorious, with connotations of avoidance, deviation, digression, sidestepping, etc. Picasso's famous formula, "I do not seek, I find," could today be substituted for a post-modernistic assertion: "I do nothing but seek." The artist is no longer an explorer, but an "exploration" in her- or himself. This involves a centripetal movement in that all possible social standards are integrated, to be arranged differently through negotiation.

Claims about the intentions and legitimizations of contemporary artistic practice are often structured around this idea of diversion that, implicitly, gives the artist the quasi-Modernistic status of a protestor, proposing new standards to replace established standards – i.e. the artist as innovator. It is easy to understand why the R&D industry integrates artistic projects, which are perceived as being potentially innovative, into its research programs. This legitimation process, cited by artistic as well as industrial actors and structured by the artistic idea of diversion, is only part of the research process. But it is a necessary veneer: it shows that the artist does not pervert himself by working with industry and, in return it, justifies industry taking risks when innovating. On the one hand, business seeks to legitimize its collaboration with artists so that it may continue to use them as a means of anticipating uses. On the other, artists seek to legitimize their work with industry so as not to be seen as sell-outs. Both actors here share the same methods: creating new uses, producing new innovations, inventing new processes. And they use the same vocabulary: innovate, invent, imagine, create, etc. Diversion may be a reality but it is also a common way for both artists and engineers to legitimize their collaboration: artists divert user manuals and engineers divert artists' ideas. We have been able to observe in several co-developments within a research and development center that this diversion may occur only rarely but that it is nevertheless used in all official external communications such as newspapers, magazines, journals, etc.

Artists are not the only ones to perform a kind of diversion with respect to some normative rule, whether consciously or not – other examples might be the murderer using a kitchen knife as a weapon, a child making a hut with covers. Nor does industry need artists to divert uses in order to invent yet more uses. However, we can better understand the collaboration between the two through the term "bricolage" from Lévi-Strauss. Although integrating the idea of diversion, bricolage is not limited to it. The way in which a dog wanders around is a kind of bricolage, as is someone surfing the Web. The bricolage between artists and engineers, usually termed "co-development," allows both sides to learn each other's culture and thus supports a cross-exchange of knowledge, but also of practices and uses. Bricolage is then a social and technical form of a "sensitive combinatorial"[11] in which the various actors must "co-develop" and collaborate but also negotiate and compromise when deciding things together.

4.   Tentative Conclusion

The types of innovation dealt with in this chapter often contain co-operations between artists and engineers entailing all that such collaboration supposes, including misunderstandings, errors, fumbling, etc. But it leads to "stabilized forms" in which new uses can emerge. These co-developments between artists and engineers proceed by "bricolage," as set out by Claude Lévi-Strauss, and their deviations generate practices of "poaching" as described by Michel de Certeau. It is these processes of research and experimentation that interest more and more industrial R&D departments because of their capacity not simply to anticipate some precise use, but rather to help reflect upon whole new exploratory fields of usage (Julien, 1996).

Looking at the story of the Fisher Price camera shows us that there is an important shift between the uses imagined by the creators and its real or end uses (artistic or not). While an artistic success may remain a commercial failure, it nevertheless shows that the social use of technical communication devices is difficult to foresee. It is for this reason that an artistic approach, when integrated into an R&D department, allows us to leave the traditional framework involving the rationalized anticipation of uses (by applied sociology, ergonomics, marketing, etc.).

The widespread success of SMS is telling in this respect. The service was originally imagined to answer professional customers and was not destined for widespread social use. It was, however, this extended use, not originally envisaged, which contributed to the commercial success of mobile telephones. Artistic practices are not, therefore, the only ones to divert intended use. In everyday life we often do this. What seems interesting in the case of the artistic uses is that these diversions are conscious, required and sometimes systematic. The use of diversion has become a practice that is asserted and assumed – it is often even the necessary prerequisite to being described as "artistic." To push a tool or a technology to its most unexpected uses, to proceed to its deconstruction then its rearrangement, to criticize traditional social uses, etc., these critical postures are conventions inherited directly from modern 20th century art with the underlying idea of the Avant-garde. There is a bond between this desired tension, caused by an artistic form of deviance with respect to dominant norms, and a prefiguring of future standards that may be seen today as "displaced" but that may turn out to be widely shared tomorrow.

---

[11] de Queiroz, J.M. Sampling stories, http://sampling.stories.free.fr/dequeiroz.html.

This quasi-systemic anticipation that is found in certain current artistic practices is also present in emergent social uses. When the users of the mobile phone adapted the SMS to send personal messages, it was done without any idea of innovation and in total anonymity. There was a powerful, forward-thinking, and structuring social force at work. Art has no monopoly over anticipation, or over change. And it has even less of a monopoly on critical attitudes. However, in contrast to non-artistic social uses, it preserves their traces by practicing diversion as an assumed, and even asserted, form of deviance. By examining artistic productions and what they set out to say, we can uncover the tangible traces of a usually anonymous, underground and dispersed process, which only becomes visible if and when it becomes widespread. Artistic experiments allow us to anticipate because they integrate this search for deviating uses into their own dynamics. One can see them, recall them and analyze them at every stage. Social uses, developed spontaneously in society, only become noticed when they are widespread, i.e. by then it is too late to be anticipatory.

References

De Certeau, M.D. L'invention du quotidien. 1. arts de faire; 1980. Gallimard, Paris: 279–296.

Deleuze, G., Parnet, C. Dialogues; 1996. Flammarion, Paris.

Lévi-Strauss, C. La pensée sauvage; 1962. Pion, Paris.

Souchier, E., Jeanneret, Y. Que signifie 'user' de l'écrit d'écran? In e-Usages proceedings, ENST, France Télécom, June 12–14, 2001, Paris.

Thely, N. Vue à la webcam. Essai sur la web intimité; 2002. Presses du Réel, Collection Documents sur l'Art, Dijon.

Chapter 9

THE MOBILE MULTIMEDIA PHONE AND ARTISTIC EXPRESSION: A CASE STUDY OF MOBY CLICK

Heli Rantavuo

1.   Many Media in One Medium

The mobile multimedia phone is often talked about in terms of the existing media that can be used with it. Press coverage, marketing, and users themselves report that the phone can be used as a digital camera (still or video), as a tape recorder, for playing games, or for making postcards, to mention a few possibilities. According to media researchers Bolter and Grusin, it is characteristic for new digital media to remediate, that is to mimic, assemble, and sometimes improve older, existing media. Seen in this light, the mobile multimedia phone can be called a remediator. The multimedia phone provides an advanced version of, for example, the camera, by adding to it the possibility of instantly sending pictures to and with others (Bolter and Grusin, 1999; for more discussion on the mobile multimedia phone as a remediator, see Colombo and Scifo in this volume.)

On the other hand, the use of mobile multimedia can be regarded as a form of communication that has characteristics of its own. Using the mobile multimedia phone is, in the end, different from taking photographs, making home videos, or sending postcards. The reasons for using it are difficult to reduce to the reasons for using other media. And the culture that surrounds mobile multimedia is different from that which surrounds other media. In other words, the mobile multimedia phone as an object, product and technology, as well as mobile multimedia communication as a phenomenon and act, carries different meanings to users than using, for example, a digital camera or an ordinary mobile phone.

In the Moby Click case study, both of the above views appear and intersect. In the case study interviews, the nine art students who used mobile multimedia in

Leslie Haddon (ed.), Everyday Innovators, 136–149.
© 2005 *Springer. Printed in The Netherlands.*

the Moby Click project often talked about the phone in relation to the features of the (ordinary) mobile phone and the (digital) pocket camera. The significance of the camera function was especially important in this project, because the students who were invited to explore the possibilities of mobile multimedia were students of photographic art and students of product design who had a professional interest in photography.

However, in the project, the students were also forming their own general definition of the mobile multimedia phone and of mobile multimedia communication. Their task was to explore what the multimedia messaging service (MMS) phone could be as a visual medium, as a fresh product that was only just being defined (and still is) in its social and cultural context. In other words, they were given the role of the innovator in the field of mobile multimedia.

In this chapter, I will examine the innovation process and its outcomes through asking how the students attributed meaning to the mobile multimedia phone and to communicating with mobile multimedia. I study the use of mobile multimedia from a cultural perspective, and more specifically, through visual culture and the culture of ICTs. The cultural dimension of a user can be summarized as the beliefs, customs and patterns of everyday life that affect the use of a product (Whitney, in McNeice, 2003). In the case of Moby Click, the particular beliefs, customs and patterns related to visual culture are, for example, notions of art and photographic art, ways of processing images and photographs, of exhibiting them, of sharing them and of preserving and returning to them. Meanwhile, the beliefs, customs and patterns related to the culture of ICTs include people's preferred forms of communication (aural, visual), modes of communication (well thought out vs. spontaneous, task-oriented vs. joking), and frequency of communication.

In the first section, I describe the project in general, the works that were exhibited and the case study. In the next section, I examine how the users in this project saw their tools, the multimedia phone and MMS messaging, how they used them during the project and why. In the conclusion, I will discuss how art students or artists are innovative users both in the case of Moby Click and more generally.

2.   The Moby Click Project and Case Study

2.1.   *The Project*

In the autumn of 2002, the Finnish national modern art museum Kiasma invited nine art students from the University of Art and Design in Helsinki to use mobile multimedia phones. The objective was to explore the potential for visual expression using mobile multimedia and to create an exhibition of the outcomes in one of the spaces in Kiasma called Mediateekki. At first, Kiasma approached students from the department of photographic art and later the invitation was extended to the department of product and strategic design. Students from this department who had a professional interest in photography also signed up. In the end, four of the students came from the department of product and strategic design and five from photographic art. Three of them were women, six of them were men. Apart from the University of Art and Design in Helsinki, Kiasma's partners in the project were Nokia, the digital solutions company Satama Interactive, and the telephone operator Sonera. The students used the Nokia 7650 multimedia phone from September 23rd to December 1st, 2002, during which time they could send multimedia and text messages free of charge (but they had to pay for phone calls).

2.2.   The Exhibition

The exhibition Moby Click was opened on November 12th, 2003. There were two works in print: *A Trip* by Ea Vasko and Liisa Valonen, where small paper prints were combined into mosaics on the wall. There was the installation *Sight/Näky* by Kitta Perttula, Antti Oksanen, and Eero Kokko, where small transparency prints were hung from the ceiling at different heights. One of the works, *Momentary Impressions: Snapshots for the Curious*, was exhibited on a TV monitor. This work consisted of a collection of nine separate series of flash-animated images, with sound effects recorded separately, after taking the photographs. Tapio Laukkanen had made four of the series, *Red/Green/Blue*, *Look into the Light*, *Waterproof*, and *Unpleasant Dreams*, Antti Hahl five, *Momentary Train*, *Cloaca Privatus*, *Having Fun with Friends*, *Solitauros*, and *Leave*.

The fourth work was one projected onto the wall, called *Visuaalista keskustelua* (visual conversation). Its concept had been created by the group and put together by Tatu Marttila and Mikko Saario. In it, approximately five students at a time held a discussion through multimedia messages around a specific theme. Visitors to the exhibition could also take part with an MMS phone that was available at the museum. Altogether seven discussions were held. Each discussion was framed by a theme and an image was chosen to accompany each theme. The themes and main images were: La Festa with Ilja Repin's painting *Suomen suurmiehiä* (great Finnish men), City as Public Space with a picture of Finland's largest construction site Kamppi located in the center of Helsinki; The Great Escape with a map of Helsinki center; Art-talk with a picture of an installation *Kreisland: mahtavan maailman alttari* (Kreisland: altar of the wonderful world) by Rosa Liksom; Injured Emotions with a map of emotional binaries drawn by Tapio Laukkanen; Open Subject – Today's Topics with a collage of magazine and newspaper headlines, and Christmas – Chasing the big Red One with a collage of images related to Christmas. Each main image was transformed into a map by adding coordinates to it and each MMS message pointed to a particular spot on the image map. The sender of an MMS thus reacted both to the unfolding MMS discussion and to the main image that accompanied the theme. The exhibition visitor could see a web forming on top of the main image with each message. The MMS discussions could be seen and participated in during the exhibition in real time when they were held. Afterward, the discussions were run as recordings in continuous loops projected onto the wall.

Keeping in mind the goal of the project, exploring the (audio)visual potential of mobile multimedia, I divide the works into two categories. The print and monitor-exhibited works fall in the category where the multimedia phone was used as a camera to make photographic art. By photographic art I mean, in this case, that each student worked on their photographs alone, the pictures were then selected and put together as the final work in small working groups and after the works had been placed in the exhibition room they remained unchanged. The other category, where the multimedia phone was itself used for mobile multimedia communication, includes only the work *Visuaalista keskustelua*. It consisted of multimedia messages (involving text and image) sent both from and outside the exhibition space and it was transformed repeatedly during the exhibition.

2.3.   The Case Study

The goal of the Moby Click case study was twofold. Firstly, it was to find out how the users in the project experienced using the mobile multimedia phone. Secondly, through this information, the aim was to understand why the final exhibition did not feature more works that made use of mobile multimedia more interactively. The hypothesis was that these particular users simply set out to use the phone principally as a camera because that was the area of their expertise.

I interviewed the students for the case study after the exhibition had opened, both individually and in the original small working groups of two or three in which the students had participated. The duration of the semi-structured theme interviews varied from 20 to 60 min per interviewee or a group of them. One theme in the interviews related to experiences of using the mobile multimedia phone, varying from technical issues to the user's emotions. Another theme referred to the exhibition: preparing it and their views on the outcome. The visual data of the case study consist of the works in the exhibition and sketches and works outside of the exhibition that the students chose to show to me. Data on the use of mobile multimedia for the students' own private purposes were derived solely from the interview material. The quotes from the interviews are my own translations.

3.   The Many Faces of Mobile Multimedia

3.1.   *Another Mobile Communication Device*

Anticipating the use of a mobile camera phone, researcher Anne Soronen (2003) had, in an earlier paper, suspected that the camera phone would be understood as being only one more version of a mobile phone. She predicted that users would attribute meanings to it similar to that of the mobile phone. According to her, the possibility of taking photographs would not essentially change the user's relationship with the mobile device, but rather strengthen or weaken some of the existing significations or meanings that the mobile phone had for the user. These significations, according to Soronen and other researchers who have studied mobile phone use (ibid.; Kasesniemi and Rautiainen, 2001; Kopomaa, 2000; Mäenpää, 2000; Raudaskoski and Arminen, 2003; Repo and Pantzar, 2003; Repo *et al.*, 2003), include the mobile phone as a status symbol, as an everyday communication device, as a tool and as a toy. The significations actually given to the mobile multimedia phone in the Moby Click project reflect these different meanings that the mobile phone can take on. The students, used to mobile communication, used to the continuous launching of new mobile phones and used to constantly taking up new ICT products, simply saw the mobile multimedia phone as just another new mobile phone model. Adding a camera in the mobile phone did not, in their view, mark the beginning of a new era in mobile communications. Rather, the students saw it as a marketing move with the purpose of bringing a sense of novelty to a familiar product. Accordingly, multimedia messaging was considered as something banal, as I will show in the next section.

"*I find that [the camera phone] is a silly toy like mobile phones were in the beginning, only yuppies have them and they get laughed at for it.*"

"*Everyone's familiar with the mobile phone, everyone's familiar with the camera, there's nothing special about the camera phone.*"

"*Besides, why do people always have to have new phones, what's the deal?*"

For those students who carried the multimedia phone on them, like they would an ordinary mobile phone, it became an everyday tool. In these cases, taking photographs became characterized by spontaneity. For example, one of the students used the camera phone as an extension to his sketchbook.

Question: *Earlier, you said that you would have photographed pretty much the same subjects with other devices as well. Do you think you would have missed something, however?*

Answer: *I think so. (With the camera phone) it's so spontaneous, right away, in a hurry quickly take a picture. It's possible to take many pictures so you can just click away and see what you've got. Of course, you can do the same with a digital camera but you don't carry it on you, do you.*

Answer: *Because (the camera phone) is always on you, like a mobile phone in general. Many amateurs don't necessarily carry a camera on them all the time, but (the camera phone) is in your pocket or somewhere at hand so in some respects it's easier to start taking pictures, you might imagine.*

One student especially enjoyed the technical simplicity of the mobile phone camera.

Question: *What became the main idea (behind taking pictures with the camera phone)?*

Answer: *Recording moments, somehow, that you don't really have to think about anything because it's such a basic, simple device anyway. You just push the button and all the technical knowledge you have about photography sinks into the subconscious. You don't need it when you take the picture as you can't influence anything anyway so you don't think about it. Mostly, I guess, composition becomes important, part (of the pictures) I outlined pretty carefully, instead of just clicking away. Moments and targets are pretty random, ones I just came across. The mobile phone freed me from the technical burden of adjusting exposure, adjusting the aperture.*

3.2.   *A Photographic Camera*

Other researchers have argued (Colombo and Scifo in this volume; Mäenpää, 2000) that in the minds of users, the predominance of telephony on the mobile phone may gradually give way to new concepts, such as communicating through images. In fact, most users in the Moby Click study were indeed more interested in the multimedia phone as a tool for photography instead of mobile multimedia. Many regarded the multimedia phone not as a phone but rather as a camera, in the context of this project. Talking about photography, the students repeatedly referred to the camera, the darkroom and the craft of the darkroom work as extensions of the photographer's body and trained eye (Lister, 1995).

As a photographer I enjoy working by hand. I have the skills needed to work with the computer, but still I think a real photograph is proofed by hand and there are no tricks made with colours.

We are photographers and print is a natural medium. We're not too interested in working on computer displays. We're just definitely not that kind of people who'd be at all interested in any kind of multimedia type of thing.

It was the interactivity, in a way, that we knew that we could use MMS-messages and that, but it just didn't interest me. I concentrated mostly on taking pictures (...) (Multimedia messaging) is not related to image. You can send them, it doesn't bother me, but I have a photography student's viewpoint, I'm interested in taking pictures, it wasn't any problem that I couldn't make calls with it.

At the same time, the students expected the camera in the multimedia phone to be of poor technical quality.

Well, of course, I knew beforehand that the resolution isn't too good, it works on a small display, precise enough to send from one phone to another. But you cannot really scale it onto a computer. I was hoping it would have been more precise, but in this project, we worked in this framework, looked at the possibilities.

Met my expectations pretty much: bad quality, bad lens, small picture.

Despite the poor technical quality of the camera, most of the students explicitly said that they set out to make photographic art in the project. At the same time, photographic art, as defined by the students, became defined as the opposite of multimedia messaging. Making and sending picture or multimedia messages was seen as an everyday activity, something that belonged to the so-called ordinary users. That was uninteresting from the perspective of someone working with images. With this view, the students adhered to the notion of photography where snapshot images were seen as being part of leisure time and home entertainment and as a plain, trivial form of expression that only features everyday topics (Slater, 1995).

(...) I sent some picture messages to my friends in their e-mail, joking, which is what the camera phone is really meant for, I think. (...) You might think taking pictures of people is kind of fooling about, if you're making art you could take pictures of something else. I don't know, I won't confess I thought like that, but maybe I wouldn't put pictures of my friends hanging out in the bar in an exhibition. At least I wouldn't. (The mobile multimedia phone) is difficult to take portraits with that would be at all nice (...)

Subjects that you photograph with (the mobile multimedia phone) are light-hearted. Here we produced art, but if I had a camera phone, I wouldn't use it as a camera but as a recording tool.

Mobile communication was clearly not inspiring innovation among the group who produced works of photographic art. The students seemed to reflect the commonly held view in Finland that the mobile phone has become an everyday, everyman's tool, so commonplace that it is almost invisible. Each time the multimedia phone was discussed as a mobile phone, or multimedia messaging was referred to, it appeared as something mundane, everyday, with a sense of banality associated to it.

At first glance, one could say that the students adopted the multimedia phone as a camera because placing the phone into the category of cameras was more attractive to them as art students with an interest in photography. Consequently, one could argue, this path kept them from innovating with mobile multimedia. Instead, they carried on working as photographers trying to cope with poor equipment.

In my view, however, the students were not merely indifferent to the possibilities of multimedia messaging. Rather, being very conscious of these possibilities, they seemed to take a stand for photographic art (as they defined it) in contrast to how they saw mobile photography and multimedia: instant, ephemeral, haphazard, fun but trivial, something that belonged to a trash-esthetics in photography. One student said that she intentionally wanted to "misuse" the device, and making good prints out of the camera phone pictures seemed to become a matter of honor for her. One could say that the students innovated with mobile image and multimedia in reverse, being, in a sense, radically conventional, as they made an effort to produce lasting artifacts out of something that they considered inherently ephemeral. (See Emmanuel Mahé's article in this volume for a further example and analysis on "misusing" communication technologies for artistic purposes.)

3.3.   *A Tool for Mobile Multimedia Art*

The Moby Click group planned the concept for the work *Visuaalista keskustelua* together. Three students continued working with the design and the rest of the group took part again later in the MMS conversations when the framework itself was set up. One of the students who were active in designing the work described the ideas that emerged around it during the process of design.

> Question: *Tell me about the work you were all involved in, how it was created (. . .).*
>
> Answer: *We had several ideas for the work. . .*
>
> Question: *Formally or do you mean topics?*
>
> Answer: *No, but Satama (Interactive) would come and make some complicated idea work, one that no-one else could put into practice and that involved multimedia messages. They were there and they told us what was possible. For example, it was suggested that with the help of the mobile locationing option we could have been seen moving on a map, we would have taken pictures and the pictures would have moved along with the person, ideas like this on how to make an MMS board just with images. We came up with several ideas, of which only one would be used and we decided that the conversation could be the most interesting one. Originally, we thought of a map with movement, but we went towards having something where we could discuss a topic and that it could be more interesting, that it would be a totally different kind of picture where we could have more varied information than in a map. We ended up with (the concept of Visual communication) where the most significant thing is that you can track the discussion and see it transform.*

Each group member took part in the MMS conversation at some point during the exhibition period. Interview statements about *Visuaalista keskustelua* and about participating in this project reflected similar attitudes toward multimedia messaging as in the case of the students' own work, although perhaps they were slightly more tolerant.

Question: *You associate MMS with certain kind of pictures you were not interested in taking?*

Answer: *Maybe not like that, but it seems it's just conversation with picture messages, having fun, but it could be something else. The discussion board is an interesting idea, all kinds of fun stuff there. On the other hand, the themes are not very conventional, what ordinary people probably send to each other in MMS-messages, if you see your mates in a bar and take pictures through the pint-glass.*

Visuaalista keskustelua was the only work in the Moby Click exhibition that the students made together and the only one where they made use of multimedia messages. The mobile phone consumer magazine Isohai noted that it was the only work where a "new kind of expression" was created (Reinikainen, 2002). It is tempting to think that there is a connection to what other mobile phone studies show: that users innovate in a group, in the mode of play and humor. (Battarbee, 2003; see also Battarbee and Kurvinen in this volume). Koskinen *et al.* (2001), having researched the use of mobile images, might also have been describing the work *Visuaalista keskustelua* when they characterized the sociability of the picture message, saying that picture messages create a common fixed point around which the group can concentrate their ideas and wit. As we saw above, the students understood multimedia messages as having fun. In addition, when participating in the MMS discussions, seven out of nine students already had their own pieces on show in the exhibition, which they held to be important, and so taking part was not guided by criteria quite as strict as those that were set for the artworks.

It also has to be noted that the most difficult technical problems, both in terms of using the phones and the network, appeared with the MMS discussions for *Visuaalista keskustelua*. This reduced the students' motivation to make the most out of their participation in the work. Students reported that they were "*in a hurry to receive and delete messages,*" because of the limited data processing capacity of the phone. Consequently, all the students took pictures to store before each discussion, trying to anticipate the conversation that would take place around the day's theme.

Question: *Discussions together . . . do they feel natural, do they feel like discussions?*

Answer: *Especially not when the technology fails and the phone jams, it's really annoying.*

Answer: *If a message arrives or gets sent later, or you don't get all the messages. Not at that technical level.*

Question: *(When taking pictures for a discussion) did you think of the discussion or the exhibition?*

Answer: *It was all very intuitive. I didn't deliberate much. I tried to think... let's see it's Saturday today, what's related to Saturday... central topics everyone could relate to. But the phone got really jammed a few times. I got ten messages and it was hard to know what to comment on.*

3.4. A Fun and Useful Tool for Private Communication

Although multimedia or picture messaging was not considered very interesting by the students when discussing the exhibition, each student had in his or her private sphere, i.e. personal life, sent MMS messages to someone outside the project, either to an e-mail address or to another camera phone. In terms of their everyday life, the students were interested in multimedia messages and reported having fun with them, making jokes, as well as the fact that such messages could be useful.

> *Maybe it's just that it's easy when the camera is there at hand and you're watching TV and you see a good or fun picture in the background (...) maybe more like jokes partly that you can send to your friends.*

Question: *Did you send a lot of messages?*

Answer: *Yeah but they were more like jokes.*

Question: *Snapshots of situations?*

Answer: *Yeah, or something from a paper like a caricature, something that's fun, a cheer-up.*

The students were also interested in using picture messages more in the future, when they would be easier and cheaper to use.

I think (mobile multimedia messaging) will change so that it will become a form of communication in a whole different way. (...) That it will become more common so that you're, for example, in a shop and take a picture like 'how's this?'. I think it suits best for that kind of use. I don't think anyone will quite so easily start making an art project like this one with it, at least.

I see no sense in taking pictures of something with the camera phone if I can't use the pictures for anything else but sending them. (...) With a camera phone I take pictures of everyday subjects when I want to say something to someone. For example, I go shopping for clothes and I want to ask someone if something looks good.

When discussing their private use of mobile multimedia, the students expressed similar fears and likings to those that has been expressed in other studies on mobile camera phone use (Colombo and Scifo in this volume; Koskinen *et al.*, 2001; Pantzar and Repo, 2002; Raudaskoski and Arminen, 2003; Soronen, 2002; Soronen and Tuomisto, 2002): the ease and spontaneity of taking pictures, taking pictures secretly, the usefulness of MMS messaging at work or in other task-oriented contexts, keeping in touch and sharing things with friends and family, and messaging during a night out.

I've always dreamed of a small device like that, taking pictures like a private detective (...) At first I might have made it seem like I was writing a text message in a bus or something, but I didn't do it so much after all.

Cos it's like that, there's been discussions that it allows you to observe some-one secretly, that people will start taking pictures of celebrities everywhere, you know (...)

You could use this in discussions at work, you could show with a picture what you mean. Some of my girlfriend's relatives live in Italy so I sent pictures to their e-mail.

For example, I was at the hairdresser's with my friend, she looked funny so I took a picture of her and sent it. (...) In a bar situation when there were a group of us I would send a message to other friends that this is where we are, this is the crowd.

The significance of "useful" messaging was more apparent in these data compared to some other earlier studies. Perhaps this was because the student users were using a real multimedia phone, not test equipment (See, for example, Koskinen *et al.*, 2001). Once the phone lost its novelty attraction, merely having fun was not interesting enough for some users. On the other hand, enthusiastic users kept finding new ways of and useful purposes for using the phone. However, the Moby Click users did not send messages to each other as a group, nor was anyone part of any other group that regularly participated in MMS messaging. Referring to the above discussion about innovation as being a form of play among many users, it is possible that this lack of group messaging decreased the proportion of time spent "having fun" with the device and geared its use to other purposes. For example, in a project called *See What I'm Talking About*, where four art students from St. Martin's in London sent MMS messages to each other, practically all of the messaging belonged to the categories of "having fun" and "sharing moments" (Banks *et al.*, 2002; Lintulahti, 2002; see also Battarbee and Kurvinen in this volume on the importance of co-experience in creative uses of the MMS).

With all the interest in MMS messaging in the field of private communication, why the dislike of using it professionally? Based on user studies carried out so far in the field of mobile visual communication (see the list of references below), on marketing and press coverage of multimedia messaging and the phone, and based on the connection between snapshot culture and camera phones, the mobile multimedia phone becomes easily defined as a device suitable for the private sphere. In the Moby Click project, the students made a clear differentiation between their professional interests, preparing an exhibition to the national modern art museum, and their private communication. With their notion of photographic art, the latter did not qualify as material for the former. In the concluding section, I will discuss the conflicting views on mobile multimedia within the context of art and within the context of private communication in terms of the students' view of themselves as artists.

4.   Conclusions

In the Moby Click project, art students were invited to innovate with the (audio)visual qualities of mobile multimedia. Considering this starting point, I find it surprising that mobile multimedia and mobile communication in general was featured only in one out of four works in the exhibition. It was certainly significant that the students had a professional interest and ambition in, even passion for, photography and that the exhibition was a debut for all of them as artists exhibiting on a national scale. Nevertheless, each of them also used mobile multimedia for private communication. Each of them had opinions about digital and mobile technology and their own ways of using it. In other words, even when preparing an exhibition as artists, they were young, urban people surrounded by visual communication and ICTs. This is the aspect that had interested me in studying the students' choices while they worked with mobile multimedia, given a task to explore and innovate with the medium.

The students were not, in my view, simply ignorant of or indifferent to the possibilities that mobile multimedia communication offered them, but instead they reacted specifically to these possibilities. Those students who did not consider mobile multimedia communication interesting or even appropriate for artistic purposes "misused" the mobile multimedia phone: they used it as a camera, made the poor image quality serve their creative purposes, and made photographic art with it. The three students, who, in contrast, were especially interested in the expressive possibilities of mobile multimedia communication, designed a piece of work that consisted specifically of mobile multimedia messaging (one of the students was part of both groups).

The expression "users as innovators," which was the original conference heading that prompted this chapter, implies that innovative users develop products further, make them more advanced, versatile or more efficient for their own purposes. In the Moby Click project, the students were, indeed, to discover the (audio)visual potential of the multimedia phone. However, what is perhaps specific to these artistic users as innovators is that they innovated in a critical way, based on their particular notions of photographic and media art. In Moby Click, the students who made print works made the multimedia phone work for them, but the result was a critical comment on the device, as well as on the age and nature of digital and mobile communication in general, since the multimedia phone was reduced to being a pocket camera. Those students who carried out the design for *Visuaalista keskustelua* also found it important that the work was technically complicated enough for no one else to put a similar concept into practice. Artistic users are likely to explore devices on a very broad scale. They are likely to familiarize themselves very well with their tools, but then they may also go beyond treating them as tools to explore the general cultural meanings given to the devices and the content that is processed with them. They may explore and innovate utilizing anything and everything from technical details to the concept of the device, as happened in Moby Click. (For other examples, see Mahé in this volume.) This mode of innovation is not necessarily in conflict with interests within the field of design or user research, but it does require an open-minded attitude, a will to engage in the process and nature of artistic work, and perhaps some more time and dedication from the researcher than is found in more conventional research methods and results.

At the same time, it is useful to keep in mind that artists work based on their particular notions of art and the art world. In other words, their exploration and innovation is characterized by what they think is good art, how it is made and how they want to position themselves against different groups and institutions working in the field of art. The Moby Click students were just in the early stages of establishing themselves as professional artists and designers and having a chance to exhibit in the national modern art museum made them think carefully about what to put on display. This resulted in a clear distinction between professional and private use of the mobile multimedia phone. In considering their own photographic works more important than *Visuaalista keskustelua* and in avoiding the use of MMS messaging in their works in general, the students relied on conventional notions of photographic and media art, which seemed to correspond with working for an important art institution for the first time.

In contrast, the mobile multimedia projects *See What I'm Talking About* carried out by four British art students (Banks *et al.*, 2002) and *Imaginary Journey, Syntymiä (Births)*, and *Situations4X* by media artist Heidi Tikka (for information on these works, see Tikka, 2004), have all produced very different mobile multimedia art than most of the Moby Click works. In *See What I'm Talking About,* the main partner is from the mobile communication industry and the MMS messages sent during the project were published as a book. Heidi Tikka has exhibited two of her latter works in the Finnish national modern art museum Kiasma, however, following a successful career as a media artist and producer. Cooperation with artists in all stages of their careers and all forms of exhibition are potentially fruitful for companies or other institutions hoping to learn from artistic work with an ICT device. However, the form of exhibition and the background of the artist (including esthetic choices and position in the art world) influence the way the artist works. Therefore, the partner who wishes to learn from the work should be conscious of and plan carefully how to set up the project in order to arrive at results that benefit all partners.

References

Banks, H., Brady, R., Jackson, J., Vernon-Kell, T. See What I'm Talking About? A Unique Multimedia Messaging Experiment; 2002. Contra publishing, Helsinki.

Battarbee, K. Defining co-experience. In Proceedings of the Conference on Designing Pleasurable Products and Interfaces; 2003. ACM, Pittsburgh.

Bolter, J.D., Grusin, R. Remediation. Understanding New Media; 1999. The MIT Press, Cambridge.

Kasesniemi, E.-L., Rautiainen, P. Kännyssä Piilevät Sanomat. Nuoret, Viesti ja Väline; 2001. Tampere University Press, Tampere.

Kopomaa, T. Kännykkäyhteiskunnan Synty; 2000. Gaudeamus, Helsinki.

Koskinen, I., Kurvinen, E., Lehtonen, T.-K. Mobiili Kuva; 2001. Edita/IT Press, Helsinki.

Lintulahti, M. Paljastan itseni. Sinä tirkistelet! Isohai, 2002; 18.10.2002–4.12.2002: 46–48.

Lister, M. (Ed.) The Photographic Image in Digital Culture; 1995. Routledge, London.

Mäenpää, P. Digitaalisen arjen ituja. Kännykkä ja urbaani elämäntapa. In Hoikkala, T., Roos, J.P. (Eds.), 2000-luvun Elämä. Sosiologisia Teorioita Vuosituhannen Vaihteesta; 2000. Gaudeamus, Helsinki.

McNeice, P. Interview Patrick Whitney: Hvorfor brugercentreret design er fremtidens design (Why human-centred design is the design of the future). Design Matters, 2003; April: 27–33.

Raudaskoski, S., Arminen, I. Mobiilipalveluiden Näkymät – Tapaustutkimus eTampereen Mobiiliklusterin Asiantuntijoiden Näkemyksistä; 2003. Tampereen Yliopisto, Tampere.

Reinikainen, P. Moby click. Isohai, 2002; 5.12.2002–22.1.2003: 15.

Repo, P., Hyvönen, K., Pantzar, M., Timonen, P. Mobiili Video; 2003. Kuluttajatutkimuskeskus, Helsinki.

Repo, P., Pantzar, M. Mediakännykkä ajoi kuvapuhelimen ohi – visioissa tarjotaan yhä puhujan kasvonilmeitä. In: Mediumi 1.3. http://www.m-cult.net/mediumi/; 2003.

Slater, D. Domestic photography and digital culture. In Lister, M. (Ed.), The Photographic Image in Digital Culture; 2003. Routledge, London.

Soronen, A. Kännyssä piilevä kamera – millaista käyttökulttuuria kamerakännykät ovat luomassa? In Mediumi 1.1. http://www.m-cult.net/mediumi/; 2003.

Soronen, A., Tuomisto, V. Mobile image messaging – anticipating the outlines of the usage culture. In Proceedings of the 4th International Symposium. Mobile HCI 2002, Pisa; 2002: 359–363.

Tikka, H. http://www.mlab.uiah.fi/~htikka/; 2004.

PROBLEMS OF RESEARCHING
AND INVOLVING USERS IN DESIGN

These three contributions raise a range of issues around identifying and incorporating knowledge about users and their inputs into the research and design process. Rosemarie Gilligan indicates the problems posed by the concept of "rural" ICT use. In so doing, she also explores the typical social science problem of measurement once a social phenomenon turns out to be far from straightforward. This is important because she looks at the type of basic research using statistics that can inform product deployment and policy. Both the chapter by Sander Limonard and Nicole de Koning, and the one by Jarmo Sarkkinen show problems or dilemmas with attempts to actually involve users in design. Limonard and de Koning do so by examining the different strategies and outcomes of projects in which they were involved. Sarkkinen takes one particular case study to show problems arising from differences between the language and logic of technical staff and those of the user. Both chapters also consider the difficulties experience during, but also the scope for, collaborations between social scientists and technical staff.

In her chapter, Gilligan sets the scene by considering standard claims made about urban–rural divides as well as a range of statistics from international studies that, at face value, show differences in urban/rural ICT use. However, the chapter then outlines problems surrounding how the very term "rural" is defined within the rural sociology literature. In fact, rural is a problematic concept for a number of reasons. The chapter outlines how rural is defined differently for statistical purposes within different countries, there are very different types of rural areas, the inhabitants of rural areas are heterogeneous and the "problems" associated with rural areas themselves vary.

One of the difficulties is that many ideas about why rural adoption of modern technology is distinctive are based on a view of "rural" as being an ideal type of community, very much attached to a traditional way of life, with long-standing norms and resisting technological change. The examples from her own studies in Ireland and elsewhere shows that due to suburbanization, modern means of transportation and mass communication such classic rural communities are dissipating. Not only do we see some move towards common patterns of living across different types of rural and urban communities. Within so-called rural settings we also see a lively interest in ICTs if they are seen as contributing to a more efficient and pleasurable way of life. Hence, the content of the concept "rural" has become multi-faceted, dependent upon the type of "rural" one has in mind. Finally, Gilligan uses Irish examples to speculate about potential "cultural" factors that could influence the rural adoption and use of ICTs. This entails looking beyond such generalized impressions of what rural life is like to consider current practices and life situations, including housing settlement patterns, living space and patterns of daily life.

Starting from a social construction of technology perspective, Limonard and de Koning critically reflect upon three Dutch projects in which they participated. In each case, they discuss the form of user analysis that was employed, the extent to which actual potential users were involved and the nature of the projects as exercises in interdisciplinary collaboration. Looking across the projects they identify some core dilemmas and possible strategies to address them. The first involves user-centred approaches that start from what potential users do now and how they use ICTs in order to extrapolate about the possible future use of innovations. The problem is that this is limiting: we cannot assume that the users will not change in some ways, and in fact the very arrival of the technology may change people's behavior. The other approach would be to acknowledge that adoption and use are fundamentally unpredictable and instead speculate about possible relations between users and the ICTs in question. The problem here is that the results may prove to be too speculative and designers may end up believing what they would like to see happen. The second dilemma involves user involvement in the project: to what extent should users direct innovation or provide feedback to the ideas proposed by technical staff? The third and final dilemma relates to the nature of interdisciplinary collaboration. To what degree should this be formal or informal, to what degree should social scientists' views about users be privileged above those of technical staff and to what degree should the different disciplines independently present their specialist contributions or instead act as one team working together throughout the development process. The authors show the pros and cons of various options.

Limonard and de Koning bring these different dilemmas together within two models or clusters. The "social shaping" cluster starts with users' current experiences, involves users very pro-actively as product co-developers and the role of the social scientist is to tap into this input, to act as the voice of the user. The "mutual shaping" cluster starts with thinking about possible future uses, involves users reacting to these ideas and the role of the social scientist is to creatively question the product development strategy. At one level, the authors acknowledge, the two models make different assumptions. The first emphasizes the belief that users are capable of articulating interests and problems and can play a strong role in shaping technologies. The second emphasizes unpredictability and the belief that we will not fully know what happens until users and the technology confront each other.

Nevertheless, the authors argue that each may be appropriate in different circumstances. This depends on the time scales for which the design is meant (present, near future or distant future). It depends on the nature of the innovation (the degree to which it is fairly radical and technology-driven, the degree to which the functionality of the technology is already specified). And it depends on the kind of user targeted (and hence how articulate they can be about what they would like). Indeed, they suggest how the two approaches may sometimes be combined. But the point is that these models, which can also be considered to provide a social learning cycle, enables those involved in product development to see more clearly the possibilities and create the space for social scientists and technical staff to work together and profit from each other's knowledge.

Sarkkinen provides an ethnographic analysis of a Finnish ICT project. He argues that even though users' views appeared to be included in the process of evaluating software, it is important to take into account the classification processes used by technical staff when providing instructions for the user-testers. The reasoning and assumptions of these staff shape the whole testing exercise, with the implication that the process is not as user-centred as it could be and the ultimate designs may be sub-optimal from a user viewpoint. Hence, there is a need for external observers to make this classification process more transparent in order to ensure that the artifact's design respects user inputs.

The chapter starts by explaining how we use classification systems, even if they are so familiar to us that they become invisible. The key point is that by organizing how we think about the world in one way, we shut out other perspectives – and this is what is happening in these test scenarios written by technical staff. Sarkkinen uses the technique of deconstruction to show how these staff are directing users to think along certain lines, through the terms and logics they use, the options they offer, etc. User could be allowed, or indeed encouraged, to think more critically if different terms, options, instructions, etc. were provided.

The key points of deconstruction are outlined and here Sarkkinen notes how tools can be seen as texts, with interpretative flexibility, as was outlined in the introduction to this book. Five aspects of the test scenario are then considered. In each of these "bi-polar" classifications, we see the understanding of the technical staff, which directs the user, and an alternative perspective that could have been offered. For example, while the test scenario considers the task of the user as being to see if he or she can "use the system," an alternative set of guidelines might have asked whether the user could "perform a task" with this software. Arguably this would be more relevant to the users, more in keeping with what they actually have to do in their working lives, for example. For each of the five classifications, the author suggests an alternative, ultimately producing an improved, revised test-scenario that would be more meaningful to the user, encouraging them to give more useful feedback for designers to consider – in this sense, empowering the user. Here again we see a novel way of involving non-technologists in the design and development process.

Chapter 10

QUESTIONING THE "RURAL" ADOPTION AND USE OF ICTs

Rosemarie Gilligan

1.   Introduction

Much research suggests that information and communication technologies (ICTs) have the potential to eliminate the "friction of distance" in terms of location and social interaction (see Graham, 1998; Lægran, 2002). Janelle (1969) used the phrase "time-space convergence" in the late 1960s to describe the ability of transport technologies to bring places closer together. He suggested that places that were at one stage relatively isolated have more contact with each other now, because the time taken to travel between locations is reduced. Moreover, communication technologies, from the telegraph and the telephone, to e-mail and the Internet, are said to be producing an even more profound transformation of space and time. While transport technologies have helped to reduce communication times, communication technologies allow simultaneous exchanges to take place. Hence, the development of cyberspace, teleworking, online shopping, and other activities such as exchanging electronic documents online, means that, in effect, it is no longer necessary for people to use physical transportation in order to access people in distant places (Graham and Marvin, 1996). As a result, ICTs have particular relevance to rural areas as these areas which have been traditionally characterized in terms of their economic and social peripherality (Skerratt, 2003; Ward, 1990). Thus, it can be argued that ICTs have the potential to eliminate the importance of physical proximity to a whole host of economic, social, cultural and political activities, thereby making rural areas more attractive places for businesses, services and people to locate.

This chapter focuses on questions of how we are to understand the adoption and use of ICTs in rural areas. Despite the availability of international statistics contrasting urban and rural adoption of ICTs, the issues involved in measuring

Leslie Haddon (ed.), Everyday Innovators, 155–167.
© 2005 *Springer. Printed in The Netherlands.*

what counts as rural are in practice complex. There are a number of problems faced by social scientists in researching "rural" users of ICTs as a group – e.g. issues of defining rural, different types of rurality, different types of people inhabiting "rural" areas, etc. The implication is that when one is researching ICT users and looking for patterns within data it is important to appreciate the realities behind those data, including the way that classification schemes are structured, a point taking up in a very different context by the chapter on Sarkkinen in this volume.

The last section takes a different turn. It speculates about different dimensions of "rural ways of life" that could shape the experience of ICTs. In this way, the chapter illustrates how we can focus on the context of use, usage in rural settings in this instance, which is more generally emphasized in the social construction of technology (SCOT) approach expanded upon by Limonard and de Koning in the following chapter.

In terms of ICT adoption and use in rural communities, it could be argued that people living in rural areas are more restricted in their everyday life activities and have less access to information, goods and services than people living in a city. Therefore, the examples below will suggest that the motivations behind why people living in rural communities adopt and use ICTs may be different to those living in urban areas. In fact, ICT use may have a greater impact on the life of a person living in a rural community than in an urban area, as the person living in a rural area is now able to access information, goods and services which were not available to him/her in the past. Understanding better the needs of people living in rural areas and how ICTs meet those needs will give a better insight into the design of new ICT products and computing applications for these users.

2.   An Overview of ICT Adoption and Use in Rural Areas

Is there really an urban–rural digital divide? To date the majority of international studies examining the use and domestication of ICTs have by and large focused on urban areas. The international discourse on the digital divide suggests that geographical location influences the take up of ICTs. According to the OECD (2001), the term "digital divide" refers to:

the gap between individuals, households, businesses and geographic areas
at different socio-economic levels with regard both to their opportunities to
access information and communication technologies (ICTs) and to their use of
the Internet for a wide variety of reasons (ibid.: 5).

Findings from the OECD (2001) reported in *Understanding the Digital Divide* show that Internet access in all the OECD countries is higher in urban areas than in rural areas. The report also points out that members of households in urban areas are more likely to work in an ICT-rich environment. Furthermore, costs tend to be higher and the quality of Internet access lower in rural regions. In general, when discussing access to and usage of ICTs, those living in rural areas are considered to be at a disadvantage because of the lack of an adequate telecommunications infrastructure and the fact that technology tends to be more expensive to buy and to maintain. Moreover, people living in rural regions tend to be late adopters of ICTs. It is, therefore, not surprising to learn that early adopters of the Internet appeared to be young, male, affluent and live in an urban area.

Another source of evidence that shows that there is an unequal take up of ICTs between urban and rural regions is the body of literature specifically addressing the adoption and use of information technologies in rural and remote areas. National studies carried out in Australia, Canada, and the USA (see Hollifield and Donnermeyer, 2003; Hollifield *et al.*, 2000; Madden *et al.*, 2000; Ramírez, 2001; Thompson-James, 1999) provide further examples of differences in ICT adoption and use between urban and rural populations. For example, Hollifield *et al.* (2000) draw on the work of other writers (Parker *et al.*, 1995) to highlight the situation of rural areas in the USA:

Rural areas had historically lagged behind urban regions in gaining access to telecommunications technologies (ibid.: 762).

The findings from Ramírez's study (2001) on the development of ICTs in rural and remote areas in Canada, show that although Canada has a very advanced ICT infrastructure overall, its rural and remote areas have less developed ICT infrastructure, services and human resources compared to urban ones. While these studies provide some clues about the urban–rural digital divide, the problems of international comparison are discussed in more detail below.

2.1.   Statistics Showing Differences in Urban/Rural ICT Use

Statistics would appear to confirm that several international countries are experiencing the type of urban–rural digital divide outlined. First, let us refer to the Flash Eurobarometer 125: *Internet and the Public at Large* (July 2002), which explored Internet access in households in the fifteen EU member states between May and June 2002. The results show that Internet access in European households is higher in metropolitan areas (45%) and urban zones (41%) than in rural areas (35%). The study also points out that:

The Internet user at home or at work is most likely to be male, in the 40–54 age category, more highly educated and living in metropolitan or urban zones (Flash Eurobarometer 125, 2002, p. 20).

Regarding daily Internet use, those living in metropolitan and urban zones are more likely to use the Internet everyday, or nearly everyday, in comparison to those living in rural areas: metropolitan (46%), urban (42%), and rural (38%).

However, where people use the Internet, be it at home, work, school, etc., the overall pattern of access modes in rural areas is similar trend to that in metropolitan and urban zones. Those living in rural areas of Europe are more likely to use the Internet at home (69%), in comparison to at work (41%), school/college (19%), public access point (10%), or via mobile phone/on the move (9%).

If we turn to other ICTs by way of comparison, Oftel, the UK regulator for the telecommunications industry (now known as Ofcom), produces quarterly residential consumer surveys on use of ICTs. Such reports show trends in mobile phone penetration rates in urban versus rural areas in the UK (see Oftel, 2002). For example, according to their quarterly residential consumer survey report carried out in August 2002, mobile ownership is surprisingly higher in rural areas (74%) than in urban areas (67%). This is in contrast to findings on Internet access and use.

Other international studies, such as the NTIA studies (2000, 2002) from the USA provide statistical evidence to show differences in Internet use between urban and rural areas. However, such studies also point out that the gap between Internet use in urban and rural areas in the USA has decreased significantly in recent years. This is similar to the findings of Hollifield and Donnermeyer (2003), who suggest that during the first 6 years after 1994, when the Internet was opened to public use, there was a large gap in Internet adoption rates between urban and rural populations in the USA and, in particular, amongst the lowest income groups. However, at the end of 2001, although substantially decreased, there was still a digital divide in the USA regarding Internet use in rural and urban areas: 52.9% of all rural households were using the Internet, compared to 57.4% of all households in urban, non-central city areas.

3.   Definitions of "Rural" and the Concept of "Rurality"

We now have to look behind the picture outlined above to see how "rural" is defined and what the concept of "rurality" consists of. In fact, there is no universal definition of "rural." And as noted in the introduction, we can see that there are different typologies of rural areas, different problems associated with these areas, different types of people who live in rural communities and different ways in which "rural" is classified for statistical purposes.

3.1.   How "Rural" is Defined in Terms of Rural Sociology Literature

The rural sociology literature deals with the issues of why it is difficult to classify "rural" for statistical purposes. Mormont (1990) argues that the "rural" is a category of thought. He suggests that it was a term referring initially to the integration of peasant communities into society as a whole. However, today peasant communities are almost completely integrated into developed and urbanized countries. He argues that the rural–urban opposition is thus also a social construct. In Mormont's view, the rural exists first and foremost as a way to analyze a society within a specific spatial context, and, moreover, to analyze the particular social characteristics while defining the spatial context.

The rural is a category that each society takes and reconstructs, and that this social construction, with all its implications, defines the object of a sociology of the rural (Mormont 1990, p. 41).

Murdoch and Marsden (1994) suggest that rural sociology developed throughout the 20th century largely around a common set of suppositions associated with the "distinctiveness" of rural life. The first supposition concerned the notion of "traditional" rural life, while the second supposition referred to the changes within the rural economy and society due to increasing integration of rural areas into modern society. The "rural" was seen as static and unchanging, while the "urban" was viewed as dynamic and evolving. But the lines of demarcation between the "rural" and "urban" have become increasingly blurred, both due to changes in agriculture and to changes in the types of people moving to live in rural areas, for example, urban commuters living in rural settings. As a result, it has not been possible for sociologists to distinguish between a typically "urban way of life" and a typically "rural way of life," leading to the difficulty in trying to develop a rural sociology and an urban sociology. Sociologists have experienced many problems in trying to establish what constitutes "urban" and what constitutes "rural" and what differentiates one from the other. Tovey and Share (2000) suggest that empirical research began to show that most places actually fall between rural and urban, and display both urban and rural characteristics; therefore, the notion of distinguishing a "rural way of life" from an "urban way of life" was rapidly undermined. Moreover, Murdoch and Marsden (1994) argue that the problems associated with the term "rural" came to be reflected in the ambivalent status of rural sociology itself (see Marsden *et al.*, 1990). Mormont (1990) suggests that rural sociology never managed to adopt a clear terminology. He also points out that rural sociology failed to provide a definition of "rural" at a global level, i.e. there was no universal explanation for what we mean by "rural" or "rural way of life."

3.2. *Different Types of Rural Areas, Problems, Rural Communities*

With regard to different typologies of rural areas, Blunden *et al.* (1998) suggest five categories of "rurality" within the EU: urban imprint zone (areas with high densities and in-migration); high amenity and advantaged areas (relatively high densities in areas with strong in-migration pressure); developed and balanced areas (areas with intermediate densities with a balance of in- and out-migration); areas with potential development (areas of low density probably with out-migration); and areas requiring economic restructuring (areas of low density with significant out-migration). These categories, which ultimately reflect their development potentials, are determined more or less by their degree of accessibility, the extent to which they have a developed settlement hierarchy, population structures in terms of numbers, age and distribution, and their socio-economic profile. Other factors that might be considered could include patterns of land ownership, proximity to urban centres (e.g. proximity of the South-East of England to London), proximity to motorways, types of agricultural industries (e.g. crop farming in Scotland to agribusiness in England), and issues relating to ICT coverage, i.e. areas where there is no coverage for the mobile phone.

It is now clear that there are different types of rural areas, but what is also important to mention is that there are different types of problems associated with each of these rural regions. For example, the European Commission identified three standard problems of rural areas in *The Future of Rural Society* (EC, 1988). The first type of problem concerns the pressure of modern development and refers to those rural areas that are just lying beyond the boundaries of large cities, such as the county of Berkshire in the South-East of England. The problems associated with this rural area include excessive development and conflicts over the different potential uses of the land. The second type of problem concerns rural areas that face social and economic decline, like many peripheral rural regions, such as the county of Shropshire that lies on the border with Wales. A decline in agriculture in these areas, which has not been replaced by new rurally based industries, means that young people, in particular, have moved elsewhere in search of jobs. The affect of young people leaving these regions leads to continued economic decline and another reduction in the quality of life. The third type of problem is a more extreme case of the second problem. It concerns the more distant and less favoured rural areas and refers to mountainous zones and certain islands. These areas have been already significantly marked by rural decline, depopulation, and the abandonment of the land.

While it is evident that there are different types of rural areas and various problems associated with these regions, it should also be noted that there are different types of people who go to live in rural settings. Urban–rural migration, referred to as "counter-urbanisation" was a key theme within rural studies in the late 1980s and early 1990s. As more and more people were starting to move out and live in rural areas in the 1970s and 1980s, this further contributed to the heterogeneity of rural areas. But what types of people live in rural communities? First, regarding the heterogeneity of rural residents, Pahl (1968) identifies six major groupings of people living in rural areas: large property owners, the salariat (e.g. business and professional people), the retired urban workers with some capital, urban workers with limited capital/income (e.g. those who are forced to live in villages, due to high cost of urban land), rural working-class commuters, and traditional ruralities (e.g. local tradespeople, agricultural workers, etc.). Such a classification of rural populations shows us that rural people are very diverse, have different expectations from the countryside and even use the countryside differently. For example, take the difference between urbanites who permanently live in rural settings and those who just stay in the countryside on a temporary basis, at the weekends, during the summer holidays, etc. In fact, rural communities are very diverse in terms of social composition, economic structure, history and culture. Therefore, as people living in rural settings come from different walks of life, it could also be argued that how ICTs are adopted and used within various rural regions could be quite different.

3.3.   The Definition of "Rural" for Statistical Purposes

When it comes to ICT statistics and rural areas, it is important to understand how "rural" is classified in order to interpret these statistics correctly and benefit from these data. Given the difficulties experienced in defining "rural" and the different types of rural areas that exist, it is not surprising to learn that rural is classified in different ways for statistical purposes, and this makes it difficult to compare the statistics from different countries. Countries such as Canada, Denmark, France, Ireland, Italy, Spain, and Sweden simply classify as "rural" all administrative zones than fall below population thresholds for urban zones. However, the thresholds adopted are considerably different between the various countries. For example, in Ireland, the census defines "rural" as all areas outside towns of more than 1500 inhabitants, whereas in Canada, the census defines "rural" as all areas outside centres of 1000 or more. In France, the national statistics service defines urban communes as those with 2000 inhabitants. This is in comparison to countries such as Spain and Italy, where areas are classified as "urban" if they have a population of 10,000 inhabitants or more – and all populations below this threshold are considered to be "rural." In Denmark and Sweden, the requirement to count as an urban areas is that there must be at least 200 people living in homes that are not more than 50–200 metres apart (Persson and Westholm, 1994; Pumain and Sant-Julien, 1992 as quoted in Hoggart *et al.*, 1995). According to Hoggart *et al.* (1995), such diversity in the classification of "rural" shows the multiplicity of rural contexts within Europe. They suggest that these differences reflect the historical development of the countryside in the different European countries, in addition to *"the physical environmental and socio-political factors that play a key role in the 'construction' of rural space*" (ibid.: 22).

4.   Urban and Rural Ways of Life

The above discussion shows how it is by no means straightforward to talk about urban and rural "ways of life." This term, like the associated term "culture" is contested and open to debate (Thomas *et al.*, 2004). But that does not mean that we have to abandon addressing this dimension at all if this is one context of people's life that may have some bearing on their experience of ICTs. Therefore, the final section is speculative in that it tries to highlight what type of research questions we might pose and on what grounds, if we wish to investigate this aspect of users lives further. As an exercise, this requires some simplification, in contrast to the more nuanced picture of rural life described above – some of this complexity needs to be suspended for the moment.

4.1.   *Housing: Settlements Patterns and Living Space*

From the outset it is evident that urban areas are associated with high population densities and many rural areas have lower population densities. This is reflected in the size and type of housing that people live in. For example, if we take the Irish case that is the focus of my research interests, it is more likely for people in rural areas to live in detached or semi-detached houses rather than apartment blocks. This means that on average the physical living space available in rural housing may well be greater than in urban housing. In which case, when it comes to the location of technology within the home, we might well speculate that rural dwellers are more likely to have the option of a dedicated study or office where they can place their computer. In fact, as rural houses are more likely to have more physical space around their houses as well they may even have a separate building that they may use as an office for their computer. As a result, the "home" computer may never enter the home, as it remains located outside the main building.

The fact that there is perhaps more living space within and around a rural dwelling in comparison to urban housing gives rise to other issues, such as the recreational area available for children and the overall safety of children. In general, the countryside is considered a safer place to bring up children, as it is safer for them to play outside. But the corollary of this, of relevance for issues of ICT use, is that we would need to investigate whether children in urban areas spend more time indoors, which could involve them spending more time on ICTs. For example, while not particularly focusing on urban–rural differences, this is captured in a British studies discussing children's "bedroom culture" (Bovill and Livingstone, 2001).

4.2.   *Difference in Daily Life Patterns*

Exploring daily life patterns provides another perspective that may help us to become aware of differences between "rural ways of life" and "urban ways of life." For instance, rural areas, such as a rural community in the North West of Ireland, often have a less developed public transportation infrastructure. People have to drive or get a lift when going to meet somebody. In particular, teenagers and young people in the community are dependent on adults for lifts if they do not drive or have access to a car. This is in contrast to living in a town where teenagers can often more easily get a bus or other form of public transport to meet their friends and are not as reliant on parents for lifts. Therefore, we would have to investigate whether this had some implications for ICT use in rural communities, to overcome any problems associated with meeting face-to-face. Teenagers, and young people living in rural areas with restricted personal mobility, may be inclined to use mobile phones and texting more as a way of keeping in contact with friends and relatives.

As outlined earlier, different rural areas attract different types of people and this influences the variety of leisure options available. In general, it could be argued that there are fewer leisure options available in rural areas and what leisure options are available stem from a demand/interest in the local community. For example, some rural communities in Ireland have no swimming pool, fitness club/gym, basketball court, tennis court, cinema or theatre – the standard leisure resources found in a town. Therefore, the computer and the Internet has the potential to offer people living in these rural communities the opportunity to pursue and develop other leisure activities which do not require such activities. Examples of such activities include having an interest in genealogy, being a fan of a particular rock band or type of music, taking an interest in Harry Potter, digital photography, compiling one's own CDs, etc.

Health is a very important part of our everyday lives and we all need information relating to our health at different stages in our lives. Some rural communities in Ireland have no General Practitioner (GP) or health centre. People living in these communities have to travel to other communities to attend a GP. However, in many cases, there may be only one GP in this clinic and no possibility of having a female GP. This is in contrast to living in a city in Ireland where there would be a much greater choice of doctors and access to more medical resources and expertise. Once again, this raises the research question of whether this makes the Internet of more interest given its potential to provide vast amounts of medical information to people living in a rural community that is not available and/or very difficult to access in a rural community. Relevant issues could be related to women's health, for example, different stages of pregnancy, or other issues such as additives in food and hyperactivity in children, diets, various cancer treatments, etc.

Another everyday life activity, irrespective of where we are living, is shopping. In rural areas there is a lack of, for example, large retail stores or chain stores that are available in urban centres. For example, in some rural communities in Ireland, there may be no supermarket, butcher, bakery, clothes shop, music store, video/DVD rental store, bookstore, bank, travel agency or insurance broker. As a result, people have less choice when it comes to purchasing products and services and they may not be able to get as good a deal as is on offer in urban retail outlets. In parallel to the argument about health, we could ask whether the Internet has the potential to offer a much wider variety of goods (e.g., CDs, furniture, books, contact lens, and other personal items, etc.) and services (e.g., flights, travel insurance, hotel reservations, campsite bookings, concert tickets, etc.) which are not available in small Irish rural communities and also at competitive prices as found in cities.

Empirically all of these differences between rural and urban ways of life may prove to be non-existent. More probably, given the earlier discussion, we may find a more complex picture, with some of the hypotheses outlined above applying to some "rural areas" more than others, and to some "rural dwellers" more than others. But if there proves to be any reality that matches these speculations, then we would actually have reasons why some "rural" dwellers may be more motivated to use certain ICTs. This would make us reflect again on the blanket claim that rural areas lag behind urban ones – there might be a more complex set of processes at work.

5.   Conclusion

This chapter began by presenting the standard assumptions and data about differences between urban and rural ICT adoption and use. It then problematized these through discussing the issues around the concept of "rurality," as there was a difference between types of rural areas and between the people who inhabit these areas, thereby highlighting the heterogeneity of the rural experience. The last section, explored some potential differences between the urban and rural ways of life. The point of the exercise, in keeping with the other interests expressed in this book, is to show what types of questions we could reasonably ask about users if we seriously want to take this urban–rural dimension into account when trying to understand people's experiences of ICTs.

Referring back to the literature on the adoption and use of ICTs in rural areas (Hollifield and Donnermeyer, 2003; Hollifield *et al.*, 2000; Madden *et al.*, 2000; Mitchell and Clarke, 1999; Ramírez, 2001), it is now apparent that we need to have more discussion of different types of rural life and the experiences of ICTs that people living in these different rural regions have. Much of the literature clearly makes assumptions that rural areas lag behind urban areas in terms of adoption and use of ICTs, and while some of this may well be justified, in this body of literature there is a tendency to simply equate "rural" with those areas that are peripheral and remote and experiencing economic and social decline. But we have seen that this is just one type of rural that we are now aware of and there is a need to address the other types of rural as well and show, for example, how urban commuters are using ICTs at home in rural areas.

Both the sections problematizing the notion of rural and the exercise speculating about rural inhabitants situations and motivations would suggest that it would be an oversimplification to assert that rural areas lag behind urban areas in terms of ICT use and adoption. Rural communities are very diverse in terms of social composition, economic structure, history and culture. Moreover, how and why ICTs are used in some rural areas is very different not only to how ICTs are adopted and used in urban centres, but also to how they are experienced in other rural areas. Rates of adoption and use of ICTs in rural areas also depends on the technology in question. For example, mobile phone penetration rates are actually higher in rural areas than in urban areas in the UK. Bearing in mind the complexity of the rural issue described in this chapter, "rural" is something that needs to be thought through very carefully.

To draw to a close, even a century ago, farmers, to most people's surprise, were surpassing city dwellers in their take up of the telephone in the USA. Fischer (1992) reminds us that it was not until the early years of the 20th century that the industry began to address the rural market in the USA. A similar pattern can also be found with regard to the early take-up of the mobile phone amongst farmers in Denmark. In addition, the take-up of digital TV in Ireland via satellite, launched in December 2002, has been far higher in rural areas than in urban areas; the main reason being that there are no cable networks in rural areas. Therefore, we need to be wary of how we approach the "rural" when discussing new technologies, and perhaps think again about our perceptions of how people in rural areas adopt and use ICTs.

References

Blunden, J., Pryce, W., Dreyer, P. The classification of rural areas in the European context: an exploration of a typology using neutral network applications. Regional Studies, 1998; 32: 149–160.

Bovill, M., Livingstone, S. Bedroom culture and the privatization of media use. In Livingstone, S., Bovill, M. (Eds.), Children and Their Changing Media Environment. A European Comparative Study; 2001. Lawrence Erlbaum Associate, Mahwah, New Jersey: 179–200.

EC (European Commission). The future of rural society. COM (88) 501 final/2; 1988. The European Commission, Brussels.

Flash Eurobarometer 125. Internet and the public at large; 2002. The European Commission, DG Information Society, Brussels.

Fischer, C. America Calling: A Social History of the Telephone to 1940; 1992. University of California Press, Berkeley, Los Angeles.

Graham, S., Marvin, S. Telecommunications and the City: Electronic Spaces, Urban Places; 1996. Routledge, London.

Graham, S. The end of geography or the explosion of place? Conceptualizing space, place and information technology. Progress in Human Geography, 1998; 22: 165–185.

Hollifield, C.A., Donnermeyer, J.F., Wolford, G.H., Agunga, R. The effects of rural telecommunications self-development projects on local adoption of new technologies. Telecommunications Policy, 2000; 24: 761–779.

Hollifield, C.A., Donnermeyer, J.F. Creating demand: influencing information technology diffusion in rural communities. Government Information Journal Quarterly, 2003; 20: 135–150.

Hoggart, K., Buller, H., Black, R. Rural Europe: Identity and Change; 1995. Arnold Publishers, London.

Janelle, D.G. Spatial reorganization: a model and concept. Annals of the Association of American Geographers, 1969; 59: 348–364.

Lægran, A.S. The petrol station and the Internet café: rural technospaces for youth. Journal of Rural Studies, 2002; 18: 157–168.

Madden, G., Savage, S.J., Coble-Neal, G., Bloxham, P. Advanced communications policy and adoption in rural Western Australia. Telecommunications Policy, 2000; 24: 291–304.

Marsden, T., Lowe, R., Whatmore, S. (Eds.), Rural Restructuring: Global Processes and Their Responses; 1990. Fulton Publishers, London.

Mitchell, S., Clark, D. Business adoption of information and communications technologies in the two-tier rural economy: some evidence from the South Midlands. Journal of Rural Studies, 1999; 15: 447–455.

Mormont, M. Who is rural? Or, how to be rural: towards a sociology of the rural. In Marsden, T., Lowe, P., Whatmore, S. (Eds.), Rural Restructuring: Global Processes and Their Responses; 1990. Fulton Publishers, London.

Murdoch, J., Marsden, T. Reconstituting Rurality; 1994. University College London Press Limited, London.

NTIA (National Telecommunications and Information Administration) and US Department of Commerce. Falling through the net: toward digital inclusion. A Report on Americans' Access to Technology Tools; 2000. US Department of Commerce and NTIA, Washington, DC.

NTIA. A nation online: how Americans are expanding their use of the Internet; 2002. US Department of Commerce and NTIA, Washington, DC.

OECD (Organisation for Economic Co-operation and Development). Understanding the Digital Divide; 2001. OECD, Paris.

Oftel (Office of Telecommunications). Consumers' use of mobile telephony; 2002. Oftel, London.

Pahl, R. Readings in Urban Sociology; 1968. Pergamon Press, Oxford.

Parker, E., Hudson, H., Dillman, D., Strover, S., Williams, F. (Eds.), Electronic Byways: State Policies for Rural Development Through Telecommunications. 2nd edition; 1995. The Aspen Institute, Boulder, CO.

Persson, L., Westholm, E. Vers une nouvelle mosaïque de la Suède rurale. Economic Rurale, 1994; 223: 20–26.

Pumain, D., Sant-Julien, T. The Statistical Concept of the Town in Europe; 1992. Office for Official Publications of the European Communities, Luxembourg.

Ramírez, R. A model for rural and remote information and communication technologies: a Canadian exploration. Telecommunications Policy, 2001; 25: 315–330.

Skerratt, S. The Implications for Rural and Regional Populations of the Irish Government's Provision of Broadband Communications Infrastructure; 2003. National Institute of Regional and Spatial Analysis, Maynooth.

Thomas, F., Haddon, L., Gilligan, R., Heinzmann, P., de Gournay, C. Cultural factors shaping the experience of icts: an exploratory review. A Report for COST269; 2004. http://www.cost269.org.

Thompson-James, M. Computer use and Internet use by members of rural households. Rural and Small Town Canada Analysis Bulletin, 1999; 1: 7.

Tovey, H., Share, P. A Sociology of Ireland; 2000. Gill & Macmillan, Dublin.

Ward, C. The Child in the Country; 1990. Bedford Square Press, London.

Chapter 11

DEALING WITH DILEMMAS IN PRE-COMPETITIVE ICT DEVELOPMENT PROJECTS: THE CONSTRUCTION OF "THE SOCIAL" IN DESIGNING NEW TECHNOLOGIES

Sander Limonard and Nicole de Koning

1.   Introduction

Participating in a long-term ICT development project as a social scientist is indeed a culture shock (as noted in Haddon and Kommonen, 2002, p. 17). Trained in performing empirical research, such researchers are confronted with other approaches, the social practices of designers and the limitations of their own perspectives. In addition, in being responsible for the "user" or "societal" part of the project, they are faced with a truckload of normative choices that will have a profound influence on the way the technology is going to be designed and introduced. Making sensible choices in a technology development environment requires a subtle and politically diplomatic way of choosing a perspective, prioritizing and maneuvering.

In this chapter, we want to share our experiences and investigate ways of dealing with these kinds of situations. We try to do this from the point of view that ICTs are socially constructed, as discussed in Section 1. The main message of this perspective is that the role and meaning of ICTs cannot be determined apart from its societal context (Bijker, 1995; Rip *et al.*, 1995). In other words, the role of ICTs in society is not primarily technologically or economically pre-determined, but rather it should be regarded as a product of society. The ICTs we have reflect various definitions of problems, concerns, power relations between people and groups and the norms and values at work in society. Taking this standpoint has major implications for the way in which the relations between the user and future ICT artifacts or systems must be understood as well as any perspective on the role of "the user" in designing ICTs. The social construction of technology (SCOT) perspective emphasizes

Leslie Haddon (ed.), Everyday Innovators, 168–183.
© 2005 *Springer. Printed in The Netherlands.*

that there are choices to be made in both the design of artifacts and systems and in the direction or trajectory of ICT development projects. If technology does not emerge from the unfolding of a pre-determined logic or a single determinant, different routes are available, potentially leading to different technological outcomes. The character of technologies, as well as their social implications, is problematized and opened up for enquiry (Reuzel and Wilt, 2001, p. 109). In short, the SCOT perspective stresses that technology development is about making normative choices and thus can be considered to be a form of politics.

When we apply this to work projects, the SCOT perspective draws special attention to the future user in two ways. First of all, if the role and the acceptance of technology are primarily determined by societal forces, this implies that any design trajectory must take into account the social context in which the ICT service or device is going to be used in order to reduce uncertainty and guide the design process. Secondly, this perspective also implies that the manner in which the context of use shapes and re-shapes the meaning of an artifact is difficult to predict at the outset of a design trajectory. Users can re-interpret intended meanings and functionalities in unpredictable ways. And the manner in which the artifact in turn influences this context of use is not predictable either. Thus, we are left with a tension between the increased need to focus on the context in which a technology has to "work," and the awareness that any claim regarding how a technology will be conceptualized and accepted is clouded in uncertainty. It is in this tension that we are exploring dilemmas and ways of handling them.

In this exercise, we are not trying simply to phase out any dilemmas that are identified. We will try to show that by acknowledging the impossibility of a single best solution in a situation that calls for one decision, setting up a specific feedback loop can serve as a useful way to deal with that situation (Hamdon-Turner, 1990; van Twist *et al.*, 1998). In this way, we may be able to transform polarized or poorly understood discussions into processes of social learning (Rip *et al.*, 1995; van Lieshout *et al.*, 2001). Instead of ending up in negotiations in which the same arguments appear time and time again, we hope that this approach, which involves thinking in terms of dilemmas, will help social scientists to organize a process of social learning: a process in which knowledge and the involvement of users, assessments of future use and the power relations between disciplines are in a continuous process of critical examination.

In short, we will identify dilemmas and propose a way of dealing with them. In our search for dilemmas, we draw on our experience of participating in three long-term ICT development projects. We worked in interdisciplinary teams of social researchers, people with a background in human computer interaction, software system architects and software engineers in order to develop innovative ICT applications. We will sketch out the problems that we encountered in working in these projects from the theoretical perspective of the SCOT. It is from this perspective that we then distil dilemmas and propose ways of handling these. By doing this, we want to show that acknowledging a dilemma enables us to overcome rigidity and polarization and paves the way for a more reflexive way of working in ICT design projects.

2.   Confronting Problems

We will now discuss some problems we were confronted with in three different pre-competitive ICT development projects. To be able to do this, our first step is to briefly describe the kind of projects from which these problems were drawn.

2.1.   *A Short Description of the Projects*

The three projects under discussion are "Media@Home," "X-Home" and "Beyond 3G." The authors participated in these projects as project members. Media@Home and X-Home were carried out by people from different TNO institutes within the Netherlands. The Beyond 3G project was carried out in collaboration with people from Ericsson. All three projects were pre-competitive, which means that the developed technology was to be applied and used 5–10 years in the future. Because the projects had these large time spans and were technology-oriented, business and financial aspects were not part of the projects. In all three projects, the overall project goal was to develop a so-called "demonstrator." A demonstrator can be considered to be a preliminary prototype that is used to demonstrate the possible uses of newly developed technology. Their primary function is to persuade companies and public authorities to develop them into marketable products or services.

Media@Home was the first and largest project in terms of budget and time span. The project was concerned not with increasing the "intelligence" of the *house* environment (the widely diffused idea of the "Smart House"), but that of the *household* (i.e. "Smart Living"). The result was the development of the Pro-Active Agenda (PAA), an ICT service that was accessible via different devices. On the basis of self-generating personal profiles, this agenda comes up with ideas regarding what to do that day, records your favorite TV programmes, and proposes meeting schedules.

X-Home stands for the "eXtended" Home and can be considered as being the sequel to Media@Home. This project was also concerned with the household, but differed in the sense that some demands other than those coming from users needed to be met. X-Home had to address healthcare issues and needed to draw special attention to personalization and security issues. Meeting these demands, the project selected "informal carers"[1] as the audience to be served. The demonstrator was a variation on the PAA, labeled the "e-buddy," and was designed to function as a virtual assistant for informal carers in their task of supporting needy family members or friends.

The approach in Beyond 3G was the exact opposite to the one in the Media@Home project: it involved no extensive research, it was technology-driven, and it was strongly linked to the other technical work. The project's aim was to improve the interoperability of different kinds of mobile ICT infrastructures (GSM, WiFi, UMTS) that were assumed to co-exist in 5–10 years from the time of the project. The starting point in this project were seven already-existing scenario's about the future "wireless world." The work package concerned with end users involved the specific task of formulating end user requirements that could then be translated into technical requirements for interoperability. The group of participants in this work package consisted mainly of engineers who were also involved in other technical activities.

2.2.   Recurring Choices

We now turn to the position and work of the social scientist. The work involving users was built up along similar lines in all three projects. In every project, the user or use of technology had to be configured, the user had to be involved to voice his or her preferences and demands, and finally the result of this work had to be integrated with the work of team members from other, mostly technical, backgrounds. On the basis of these tasks, we discerned three different stages in every project: user configuration, user involvement and interdisciplinary co-operation. Below, we will discuss problems occurring in each of these stages.

2.2.1.   User configuration

The task of user configuration consists of selecting a target group and a context in which a technology will be used and then describing the possible future use of this technology. During this process, different design trajectories are possible, each with their own advantages and disadvantages. Within the Media@Home project, the researchers started from research on the present context of the household – what they did and how they used ICTs. On the basis of this, narratives were written that described prospective future situations in which

---

[1] Informal care-takers are people from the social network of a patient who assist him or her in their daily activities: the household, taking care of administrative issues, hospital visits, etc. This definition does not include professional care-takers. Informal care-takers can include spouses, family members, friends and neighbors.

family members would use the PAA in their everyday lives. The advantage of this exercise was that it gave a structured, demarcated and detailed image of the present context of use. However, this meant that any future uses that were anticipated were derived from and framed in terms of a rigid typology derived from the present situation. In other words, there is an extrapolation assuming daily practices, preferences, etc., stay the same. This is a limitation, since we know, for example, there is no guarantee that attitudes toward ICTs and the symbolic value of ICTs will, in fact, stay the same. So, despite the solid foundation of knowledge generated concerning the present situation, the social scientists in Media@Home were stuck with a problem or a discrepancy. Taking the present context as a starting point does not suffice, because, to take another example, we already know that the introduction of a new ICT service will influence both the user and the context in which it is going to be used. Yet it is only from the present situation that we can draw any factual conclusions. Somewhere in the description of the context and possible use of ICTs, we need to reflect on, and maybe even fantasize about, possible changes in use that may arise following the introduction of a new technology.

The Beyond 3G project team started with this last thought in mind. The work focused almost exclusively on future possible uses, without paying much attention to how users use mobile networks now. The starting point for configuring the context of use and the future use of these wireless infrastructures was the scenarios developed by large companies and international research organizations that already existed. In discussing and analyzing these scenarios, certain examples of uses were selected. To a large extent, *the foresight exercise was a social process*, in which the group selected what they regarded as being relevant elements from several images of possible futures. The advantage of not dealing with the present situation is that it opens up the possibility of providing detailed accounts of possible future situations. A major disadvantage lies in the relatively weak methodology underlying the steps in this project. As a consequence, when writing out the narratives, project members were inclined to confuse possible futures with desired futures. The freedom in writing these narratives opened up the possibility for personal preferences to dominate or arbitrary decisions to be taken.

The problem in configuring a future context and future use basically comes down to a problem of foresight. Do we start from the present situation and reflect on how a certain technology might change this situation? Or do we start by fantasizing about what the future might look like and then investigate how feasible these "made up futures" are?

2.2.2.   User involvement

Users were involved in different ways in the three projects. In Media@Home and Beyond 3G, users and user groups were interviewed and participated in focus groups. They were involved in a *validating* capacity: In Media@Home, project members proposed ideas or presented assumptions to the families to get their reactions. In Beyond 3G, interviews with representatives from professional user groups were held in order to validate those aspects of the professionals' work of relevance to the technological infrastructure that could support their work. In this way, a factual and detailed picture could be drawn of the present context of use and the perception of the technology under development (the PAA in Media@Home and heterogeneous mobile networks in Beyond 3G). Despite these advantages, this approach left the potential users free of obligations or engagement. The users considered discussing the PAA or the use of mobile networks to be fun, nothing more.

The X-Home project team tried to give potential future users more of a steering role: the everyday problems of informal carers served as the starting point for thinking about design options. Potential users were asked to identify problems for which the e-buddy, the virtual assistant that was developed in X-Home, could offer some kind of solution. In addition, at a later stage, these participants were asked to provide their reactions to the specific solutions that e-buddy offered. It was a useful starting point in certain respects, but as they were asked to think about what the e-buddy could offer them the representatives of the user groups had trouble imagining how they could contribute to the development process. How could they be of any help if they did not understand what a prototype, which was not yet fully developed, could actually do? This misunderstanding led to the limited involvement of users and an end product that had a distinctly "technology push" character.

The problems we encountered in these projects had related to the opportunities arising from, but also limitations of involving, lay users or user groups. On the one hand, their perspective needed to be taken into account because the ICT product under development had to fit into their everyday lives, even if the functionality offered by the technology only played a minor role. On the other hand, users were often limited in their ability to indicate how they wanted a technology to be developed, because they lacked the appropriate technological know-how.

2.2.3.   Interdisciplinary co-operation

Disciplines can work together on many different levels. The interdisciplinary co-operation in Media@Home consisted largely of staff from different backgrounds discussing the results from the project management team. No "user requirements" or other documents for discussion were used to transfer the results in a more formal way. In other words, the interdisciplinary co-operation was first and foremost a social process. This social transfer of user-related knowledge worked very well in the short-term. Using the terms "everyday life" and the messages from the empirical research proved to be very powerful in terms of influencing the functionality of the application. At a later stage of the project, however, this strategy for transferring such social knowledge proved to be too informal. The user-related work in Media@Home mainly produced appealing images, but in practice it had little effect on the development of the technology.

Within X-Home the co-operation between different disciplines took place on a different level, that of formulating requirements. The information generated in the configuration and validation phase was translated into user requirements. After these were formulated, the engineers who had to build the demonstrator protested against the weight being given to these requirements. A discussion followed. Should the requirements play a prescriptive role, serving as pre-conditions when building the application? Or should they be treated as a tool for monitoring and evaluating the process of building the e-buddy? The project management chose to follow this last course of action, thereby limiting the involvement of users. While this issue relates to the previous discussion of user involvement, it clearly has implications for relations between disciplines.

In Beyond 3G, people from other disciplines (all of them engineers) were actively involved in this "user" work package. They were given the task of selecting elements from the scenarios, writing the narratives and formulating user requirements in order to optimize the knowledge transfer from this work package to the others. The task of the social scientist was to guide the other project members, not to prescribe what they should build or design. An advantage of this method is that the information about users was generated by the same people who had to use it. The other side of the coin, however, was that the engineers who participated on the "user side" perceived these activities as being merely an intermediary stage, a task that had to be carried out in order to start the "real" work.

3.   Three Dilemmas

Looking at these projects, many complex situations occurred that did not allow for one best course of action. The SCOT perspective showed that there is a tension between not being able to predict future use, but at the same time acknowledging the need to focus on the future context of use in order to evaluate whether new ICTs will be successful. In each phase of the projects, we have just discussed, this tension can be regarded as being a specific dilemma. In the next section, we will isolate the dilemmas from the configuration, validation and participatory phase of the projects. At the same time, we know that we are not the first to notice them. So in order to avoid a naive discussion of the problems in technology development, we will discuss them in combination with earlier observations and remarks made in the existing literature. By raising these dilemmas to a more general level of discussion, we want to present a more generally applicable way of dealing with problem situations.

3.1.   The Configuration Dilemma

In the configuration phase, the dilemma was one of foresight. On the one hand, we need to focus on the context of people's everyday life if we want a technology to be accepted by its target group. However, on the other hand, we know that any claim about how a technology will be taken up is full of contingencies. In choosing a course of action in the configuration phase, two starting points emerged, summarized in Table 11-1.

Table 11-1. The possible starting points in configuring the future use of ICT technology

Present socio-technical context of use	Future use of a technology in context
Need to focus on context of use	Need to recognize uncertainty
Projective research	Prospective research
Extrapolating from current situation	Exploring the future situation

The first starting point (the left side of Table 11-1) is the present context in which we pre-suppose the ICT under development is going to be introduced. It rests on the first message from our SCOT perspective – the need to focus on the context of use in which the new technology is to be accepted. Media@Home was a project that was organized in this way. The present situation and its dynamics were used to cast some light on how a technology might be accepted. People concerned with "user-centerd design" advocate this point of view when they talk about designing for a "technologically ignorant" user (Chrisler, 2005, p. 21). The other starting point (the right side of Table 11-1) is the future context of use, which assumes the future ICT is already in use. This starting point rests on the other viewpoint that states that we, by definition, cannot know how users are going to accept and appropriate newly introduced ICTs. The configuration phase in Beyond 3G was good example of this approach. Here, the flexible and unpredictable nature of the process of technology acceptance is highlighted. It pre-supposes that future use cannot be determined from looking at the past. This perspective advocates creativity in order to be able to anticipate any unexpected kinds of use. In addition, the technology that is under development is taken into account, which enables the social scientists to elaborate more on the possible interrelationships between that user and technology. In short, the dilemma consists of the choice between starting from the existing socio-technical context or starting from a non-existing future context in which it is assumed that the ICT in question has already been accepted.

3.2.   The Dilemma of User Involvement

The second dilemma concerns the way in which users are involved. Here a variant of the dilemma articulated by Collingridge (1980) comes into play. Without having a fully developed ICT device at their disposal, users do not have a clear-cut idea of what they require, want or need. Users articulate their needs according to the state of development of the technology, according to how finalized it is. The dilemma involved is the following: at a stage when it is still possible to steer the technology in different directions, knowledge of the requirements, needs and wants of the user remain very limited. This dilemma contains a cognitive as well as a socio-political element (Rip and Schot, 2002, p. 156). The cognitive element again lies in the field of foresight. The function-alities originally envisaged for a technology differ from the ones that eventually become dominant. Even if we use a "context of use" approach, this does not guarantee user acceptance in any way. In order to be accepted, any given ICT re-quires some kind of re-conceptualization by the people who are going to use it. In this process of "stepping into the wider world" (Rip and Schot, 2002, p. 163) the socio-political dimension becomes apparent. Technological development may seem like a matter for insiders – the project members. However, in the end, the technology will be exposed to outsiders. Therefore, the fact that users ultimately act as co-producers of the role of the new technology and therefore act as stakeholders in the project has to be taken into account in the early stages of the project. Looking at the projects from the SCOT perspective, the courses of action are limited to two options (see Table 11-2).

Table 11-2. Two possible courses of actions in involving users

Pro-active user involvement	Reactive user involvement
Problem- or demand-based design	Design based on vision or ambition
User as the principal client	User as one of the stakeholders
User as co-creator and co-producer	User as co-producer

The left side depicts an approach that puts the users on a pedestal. They act as the guide in determining the functionality of the ICT under development. Users are at the center of the design process, actively determining the functionality of the ICT technology. This approach was employed in the X-Home project, where we asked representatives of users to explicate their problems, needs and wishes. The other option, on the right, is based on the combination of the future user and the future technology. Here, users have a more passive role, in which they give their comments and discuss the findings and propositions that the researcher or designer comes up with. In Media@Home, users were given this rather passive role. In this role, they validate the findings of the researchers and approve or disapprove of what is offered to them. The dilemma thus consists of the choice between a pre- and pro-active role for users versus a more reactive involvement.

3.3.   The Dilemma of Interdisciplinary Co-operation

The third dilemma is a socio-political one: project members have different backgrounds and use different vocabularies. How can the work that is carried out on the user's side be properly accounted for in the development of a technology? Here, knowledge generation and collectively making the project are the two poles of the dilemma. We will characterize the dilemma using the metaphors of the "laboratory" and the "development arena" (Jørgensen and Sørensen, 2002) (see Table 11-3).

Table 11-3. The organization of interdisciplinary co-operation

The laboratory	The development arena
Knowledge before participation	Participation before knowledge
Black-boxing of research findings	Collectively constructing research results
Social researcher as scientist	Social researcher as project member

The laboratory is taken as metaphor for the approach on the left. It functions as a space for reducing and ordering processes that are too complex to be understood in "real life." When the processes are ordered in the laboratory, they can be translated and reproduced outside (Latour, 1988). The laboratory is used as a confined space that produces a certain kind of authority in terms of knowledge and discourse, e.g. the way that matters are discussed and analyzed. The Media@Home project was a nice example of this approach. Here, knowledge was constructed independently of the other project members and then used to organize other activities in the project. In X-Home, the knowledge was translated into a requirements' document, which acted as an interface between disciplines, but served a similar "authoritarian" role as well. This approach pre-supposes a strong belief in the knowledge claims made by social scientists concerning the future context of use and future user wants and needs. The major disadvantage of this approach is the transferability of the findings. Because the knowledge is already "blackboxed" – i.e. how it was derived is not visible to outsiders and open to debate – the other project members will not easily commit themselves to the way in which this knowledge then organizes their work. The other "horn" of the dilemma is that of the development arena. The development arena can be thought of as a space in which several "actor worlds" are brought together through looking at the same problem area (Jørgensen and Sørensen,

2002, p. 208). Here, the social scientist does have a role as a messenger of the truth but rather he or she is simply one of the project members and is steered by the overall project strategy or concept. The emphasis is on co-operation and interdisciplinary teamwork. Beyond 3G was organized in the spirit of this approach: engineers who were going to build the application actively participated in examining scenarios and drawing up narratives. This approach ensures that the insights generated about users and the context of use are then represented in the technical work, because the engineers also participate in the social science research and vice versa. On the other hand, the quality of these findings may vary due to the fact that engineers may have another, sometimes overoptimistic, view about future uses of ICTs.

3.4.   *Mapping Dilemmas from the SCOT Perspective*

Back to the SCOT perspective. We began investigating the projects from the paradoxical tension between the need to focus on the future social context of use and the acknowledgment of the unpredictability of the way in which users will accept and appropriate new ICTs. It is in this tension that we identified the three dilemmas and it is this same tension that we now use to map them (see Table 11-4).[2]

Table 11-4. Mapping dilemmas from the SCOT perspective

	"Social Shaping" cluster	"Mutual Shaping" cluster
	Need to focus on the (future) context of use	Recognizing the inability to predict future use
Configuration	Present socio-technical context of use	Future use of a technology in context
User involvement	Pro-active user involvement	Reactive user involvement
Interdisciplinary co-operation	"Laboratory" strategy	"Development arena" approach

By mapping the positions of each dilemma in this way, two value clusters appear. The two columns represent the two ideological positions already present in our discussion of the SCOT perspective. However, having examined the projects we can now flesh out these two positions and specify them for each phase of a technology development project. This is relevant because an important element in dealing with these dilemmas is timing and sequencing

---

[2] We need to note here that the projects from which we draw the dilemmas do not neatly fall into one cluster or the other. For reasons of convenience, we worked with the extracted dilemmas instead of the project descriptions or the recurring choices.

the management of the different dilemmas. We can only sequence them in the right way if we have a grasp of the values on which they are built.

3.5.   The "Social Shaping" Cluster

We label the first value cluster (the left column in Table 11-4) the "social shaping" cluster because it reflects a strong belief in the abilities of end users and their representatives to actively control technology development. Supporters of this view pre-suppose a relatively high level of problem or demand articulation among users, which makes it easy for researchers to "tap" the information from the users and to cast light on the future use of a technology. Such a belief in the abilities of the users to predict their own behavior and use legitimizes social scientists presenting their findings as relatively stable "facts." This enables these researchers to use the analysis of the cluster as a tool to steer the innovation in a certain direction. From this viewpoint, the role of researchers is to represent the "voice of the user." They act as a serving hatch for the people who are going to use the technology that is under development and have the task of ensuring that users' problems, needs and wishes are accounted for.

3.6.   The "Mutual Shaping" Cluster

We label the second value cluster (the right column in Table 11-4) the "mutual shaping" cluster because the central assumption is that the relation between the user and the ICT technology is determined only when they are confronted by each other. Users are perceived as being unpredictable subjects who accept and appropriate technology. Therefore, predictions of future use are hard to make. The ambition of foreseeing future use is abandoned and exchanged for *anticipating* future use. In this anticipation exercise, users are one of the stakeholders who have an interest in anticipating the use of technology. They are asked to react to possible futures so that the project members can formulate strategies to manage unexpected or non-use. From this viewpoint, social scientists take a creative role and have the task of coming up with images and narratives concerning possible future uses. Here, other project members are perceived as being important stakeholders too. The role of the social scientists is now limited to testing the strategy that the project management or the visionary behind the project has come up with. This is a non-authoritative role. The social scientist represents contingency and has the task of questioning the strategy and of enticing the project management to take on different perspectives and experiment with their own strategies.

With these two value clusters, we are now ready to sequence the dilemmas and propose a configuring/involving users/co-operating cycle. This enables us to time the use of the different conflicting values in the project. We can do this by arranging the clustered dilemma positions in a circle.

4.   Strategy Formation

The strategy in dealing with the three dilemmas is represented in the learning cycle in Figure 11-1.

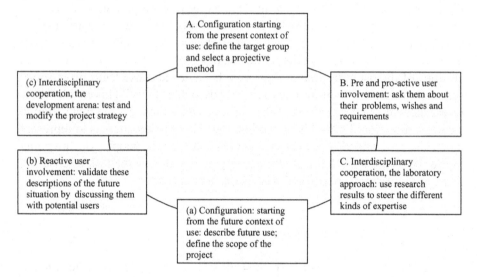

Figure 11-1. Dealing with dilemmas.

The text blocks A, B and C represent the "social shaping" view in the different phases of the project, whereas the text blocks with the small a, b and c represent the "mutual shaping" value cluster. The combination of the capital and small letters represent the specific dilemmas discussed earlier. This cycle offers a sequenced methodology for dealing with different dilemmas. The only rule in using this tool is that it has to be run through in a clockwise manner.

We will briefly walk through this learning cycle. We start at the top, but this starting point is artificial since we have to start somewhere. Firstly, a theory and a methodology to characterize the target audience and cast light on the future context and future use has to be selected (activity A). Then, a foresight study can be carried out in which the problems, needs, wishes or requirements function as the (partial) basis of this exercise (activity B). The results can then be used to actively steer and organize the work of others in the project (activity C). At this stage, others in the project have to be able to indicate what the ICTs in question have to offer that is of value to the targeted user group. When this socio-technical "scope" is defined, the social scientists can take their more critical and creative role by drawing up unexpected, weird, funny or distopian futures (activity a).

After walking through these possible futures with users, (activity b) they can then test the project's strategy or binding concept by confronting it with these prospective futures (activity c). It is then up to the "concept manager" or the project management to modify the strategy or concept behind the project. A part of this strategy formation may involve re-conceptualizing, specifying or changing the target group, which leads us to activity A again.

4.1.   Where to Start

The point of departure in the cycle is dependant on the project strategy, the time horizon, the ability of the user to articulate his or her needs and the level to which the functionality of the technology is specified. For example, when a project strategy is technology-driven, the first contribution you can make as a social scientist is to take a critical stand and test the expectations and preliminary outcomes of the project by starting at the left side of the circle (activity b). This enables you to influence strategy and maybe get into a position to negotiate a more prescriptive role for the "user part." Another factor is the time horizon. If a project has a short time-to-market, users will probably have a more crystallized view on what they need, want or require, so the starting point can be the top of the circle (activity A, maybe even B). The kind of user group also determines this level of problem or demand articulation. Professionals in the care domain may have a more articulated view on how ICTs could help them in doing their job then is the case with households. Finally, if a project is organized around expertise instead of an external driving factor such as an assignment for a customer, a common starting point is that of defining the scope of the project (activity C in combination with activity a), in which the different kinds of expertise present in the project are taken as resources for developing a common territory or arena.

4.2.   How Can This Cycle Serve as a Tool?

In the first place, this loop can be used as a resource in *sequencing* the different approaches in a project. Selecting a specific kind of foresight method implies a specific kind of user involvement and a different kind of strategy or role in relation to the other parts of the project. It can be used as a basis for designing work plans, but also for *evaluating* activities performed in projects. Inconsistencies in the values underlying different courses of action can be identified and corrected, which leads to a solid and coherent way of handling dilemmas. The use of the requirements in the X-Home project was an example of such an inconsistency. After a projective study was carried out, the requirements that were extrapolated were used to test and verify the outcomes of the work of the system architects and software engineers instead of determining the very outcome of their work. By coupling different activities in different phases of the project in this way, we can overcome these inconsistencies and refine the steps, instruments and interdisciplinary co-operation in a reflexive way.

4.3.   *A Note on Thinking in Terms of Dilemmas*

By walking through this loop several times during a project, we can bend the vicious circle of never-ending discussions into virtuous ones and engage in a process of social learning. Thinking in terms of dilemmas is an approach that thrives on the fact that we cannot derive from theory what action we have to take. It is a practical approach in which the process gives order to the parts rather than the other way round. However, we need to be wary of a blurry discussion in which buzzwords like "integration" and "synergy" prevail. Thinking in terms of dilemmas sets the stage for negotiation, politics and confrontation, activities that require specific skills and attitudes. Before engaging in such a process it is important to have a common interest from which to start. This may be funding-related, but it could also be an ambition to contribute to world peace. Finally, we need to stress that the goal of this chapter is to find a way to deal with dilemmas when they force themselves upon social scientists. We never had the intention of presenting an "ontology of dilemmas," defining every problem as a field of tension. When properly applied, the methodology in this chapter can even be used to remove or reduce the number of dilemmas. By explicitly problematizing certain situations at a certain stage in a project, we open up the possibility of dealing with them in a constructive way: a field of tension in itself.

References

Bijker, W.E. Of Bicycles, Bakelites and Bulbs. Towards a Theory of Socio-Technical Change; 1995. MIT Press, London.

Chrisler, K. A user-centred approach to the wireless world. In Tafazolli, R. (Ed.), Technology for the Wireless Future; 2005. Wiley, Chichester.

Collingridge, D. The Social Control of Technology; 1980. Pinter, London.

Haddon, L., Kommonen, K.-H. Interdisciplinary explorations: A dialogue between a sociologist and a design group. Report for COST269 from Discussions with the ARKI Research Group in the Media Lab, University of Art and Design, Helsinki, Finland; 2002. Available at http://cost269.org

Hamdon-Turner. Charting the Corporate Mind. From Dilemma to Strategy; 1990. Blackwell, Oxford.

Jørgensen, U., Sørensen, O. Arenas of development: A space populated by actor-worlds, artefacts and surprises. In Sørensen, K.H., Williams, R. (Eds.), Shaping Technology, Guiding Policy. Concepts, Spaces and Tools; 2002. Edward Elgar, Cheltenham.

Reuzel, R.B.P., van der Wilt G.J. The societal context of health technology assessment. In: TA-Datenbank-Nachrichten, 4(10), December 2001, 106–111.

Rip, A., Misa, Th.J., Schot, J.W. Managing Technology in Society: The Approach of Constructive Technology Assessment; 1995. Pinter, London.

Rip, A., Schot, J.W. Identifying loci for influencing the dynamics of technological development. In Sørensen, K.H., Williams, R. (Eds.), Shaping Technology, Guiding Policy. Concepts, Spaces and Tools; 2002. Edward Elgar, Cheltenham.

van Lieshout, M., Egyedi, T.M., Bijker, W.E. Social Learning Technologies. The Introduction of Multimedia in Education; 2001. Ashgate, Burlington.

van Twist, M.J.W., Edelenbos, J., van der Broek, M.G. In dilemmas durven denken. Tijdschrift voor Management en Organisatie; 1998, 52(5), October. Samsom Bedrijfsinformatie, Alphen aan den Rijn, 7–23.

Chapter 12

TEST SCENARIOS AND THE EXCLUDED USER

Jarmo Sarkkinen

> *"To classify is human. Not all classifications take formal shape or are standardized in commercial and bureaucratic products. We all spend large part of our days doing classification work, often tacitly, and we make up and use a range of ad hoc classifications to do so."* (Bowker and Star, 1999, 1–2)

1.   Introduction

Users can be extremely helpful when information and communication technologies are being evaluated since they have a knowledge of their everyday practices in the workplace and at home where the new technology is supposed to be used. When involving users in technology evaluation, one of the main concerns is how to empower these users to make their knowledge visible to designers. The related concern is how to teach the designers to treat users as empowered partners and how to widen the scope of the system testing stage to include the users' perspective as well. Finally, the whole issue turns out to be a matter of augmenting the users' own technology evaluation procedures. The purpose should not be to teach the users to read engineering tools such as Information Engineering diagrams, in contrast to what Martin (1990) suggests below:

> *These four diagram types [Information Engineering diagrams] are a basis for clear thinking and can help users to structure their ideas about systems, and, where appropriate, build procedures . . . Experience has shown that end users can be taught how to read (but not necessarily create) these diagrams in a half-day training course* (Martin, 1990, 102; underlines in Beath and Orlikowski, 1994, 367).

Engineering diagrams, as embodiments of the software engineering perspective, are akin to what has been called a "technology of classifying" (Bowker and Star, 1999), human-made tools capable of organizing entities into

Leslie Haddon (ed.), Everyday Innovators, 184–199.
© 2005 *Springer. Printed in The Netherlands.*

categories. One such technology is the International Classification of Diseases, which places a huge number of diseases in pre-specified categories. In contrast, engineering diagrams are more implicit classifiers since they tell only indirectly what qualities matter in the technological development. Moreover, they do this in engineering terms and by doing so exclude the way that users perceive technology. Users need to be free from constraints such as this, imposed by the engineering tradition, through using what could be called a "technology of empowerment." This technology could augment the users' own classifications of what is significant in the assessment of a technology. We also need to integrate this technology of empowerment into the very infrastructure of technology development.

Deconstruction is a key approach for tearing apart the texture of the technology of classifying provided by designers. According to Norris (1991), the purpose of deconstruction is to examine cultural artifacts with "*an eye sharply trained to look for (built-in) contradictions*" (p. 137). The approach will be elaborated later, but essentially it challenges and makes visible the assumptions being made by designers. Truex *et al.* (2000) has deconstructed the whole concept "methodical information systems analysis" and Beath and Orlikowski (1994) have used this approach to tear apart one system development methodology. The objective of the current chapter is to deconstruct one particular software testing tool, a test scenario. This deconstruction discloses the embedded, opposing and mutually exclusive classifications built into a specific test scenario, revealing both the users' classifications and the designers' classifications. The aim is to show which of them is included and which is excluded and, indeed, visible only to a critical researcher. The conclusion of this analysis will be that "user-centered" classifications are marginalized. If these could be included, embedded in technology of empowerment and used during the earlier phases of the technology construction, users could be given the opportunity to engage in a more constructive dialog with designers. Scenarios need to be used more as a basis for communication between these stakeholder groups to support both "*reflection* and *action*" (Bødker, 2000, 62, italics in the original), instead of, as now, using them to provide merely descriptive "technology-centered" accounts (cf., Hertzum, 2003).

2. Classifications in Different Social Worlds

Information system development tools become meaningful through their utility value, through what they help to achieve. In this sense, they are different from artwork, which can be meaningful without any instrumental value. Furthermore, what is meaningful when using a technology development tool is dependent on the built-in intentions of its creator. Meanings do not just "*lie in (that) object*" (Hall, 1997, 24), but they reflect the way its creator tends to manage a piece of the surrounding world (e.g. a new information system). They mean what their creator "*intends they should mean*" (ibid., 25), that is, how they should be used meaningfully. Their "*private intended meanings*" (ibid., 25) are imposed on the users of this tool through built-in classifications.

Bowker and Star (1999, p. 10) define the term "classification" as "*a spatial, temporal, or spatialtemporal segmentation of the world.*" For example, an engineering diagram can illustrate a potential future (not the past) system in terms of interactions between system components. Bowker and Star (1999) divide classifications into either symbolic or material ones. A classification thus denotes metaphorical or literal boxes in which entities in the world can be put. Bowker and Star emphasize that these classifications simply become invisible to people when they are immersed in their everyday duties. Because the categories then seem so "natural" or obvious, this explains this invisibility: "(t)he more at home you are in a community of practice, the more you forget the strange and contingent nature of its categories seen from the outside" (ibid., 294). This may explain why the users may have trouble understanding tools introduced by designers.

Two examples of classifications are given next. The first example from everyday life demonstrates this naturalization of a symbolic (here verbally presented) classification. We hardly ever contemplate what it means to say "I hate you." There are at least four classifications embedded in this sentence. First, the word "I" says that it is the speaker who hates the other person. Second, this person appears to have a strong feeling of dislike for this other person. Third, the sentence says that the speaker hates the particular person with whom he or she is. The sentence is a spatiotemporal segmentation of the world coming into being in the "topography" of emotions at that particular moment in time. Finally, the sentence as a whole excludes the possibility that the speaker would love this other person.

The second example illustrates the naturalization of a symbolic–material classification system for a payment plan (Figure 12-1) taken from the project that was studied. Payment plans may be labeled as accepted ("Hyväksytty"), created ("Perustettu"), or scanned ("Skannattu"). For the project members,

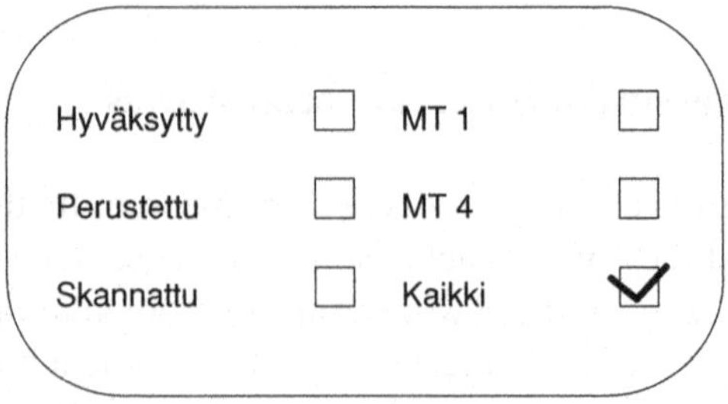

Figure 12-1. A classification system.

this classification system became natural during the project since it was used frequently in the talk and screen layouts constructed by the designers. From the users' viewpoint, however, there may also have been other unarticulated ways of classifying a plan.

Symbolic and material classifications are not innocent intermediaries. Bowker and Star (2000, 156) emphasize that *"each category valorises some point of view and silences another."* That is, if we offer one set of options this excludes other possibilities. As in the previous example, classifying a payment plan as accepted, created, or scanned excludes the possibility of other categories such as (hypothetically) "pending" or "deferred."

Different social worlds (e.g. those of accountants and designers) have their own classifications. These classifications are capable of framing how we talk and write *"the past and the sequence of events in the present"* (ibid., 161). By suggesting how to perceive the past and the present, the classifications used may also impose a view of how things should be done and understood in other social worlds if used by members of these different communities. For this reason, it may be incautious on the part of designers to ignore moral choices embodied in the tools that may be capable of *"craft(ing) people's identities, aspirations and dignity"* (ibid., 148). We need to see behind the tool to tear its built-in classifications apart, to see how tools are coupled to the technologists' view or users' views, and especially how tools are biased toward certain social worlds rather than others.

3.   Deconstruction

Each textual or visual object contains a counterpoint. Such binary oppositions involving pairs of terms or objects can also be found (Encyclopædia Britannica, 2003) in every technology development tool. Each binary opposition includes one term or object and excludes another. The term "bipolar classification" is used from this point forward. To mention a few fundamental bipolar classifications, there are philosophical ones such as nature/culture, speech/writing, mind/body, presence/absence, inside/outside, literal/metaphorical, intelligible/sensible and form/meaning (Encyclopædia Britannica, 2003). Potter (1997) gives another set: white/black, men/women, masculine/feminine, upper class/lower class (p. 235). In a technology development context, we can note such oppositions as practice/system, user/designer, use/technology construction and amethodical/methodical (Truex *et al.* 2000).

Deconstructing a term, a text or an object means to tear it apart. The aim is to challenge the existing binary classifications and to emphasize that these classifications are in fact hierarchical. In other words, one pole of each binary classification is emphasized as being "primary," "fundamental" or "dominant" in some regard. Thus, it is a privileged pole; it is superior to the "sec-ondary" or "derivative" pole (Encyclopædia Britannica, 2003), which is, for this reason, marginalized. The dominant poles in one of our examples are empha-sized in bold as follows: **system**/*practice*, **designer**/*user*, **technology construc-tion**/*use*, and **methodical**/*amethodical*. However, the task of the researcher in the deconstruction process should not be to challenge the moral choices made by the creator of the text in question (Beath and Orlikowski, 1994). Decon-struction should only make visible which poles are privileged and which are marginalized.

Jacques Derrida's contribution to deconstruction is indisputable. His decon-structive approach involves a critical investigation of *"the ambivalences, or, more accurately, the self-contradictions and double binds, that lie latent in any text"* (Cooper, 1989, 481–482). The purpose is neither to invert the opposition nor to challenge its existence (Encyclopædia Britannica, 2003). Deconstruct-ing a hierarchical binary does not mean simply replacing the privileged pole with the marginalized one. Instead, it means "overturning" the opposing poles to demonstrate that they actually *"contain their own opposites"* (Cooper and Burrell, 1988, 98) or *"inhabit each other"* (Cooper, 1989, 483). That is, the re-searcher should not decide which one of the two opposites is more legitimate. The aim is to augment both and to show, one way or another, how their mutual order appears to him or herself. The future readers of the same text or object can later decide what the order of the opposites *should* be.

Every conceptualization of a thing is *"inscribed in a chain or in a system within which it refers to the other, to other concepts, by means of the systematic play of differences"* (Derrida, 1982, 11). Deconstruction is what everyone of us needs to do when interpreting everyday objects. It is a matter of "différance" (with an *a*); it is *"a conceptual process"* (ibid., 11) in which one person attaches meanings to an object, making it meaningful. Making things meaningful means to produce bipolar classifications or "differences" (with an *e*) that are only created temporarily (Derrida, 1982, 14). This impermanence implies that to produce one particular bipolar classification is also to commit to "an act of deferring" (Encyclopædia Britannica, 2003) since bipolar classifications cannot be defined once and for all but they are "deferred in time" (Cooper, 1989). In other words, interpretations of classifications depend on the future reader. They cannot be simply given to this reader by someone else. Each future reader always has to re-interpret the relationship between the opposite poles and to construct them either as privileged or as marginalized. Provocatively said, it is *"the reader who writes the text"* (Woolgar, 1994, 205).

In this chapter, a broad definition of the term "text" is used. Tools can also be thought of as texts (Woolgar, 1991, 1994). Deconstruction-différance is therefore useful for the deconstruction of these tools. To say that tools can be thought of as texts is to say that they are "interpretatively flexible" like texts, but still only a limited set of readings are possible (Woolgar, 1994, 205). Tools can often contain both textual (i.e. written) and visual elements. Moreover, tools, like texts, contain the type bipolar classifications noted above that reveals *"(the past) presence (of the original writer) in its absence"* (Derrida, 1982, 9) to the future reader(s).

4. Introducing the Tool

As a member who had been permitted to occupy the position of an independent ethnographer in an industrial software development project, I was offered by the other members access to the tools used during the system testing phase. In this study, the purpose is to deconstruct one test scenario sequence. This particular tool was chosen since scenarios are also widely used in the usability testing. The designers supposed that test scenarios help software testers, most of whom were end users, to test the correct things and to find errors in the program code. According to the designers, test scenarios were meant to encompass "only" a "minimum" number of functions for testing the system to see if there were errors in the program code. Thus, scenarios were not assumed to contain every possible use of the system. The designers said that the users were expected to complement these scenarios. The chosen scenario is presented in Figure 12-2.

I focus not on the details of the working context, since that would be distracting, but rather on the components of the deconstructed test scenario. Attention is first given to how the scenario classifies the target area at first sight. Only then is the scenario deconstructed to find out its ambivalences, self-contradictions and double binds. The test scenario (Figure 12-2), introduced by the designers, contains the following surface structure. The scenario includes the "header" section, the name of the tool. It also implies the purpose of the scenario. The second section from the top provides background information including, for example, the name of the development project, the present stage of that project, the focus of the test scenario, and other commonly unused fields such as compiler, date, page, and duration. The section that will be deconstructed includes steps to be taken by the tester, what functions each step contains and what input the tester is asked to enter into the system and, finally, what outcome is anticipated and what may happen if things go wrong.

5. Deconstructing a Test Scenario: Introducing Five Bipolar Classifications

Five bipolar classifications were deconstructed: **linear input–output process/** *non-linear process*, **using the system/***performing the tasks*, **producing the outcome/***understanding the outcome*, **textual presentation/***visual illustration*, and **errors-as-detected/***breakdowns-as-experienced*. Each bipolar classification is discussed in the following subsections. The first terms in these classifications

TEST SCENARIO

Project	: XXX .	Compiler	:_____.	Page	: 1 .
Stage	: System testing V3 .	Date	:_____.	Duration	: h .
Focus	: Payment procedures for supervisor				

Test Scenario	Function/input	Anticipated outcome/detected error
	Logging on the system	
1	Enter the user name 'supervisor' and password 'xxxx1/avustus' to log onto the system and open the 'Payment' main menu.	The screen opens successfully.
	The 'Document identification' list	
2	To start the handling of the scanned documents, open the handling screen by pressing the 'Document identification' button in the 'Payment' main menu.	The screen opens successfully. All search limits remain empty. There are no rows in the list. The 'Fetch' and 'Close' buttons are in use.
3	Launch the retrieval of the scanned documents on the screen by first setting the desired search limits and then pressing the 'Fetch' button.	The desired data appears in the list, and they are in accordance with the search limits. If rows were retrieved, the uppermost row appears active (i.e., it is highlighted). If rows were not retrieved, an error message appears on the display. The list remains empty and there are no empty rows in it. The rows have been sorted by scanning date and within it by organization name by default. The user may sort rows not only by these two attributes but also by status. To change a particular sorting mode, the user selects a column. The contents of the list may be copied onto the clipboard by pressing 'Ctrl + C'. The 'Documents' button becomes active.
4	Select a row in the list by clicking the mouse and display the documents by pressing the 'Documents' button.	The viewer opens and the documents are displayed. Inspect the documents.
5	If the documents form a new payment request, try to create a new payment request by clicking the 'Payment Request' button.	The button is inactive for those users who have logged on with the supervisor login.
6	If the documents form a new payment plan, try to create a new payment plan by clicking the 'Payment Plan' button. Then, choose a target and a supervisor whose queue of work objects you choose to send it to.	The button is inactive for those users who have logged on with the supervisor login.

© YYYYY version 1.11   File: SvsMak TarkastajanTestitap.doc   Changed: 28.05.2001 12:16

Figure 12-2. The original test scenario.

were found to be dominant, whereas the second terms were derivative and inferior to the first poles. At the end of the current chapter, new revised test scenario steps are suggested in order to include the marginalized poles in the usability testing.

5.1. *Linear Input–Output Process/Non-linear Process*

First, the bipolar classification "**linear input–output process**/*non-linear process*" was deconstructed. This is one of the most remarkable classifications since it fundamentally frames how the user should perceive the use of the new system. It frames how the user needs to use the system. The idea that was stressed in the above classification, **linear input–output process**, is in fact the perspective that is to the forefront, or is "privileged," in the deconstructed scenario. In contrast, the alternative view that the scenario could involve a *non-linear process* is not present and is marginalized. And it is deferred to the reader, i.e. left to the reader to think of this for him or herself. Let us see how this works in a little more detail. The scenario is composed of clearly articulated instructions for taking particular steps in a pre-given and predictable order. In the deconstructed scenario sequence, six steps are presented in a linear fashion. Each step contains an input–output pair. It is assumed that the user enters the desired input into the system to achieve some output. No extra branches in the linear progression that is presented here are allowed to occur during the use of the system. For example, users are not expected to visit any screens other than the "Document identification" screen in step 3.

In this step, the user is expected to fill in the desired search limits and, after this, he or she enters these limits as input into the system by pressing the "Fetch" button. This launches the retrieval of the desired documents on the screen. However, we can ask what would happen if the user needs to check for some other data on another screen before setting the search limits. The process may also be an unpredictable non-linear one. There may be several, even probable, "branch moves" before the user is finally ready to press the "Fetch" button in order to retrieve the data as output on the screen.

5.1.1. *Suggestions for the future*

Taking into account the *non-linear process* member of this first bipolar classification can help users who act as testers. It is not sufficient to provide the users with test scenario steps emphasizing only the linear progress. Instead, users need to be encouraged to envision and test alternative, non-linear routes, as well. Users could be encouraged to consider potential alternatives if these instructions were supplied by the surface structure of the test scenarios.

5.2. *Using the System/Performing the Tasks*

Deconstruction also helped to recognize the "**using the system**/*performing the tasks*" bipolar classification. It became obvious to me that the "**using the system**" assumption is privileged over its counterpart, the "*performing the* *tasks*" assumption. The superior–inferior relationship shows a clear distinction between the system as an end in itself and as an instrumental tool. What is emphasized by the privileged member in this classification is that there is a collection of functions built in the system that need to be used by the user in order to command the system to function in desired ways. Real documents and payment plans are discussed only in the abstract in the present scenario. No real instances of them are mentioned. Real tasks with real data are not mentioned at all. In contrast, what is implied by the alternative "*performing the tasks*" view is that such details of people's actual working procedures and working situations are important and need to be taken into account.

Each step of the scenario follows the privileged view. The following examples illustrate this. Each scenario steps (2–6) explains how the user can command the system. The attention here is centered around the "Document identification" list. What the user is expected to do is to use the functions provided by the list screen. How the functions provided by the list screen help the user when he or she is actually performing real tasks is not mentioned. This function-centered view is apparent when the instruction "start on the handling of the scanned documents" is examined together with the specification "pressing the 'Document identification' button." We see it when the instruction "[l]aunch the retrieval of the scanned documents" is studied together with "pressing the 'Fetch' button." And it is apparent when the instruction "try to create a new payment plan" is studied by "clicking the 'Payment Plan' button." These examples show how the user is only expected to use a certain system functions at one moment in time. The scenario, however, forgets to explain how these functions actually help the user to perform his or her tasks.

5.2.1.   Suggestions for the future

The recommended starting point for building scenarios for the usability testing would be to emphasize users' tasks rather than how to use the system's functions. The constructed task scenario steps would then emphasize how the user could utilize the new system in order to perform concrete tasks belonging to that user's job description.

5.3.   Producing the Outcome/Understanding the Outcome

Deconstructing the test scenario uncovered a dichotomy between "**producing the outcome**" and "*understanding the outcome*." Of the two perspectives, "producing the outcome" appears to be privileged, whereas the alternative approach where "understanding the outcome" is more important is once again a matter that is left to the reader to suggest. From the privileged standpoint noted above, the scenario is a collection of steps, each of which, if taken, produces a certain outcome – for example, a list or a document is displayed on the screen. That outcome would appear to be an end in itself. The dominant "**producing the outcome**" pole implies that there is a set of predictable outcomes in the system. These outcomes are assumed to ensure the seamless performance of a set of tasks. The potential unintelligibility of any such outcomes is assumed to be a minor concern to users according to this privileged view. The marginalized view would be that it is more important to emphasize how the user understands the outcome of the system than to describe how these outcomes are produced.

Some instances of the "**producing the outcome**/*understanding the outcome*" bipolar classification are presented next. First, step 1 says that "(t)he screen opens successfully." However, what this word "successfully" explicitly means is not told. How should it be understood? The utterance says that the screen opens but it does not specify how and why it actually opens. We can also ask whether other screens should open simultaneously. Second, step 3 states that "(i)f rows were retrieved, the uppermost row appears active." How does this active row help the user to understand if something is, in some sense, correct? Could there be other, even more helpful, explanations? Finally, step 4 says that "the documents are displayed." How are they displayed? Is their arrangement understandable to users? Does this arrangement help the user to perform his or her task? Should the documents be displayed in alphabetical or any other particular order? What is common to these three examples is that they focus on the outcome itself. The intelligibility of the outcome is, however, not emphasized at all.

5.3.1. *Suggestions for the future*

The marginalized "*understanding the outcome*" view needs to be augmented. Unlike the test scenario that merely illustrates what outcomes there will be after doing something, an alternative scenario could include catalytic questions for stimulating the users' own critical assessment procedures. With these catalytic questions, users could be encouraged to challenge any unclear outcomes.

5.4. *Textual Presentation/Visual Illustration*

The scenario makes a distinction between the two ways of demonstrating the scenario steps. The "**textual presentation**/*visual illustration*" bipolar classification is embedded in the scenario and the dominant idea of "**textual presentation**" assumes it is sufficient to present the instructions in written form. The scenario has been constructed from a designers' standpoint. The designers are familiar with the system language being used and how the system parts interact. Representing the uses of the system with these textual instructions also assumes that those who will use the system would be familiar with the system language and agree with how the system is supposed to work. In contrast, the marginalized and deferred *"visual illustration"* view recommends using visual images to show the steps. It would be insufficient to present the users' tasks as written instructions. The scenario steps presented in a technical language could, in the worst case, serve to prevent users thinking critically about the steps from their own perspective. In contrast, as a richer communication medium, some sort of visual illustration could be more thought-provoking and could stimulate users to reflect upon the system uses in the context of their own work practices.

5.4.1.   Suggestions for the future

The designers could support a user's own classifications during the usability testing if they build the *"visual illustration"* into the constructed scenarios. Visual illustrations could make the use situations being demonstrated more concrete and stimulating for the user testers. Unclear tasks could be discussed with the designers. The aim, however, is not to overshadow textual presentations. Written instructions are also needed in the usability-testing context to explain visual illustrations.

5.5.   Errors-as-Detected/Breakdowns-as-Experienced

The scenario privileges the first member of the **"errors-as-detected/** *breakdowns-as-experienced"* bipolar classification. The scenario assumes that an error appears only if something, for some reason, goes wrong with display-ing the expected output. Errors thus follow from the inability of the system to respond to a given set of inputs. It is then possible that something is either wrong with this input itself or with the program code. The column "anticipated outcome/detected error" in the scenario explains that errors are assumed to be observable only through the output of the system. An indication of this is step 3 saying "[i]f rows were not retrieved, an error message appears on the display." According to the privileged **"errors-as-detected"** view, users acting as testers are simply assumed to be trying out different functions of the system. After running into an error, it is either fixed or forgotten.

According to the alternative *"breakdowns-as-experienced"* view, break-downs in performing the tasks are more salient than errors in producing output. If things go as expected, a tool remains invisible to the user but it becomes vis-ible if there is a breakdown in performing a given task (Winograd and Flores, 1986). Breakdowns are deeply experienced rather than just observed. Further-more, breakdowns may profoundly affect the user. As an example of a situation of this sort, it may be very disruptive if users are forced to perform tasks in an illogical order. However, when deconstructed we can see that the scenario ig-nores the *"performing the tasks"* view. It does not encourage users to recognize breakdowns. It is perfectly sufficient if the system can function faultlessly, that is, if it can display the expected output.

5.5.1. Suggestions for the future

In order to support usability testing activities, users need to be stimulated to identify things that are likely to lead to a breakdown in the performance of tasks. As one alternative and potential implementation to be embedded in each step, users could be provided, for example, with a piece of text containing a listing of all recognized breakdowns.

6. Revised Test Scenario

A revised version of step 3 of the original scenario is presented in Figure 12-3. The marginalized poles of the five bipolar classifications have been added. Augmenting these marginalized poles can enable the designers to engage more fully in a constructive dialog with users and to encourage users to become more absorbed in usability testing. The primary argument for augmenting the marginalized poles of the five bipolar classifications is that users are more likely to be acquainted with them than with the dominant engineering views since carrying out their daily jobs involves dealing with that sort of "user-centered" classifications to a great extent.

The linear input–output process was too narrow and for this reason the view that use can be a *"non-linear process"* is taken into consideration in the alternative scenario. This encourages users to think up unpredictable ways of performing the tasks. There is a text field, a space where users may verbalize their specific preferences as regards the step at issue. The question "What else would you need to do, see or know here?" treats users as competent subjects. In other words, they are allowed to gain mastery over the process. This means that they are the ones in control of improving the user interface. The contents of the text field provide the designers with suggestions. The designers can then, based on this information, re-consider, for example, the ways in which users could move from one screen to another.

To augment the marginal *"performing the tasks"* view, the aim of using the system is once again illustrated from the perspective of a competent subject. This view also requires us to rephrase the written instructions. Rather than describing these textual instructions in confusing "system" terms, they are described from the user's perspective in the "What I do" field.

The outcome is not just described, but users are encouraged to challenge it. This is supported by a set of questions intended to encourage the user to evaluate critically the suggested system and its user interface. In order to make a clear link between the scenario and the system itself, the steps to be taken are

TEST SCENARIO

Project   :   XXX   .   Compiler   :_____.   Page   : 1 .
Stage   : System testing V3 .   Date   :_____.   Duration :   h .
Focus   : Payment procedures for supervisor

Step	What I do	What I get	How I feel
3	AIM: I need to know how many scanned documents have been stored in the system. I want to limit the results only to those documents that have been scanned but not yet handled.	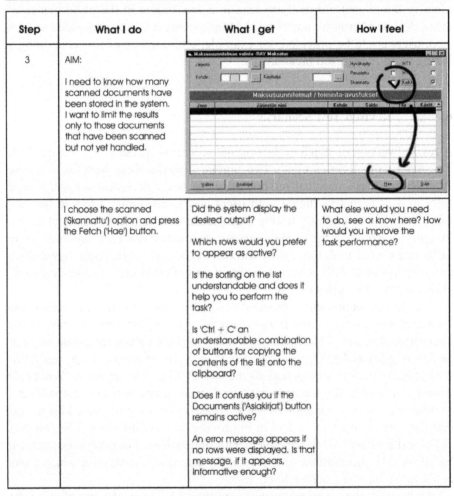	
	I choose the scanned ('Skannattu') option and press the Fetch ('Hae') button.	Did the system display the desired output? Which rows would you prefer to appear as active? Is the sorting on the list understandable and does it help you to perform the task? Is 'Ctrl + C' an understandable combination of buttons for copying the contents of the list onto the clipboard? Does it confuse you if the Documents ('Asiakirjat') button remains active? An error message appears if no rows were displayed. Is that message, if it appears, informative enough?	What else would you need to do, see or know here? How would you improve the task performance?

© YYYYY version 1.11   File: SvsMak TarkastajanTestitap.doc   Changed: 28.05.2001 12:16

Figure 12-3. The revised version of the scenario.

also presented as visual illustrations. In this way, the abstract system terms are now in the background, whereas the users' language is foregrounded to some extent. Textual instructions are merely used to support the visual illustration. Users are also encouraged to talk about any breakdowns they run into. For conveying this knowledge to designers, users are provided with a separate comment field.

7.   Discussion

The test scenario reflects typical software engineering conventions when searching for errors in the program code. These conventions are to ensure that the program would function faultlessly in production. Deconstruction-différance‖ (with an *a*) provided the appropriate tools for understanding how this scenario classifies software testing. Precisely put, the analysis led to the identification of five bipolar classifications, each of which rules *in* one particular way of classifying and rules *out* another. The bipolar classifications embedded in the scenario are **linear input–output process**/*non-linear process*, **using the system**/*performing the tasks*, **producing the outcome**/*understanding the outcome*, **textual presentation**/*visual illustration*, and **errors-as-detected**/*breakdowns-as-experienced*.

The privileged members of these classifications come from the engineering world. In order to construct a technology of empowerment, an alternative test scenario for involving users, the marginalized counterparts were foregrounded. However, there is no intention to replace the original test scenario. It is certainly useful in finding out what is wrong with the program code. My purpose has been to support usability testers, who are normally users, by providing them with a tool grounded upon the more user-centered classifications. It is relevant to assume that the alternative test scenario is more useful in the evaluation of user interfaces and their appropriateness than the original scenario used for engineering purposes.

It is worth remembering that I have only deconstructed the test scenario used for testing the program code. This probably delimited my possibilities to recognize all relevant classifications. However, those unrecognized classifications that we do not know yet could also support the users' processes of searching for breakdowns in uses of systems. Therefore, the present classifications should be conceived merely as groundwork. The recommended classifications should be critically assessed in real usability inspection sessions to ensure their validity. Future studies are also needed to show how users would deconstruct tools in real usability inspection situations to uncover other appropriate classifications.

Being conscious of those classifications that can be used in the usability testing scenarios would help avoid the risk of delimiting what testing approaches the user testers want to adopt in practice. Future studies are needed to examine critically classifications since it is quite clear that classifications can impose an unwanted procedure on users. In fact, a procedure of some sort is always imposed. For this reason, the aim should be to ensure that testing tools prioritize the procedure that would confirm the users' position. The consequence of overlooking the significance of classifications is that the scenario may fail to support the process of searching for breakdowns in the uses of systems. The scenario may even become a technology of classifying, which may classify not only the procedure but also user testers who are involved in the usability testing. If the original scenario had been used in a usability inspection session, users would have felt they lacked certain qualifications. One reason for feeling this way is that the scenario implies that users cannot test the system without instructions. If a tool "acts" this way, users are very likely to put this sort of tool to one side and feel mistreated.

However, test scenarios are surely not capable of dictating what one can do with them. For example, it was observed in one of the software testing sessions that some users were testing the system without utilizing the test scenario even if some of the others followed its steps literally. Despite the fact that classifications alone cannot steer the process, we need to be careful with the classifications that we build in usability testing scenarios. What is worth emphasizing is that we should avoid building technology for classifying, which may even degrade the user population. Instead, we need to build tools that could be called technologies of empowerment, enabling users to gain mastery over the usability inspection process.

References

Beath, C.M., Orlikowski, W.J. The contradictory structure of systems development methodologies: deconstructing the IS-user relationship in information engineering. Information Systems Research, 1994; 5: 350–377.

Bødker, S. Scenarios in user-centred design – Setting the stage for reflection and action. Interacting with Computers, 2000; 13: 61–75.

Bowker, G.C., Star, S.L. Sorting Things Out; 1999. The MIT Press, Cambridge, MA.

Bowker, G.C., Star, S.L. Invisible mediators of action: classification and the ubiquity of standards. Mind, culture and activity, 2000; 7: 147–163.

Cooper, R. Modernism, postmodernism and organizational analysis 3: the contribution of Jacques Derrida. Organization Studies, 1989; 10: 479–502.

Cooper, R., Burrell, G. Modernism, postmodernism and organizational analysis: An introduction. Organization Studies, 1988; 9: 91–112.

"Deconstruction." Encyclopædia Britannica. 2003. Encyclopædia Britannica Online: http://search.eb.com/eb/article?eu=30194; June 18, 2003.

Derrida, J. Margins of Philosophy; 1982. Harvester Wheatsheaf, New York.

Hall, S. The work of representation. In Hall, S. (Ed.), Representation: Cultural Representations and Signifying Practices; 1997. Sage, London: 13–74.

Hertzum, M. Making use of scenarios: a field study of conceptual design. International Journal of Human-Computer Studies, 2003; 58: 215–239.

Martin, J. Information Engineering, Book III: Design and Construction; 1990. Prentice-Hall, Englewood Cliffs, NJ.

Norris, C. Deconstruction: Theory and Practice, 2nd edition; 1991. Routledge, London.

Truex, D., Baskerville, R., Travis, J. A methodical systems development: the deferred meaning of systems development methods. Accounting, Management and Information Technologies, 2000; 10: 53–79.

Winograd, T., Flores, F. Understanding computers and cognition: a new foundation for design; 1986. Ablex Publishing Corporation, Norwood, NJ.

Woolgar, S. Configuring the user: the case of usability trials. In Law, J. (Ed.), A Sociology of Monsters: Essays on Power, Technology and Domination; 1991. Routledge, London.

Woolgar, S. Rethinking requirements analysis: some implications of recent research into producer–consumer relationships in IT development. In Jirotka, M., Goguen, J.A. (Eds.), Requirements Engineering: Social and Technical Issues; 1994. Academic Press, London.

THE POLITICS OF USER INVOLVEMENT
IN PROGRAMES OF INNOVATION

The chapters by Marja Vehviläinen and Somya Joshi follow on from a key interest of the previous section in the problems of involving users in design, but now the focus is on public projects and policies. Many of these public projects take place against the backdrop of wider political discussions requiring more democracy and social inclusion and referring to citizens and to communities, not just to the consumers considered by firms. Hence the emphasis on "participation" and "consultation," rather than just the commercial interest in getting "user feedback for design." Vehviläinen's analysis of policies and Joshi's study of a particular project provide critical assessments of how much these aspirations are addressed and realized in reality. They show how this area of innovation adds to the notion of the active user but also reveal the limitations of that role.

Vehviläinen first outlines a vision of "equal agency," whereby everyone can participate in helping to shape ICTs on an equal basis. This requires us to appreciate that they can only do so on the basis of their "situated knowledge," the knowledge, priorities and perspectives developed through their previous experiences. In setting the scene for the main argument, Vehviläinen like some of the other authors in this book, refers to a perspective that sees technology as a text. Finally, she questions views that see expertise as simply objective, the "truth," or neutral knowledge. Instead, it is always based in people's other social experiences. This becomes important when she later questions the role of technological experts as being the main people defining the directions in which innovation should occur.

Vehviläinen provides an overview of the different meaning of "equality" in general at different historical periods, finding parallels with different understandings of what equality means in terms of who has the right to influence the development of ICTs. The mainstream assumption is that it is the technological professionals who should predominate in this matter. She then uses her interview and documentary evidence to provide a retrospective analysis of four main alternative approaches to technological development that have evolved in Finland. These all, in different ways, aimed to encourage the participation of ICT users as equal agents in the innovation process. However, she shows how they have very different understanding about the nature of "equality" and "agency," reflecting their wider perspectives on and knowledge about the social world. In practice, most of these approaches tend to favor some users over others.

Joshi's chapter looks at the role of technology in an attempt to foster local participatory decision-making. The study provides a good illustration of the problems of different types of "expertise" and the inequality of the different parties in the decision-making process, as signalled above by Vehviläinen. Joshi's chapter deals with a case study of a British project involving the use of virtual and augmented reality technology. The project aimed at providing a tool for involving, and thus empowering, a local community in Salford, near Manchester, which was at the time undergoing regeneration. The author questions the type of participation that was taking place, suggesting this was a case of technology transfer rather than involving effective input from local people. She asks whether participation was really only token.

Joshi uses activity theory to examine the viewpoints, assumptions and values lying behind such technological systems. She outlines the theory and returns to consider some of its features in the conclusions. But at this point she notes how this VR project counted as one activity system, interacting with another one, the regeneration project – each having their own notions of desired outcomes. Sometimes these notions were contradictory. For example, while the project may in principle, or at least in its mission statements, have aspired to fostering greater community involvement, the project designers also wanted to keep control over the innovation process.

Although it is a slightly different theoretical framework from many of the others covered in this book, activity theory has many parallels with them. Joshi describes designers configuring the user, i.e. making design decisions based on assumptions about the latter, and users bringing with them own perspectives to the innovation. In the project we actually see a mismatch between the two over the issue of how much users wanted to interact with the system offered rather than merely navigate through it.

Joshi outlines problems of defining end-users, illustrating this with the actual differences that emerged in this project, and also problems of defining the very communities to be consulted. While some of those organizing the consultation wanted to be sensitive to the feedback of this specific set of users, others wanted to generalize from it. There were also problems in the consultancy process as, compared to other stakeholders, the users consulted brought fewer skills and resources to the negotiations, as well as being constrained by time and other limitations. The author argues that all these factors need to be appreciated and addressed, if users are to engage more fully in this process, and activity theory can provide a wider framework for achieving this.

Chapter 13

THE CONSTRUCTION OF "EQUAL AGENCY" IN THE DEVELOPMENT OF TECHNOLOGY

Marja Vehviläinen

1.   Introduction

The process of technology development involves numerous groups of people. All societies in the world are currently mediated by information and communication technologies. All groups are not, however, similarly positioned in relation to the technology. There are digital divides between the poor and the rich, women and men, well educated and the others, and also between entire societies in the North and the South. Technology benefits the activity of some particular groups more than others. Hence, moves toward greater equality and equal agency are important objectives in technology research and development.

The question of equal agency has been discussed in the context of technology development ever since the socio-technical projects in British coal mines in the early 1950s (Trist and Bamforth, 1951). The socio-technical school has often discussed the matter in terms of user participation, arguing that it is neither profitable nor right to exclude workers from the planning and development of technologies and work practices. Groups of workers should be involved in the development process. This idea has been applied to information technology by, for example, Enid Mumford, who had already started working with information technology development in the United Kingdom by the turn of the1970s. The famous Scandinavian participatory design projects, for example, UTOPIA and DEMOS, also owe much to socio-technical thinking, although the Scandinavian model differs from the UK version by, for example, giving a significant role to labor unions.

Partially joining these traditions of user participation and partially developing them further, I consider people as actors who view the development of technology from the starting point of their bodily experiences and life

Leslie Haddon (ed.), Everyday Innovators, 203–217.
© 2005 *Springer. Printed in The Netherlands.*

histories, i.e. from their "situated knowledge" (Haraway, 1991; Suchman, 1987). They do not simply react to the suggestions made by other groups of people, experts, as often happens in user participation. They actively formulate views about technology as a social process from the starting point of their own situated knowledge. Equal agency in the development of technology means that all these people, for example, in various hierarchical positions, in both genders and in all race groups, have a chance to put technology to use and to develop technology in such a manner that it benefits them in their particular situations. Situated knowledge and social experiences are at the center of equal agency.

However, discussions of user participation and equal agency, despite their long and influential history, have neither spread systematically nor linearly to the practices of and research on the development of information technology. Quite the contrary. It has developed toward my own vision of equal agency in, for example, the computer supportive co-operative work and gender and technology research communities. Yet it has not become "mainstreamed" in information technology development. In particular, the social aspects of information technology have remained underdeveloped and user participation and equality in the development process have only gradually come to be seen as social phenomena within the international research community looking at ICT development. Social relations involving power, inequality and the exercise of knowledge, even though they are the core problems in equality issues, have often been left unnoticed or only partially elaborated.

In order to emphasize the social processes and the particular starting points of people, their situated knowledge, I refer to technology as textuality by applying Dorothy Smith's (1990) theory of institutional textuality (Vehviläinen, 1997). Technology texts include artifacts such as computers and other devices, programs, e-mail messages and media descriptions of technology. The research questions in this approach focus on the social practices of interpreting and producing technology texts. The use and development of technologies intertwine when people interpret and produce technology texts in their everyday practices. The "use" or "development" of technology, however, only occasionally become the primary organizers of people's activities.

Technologies entail skills and expertise. In order to carry out technically mediated practices people need to have expertise in technologies. Expertise, in Smith's framework, is a fundamentally socially organized phenomenon produced in people's everyday practices rather than being an entity, a thing, possessed by individuals. There is no sole objective or universal knowledge called "expertise" that is detached from people's situations in the social world. Therefore, the researcher needs to take the standpoint of particular socially located groups of people. I take the standpoint of a user who also takes part in the development. In my mind, it may be better to think of this person as female, old, colored, less educated, working class, not taking part in paid work, located at the periphery of society – rather than a male, young, white, well educated, middle class, in a permanent job, located in a global center – if we want to challenge the hegemonic cultural images held by the developers of technology.

In this chapter I examine four approaches that have been used in the development of information technologies and technically mediated practices. The approaches have all paid attention to the question of equality and user participation in Finland. The first approach arises from the strong leftist movement in Finland in the 1970s, an activity theory approach to work and technology development. The second one builds on the first approach and further supports the expression of multiple voices through socio-drama plays. The third is a national information society strategy – from 1998 – that aims to develop equal access to information and new technologies in society. The fourth one is a North Karelian regional information society strategy. It engages with the national equal access approach but aims to make room for some influence by a locally situated agency.

My aim is to explore the differences in user participation and equality in these approaches. How do they deal with the social world? Do they mainly ignore it or do they provide tools for acknowledging the social differences and the inequalities embedded in them? Are they sensitive to social hierarchies and differences in the practices through which people strive for equality?

I am especially interested in the social construction of expertise, including the understanding of knowledge, and its connection to agency and equality. How is expertise defined in information technology? What kind of activity and which groups does a particular understanding of expertise support? Does it support all those developing and using information technologies equally or is it only some particular groups of the society that are primarily supported? My assumption is that those approaches that acknowledge social relations and inequalities, as well as the situated knowledge connected to them, contribute more to creating broader equality in technology development than do other approaches.

The chapter is based on my previous research and empirical material collected for various articles and books (Vehviläinen, 1994a, b, 1997, 2002; Uotinen *et al.*, 2001). I have assembled documents on the four approaches and interviewed various actors involved in the development of these approaches as well as people involved in practical development work. In the North Karelian case I have, together with Sari Tuuva and Johanna Uotinen, also interviewed people who deal with development in their everyday lives. In this chapter I take a retrospective look at the construction of equal agency in the practices of this technology development.

2.   Agency, Equality, and Expertise

Equality has been one of the most central of citizen rights in most Western societies since Greek antiquity. The meaning of equality has, however, varied greatly according to the different ways in which societies have been structured. In Greek antiquity it covered only some thousands of free men whereas the enlightenment made the right of equality available first to all adult men and, later during the 20th century, to women.

Political scientists, for example, Ruth Lister (1997) and Bryan Turner (1993), point out that the rights of equality originating from the enlightenment do not necessarily lead to equal agency. Universal rights are self-evidently necessary for equal agency, but they are not sufficient for it. The way in which wider social order intertwines with people's everyday lives has a huge influence upon their chances of achieving equality. The ones in favorable social positions, such as Western well-educated white men, generally achieve equal rights more easily than any other groups. The nature of the social order that is embedded in the very practices of people is the most important element determining the extent of equal agency.

Equality is not a question of individual choice, as the liberal enlightenment ideology tends to emphasize. Rather, it is a social process and a question of practices and institutional support. Groups that do not have such a favorable position may need special support and perhaps special rights in order to accomplish equal agency. The focus moves from talk of equal and universal rights to that of people acting in various positions in society and to their chances of achieving equal agency from different starting points. Hence, an analysis of social orders and social differences as well as situated knowledge becomes a crucial tool in the studies of equal agency.

In current societies equality and agency are understood in multiple ways. The liberal citizenship of the enlightenment with its emphasis on individuals' equal rights is alive and well. Simultaneously, there exist understandings that focus on the communal and social nature of agency. These understandings stress the importance of institutional support and the role of the welfare state.

By drawing from feminist political science and technology research, especially Donna Haraway's (1991) notion of situated knowledge, I suggest a vision of "situated equality" (Vehviläinen, 2002). This approach allows for one's own agency from the starting point of one's local situation and situated knowledge. Universal rights are important, but this agency takes shape according to the nature, and contradictions, of situations, societal relations and differences as well as cultural interpretations. Agency is communal rather than individual and deeply rooted in the societal order. In situated equality people can become equal from their situated positions by using their situated knowledge.

As noted earlier, the use and development of technology always require specific know-how, expertise, but this is connected with questions about who has power. Here, I focus on expertise: Which groups are seen to have expertise? What kind of knowledge is counted as expertise?

It seems that the information technology expertise is repeating the general historical pattern. The equality of antiquity applied to just few men while the move to the enlightenment expanded equal rights to all and then the welfare state provided situated equality to particular groups (e.g. disabled, single parents). From the 1950s all the way to the 1980s information technology was mainly developed by information technology professionals. They were a small group consisting mostly of males who gradually developed institutional professional education and practices of their own. I have studied the codes of ethics of two international associations of information processing professionals (ACM and IFIP) from 1972, 1989 and 1992 (Vehviläinen, 1994b). These codes define expertise as residing solely in the information technology professionals themselves. This is particularly true in the 1970s codes. The more recent codes suggest that professionals should strive toward a new task – taking care of user participation. The authors of these codes seem to be aware of the research on and development of user participation both in the United Kingdom and Scandinavia in the 1970s and 1980s. The greatest responsibility for and power as regards the development of information technology stays, however, firmly in the hands of the information technology professionals. These codes are not particularly useful. They do not provide nearly enough tools and they should be drawing attention to the nature of the social world in which technologies are being used and developed. Instead, the activity of the professionals is based on what is perceived as being objective knowledge, which in turn legitimates the professionals' control over the development process. I consider this understanding presented in these codes of ethics as constituting the mainstream (or Greek antiquity) definition of equal agency.

This mainstream understanding has been challenged by various research traditions and development projects. Here we find an emphasis on the equal access to information technologies for all people, comparable to the universal rights of the enlightenment. Situated agency has also been introduced. It is these alternative approaches that I explore in this chapter. I start by presenting an approach that challenged the power of information technology professionals in the 1980s.

3. Activity Theory Based Approaches in the 1980s

Alternative approaches to information technology development have been rare in Finland. The Scandinavian participatory design movement was hardly noticed in the 1970s and the 1980s, Pertti Järvinen's research being one of the exceptions. In Finnish society there has generally been little room for more than one dominant understanding of the design process at a time. There are only 5 million inhabitants and the country has been heavily dependent on a few industries, mainly on forestry industries and recently on information technology industries lead by Nokia, the mobile phone company. One hegemonic discourse has prevailed, shutting out all others, and perhaps this situation is distinct from most other countries. A strong leftist movement in the 1970s produced one alternative discourse, and this influenced the development of information technology in the 1980s – even at the level of the ministry committee.

The Ministry of Finance committee for information processing planned an educational program for "persons responsible for information processing" (known as "PRIPS," tietojenkäsittelyn vastuuhenkilö, TIKVA in Finnish). The committee recognized the problems of the mainstream notion of equality and suggested novel solutions:

> *The problem of information processing development has been that development work has been separated out and given to computing professionals and developers who do not have expertise on the contents of work activity. (. . .) The development of information processing was to be integrated seamlessly into the development of the whole organisation.(. . .) (PRIPS) would be experts in the content of activities in their own organisations; designers and developers who are able to "interpret" between line administration and computing professionals and mastered both concepts. (. . .) (A PRIP) would not be an information technology expert, nor would she or he necessarily have thorough basic skills in information technology while entering the PRIP training. (. . .) The development of information processing presupposes a more fundamental analysis of activity systems. (. . .) Therefore, the educational programme needs to take both activity system and information processing development into consideration simultaneously* (Tietojenkäsittelyn, 1986, pp. 4–5).

The Finnish state administration planned – and in some measure also managed – a radical move to transfer the expert power of information technology professionals to the experts and developers of work activity processes. This move was based on a research tradition called the activity theory approach. Leontjev and Engeström were referred to as providing its theoretical roots. This approach emphasized the importance of the scientific analysis of work processes, including both societal and historical orders. The approach not only shifted the location of expert power but it also defined agency in a social context. Workers were actors and members in a historically evolving work process organized according to particular social relations. These main actors were not technical experts but rather people who knew the work processes. Not all workers, however, achieved positions as PRIPs, but there was an assumption that PRIPs, who understand the work processes, can better (than technical experts) take people's work into account. Since the approach assumed that scientific objective knowledge was possible, the PRIPs were able to produce an appropriate analysis.

In this case, although the expert power was shifted, it was still experts, the new kind of PRIP experts, who gained power. The expert position as such was not challenged and agency in terms of influencing the development of technology was not spread to all equally. The analysis, assuming objective knowledge, did indeed capture important facets of the work activity. But the perspectives of those working in the lowest levels of organizational hierarchies tended to be forgotten (Vehviläinen, 1997).

4.   The Socio-drama Approach

This disparity in workers' expert positions was recognized by Eeva Piispanen, a member of the PRIP committee. In an extensive oral work history interview (Vehviläinen, 1994a, b) she told me about the committee work and her own personal view:

> *We were very ambitious. We read everything on Frigga Haug's PAQ, on the effects of automation, on the activity theory approach to work development. There was a hard ideological fight. We studied and argued a lot. (...) I had a personal dilemma. I could not accept everything in the activity theory approach. It denied the individual. It forbade talking about people's experiences.*

Together with a colleague she set out to develop a further approach based on socio-drama (Piispanen and Pallas, 1991) in order to redefine the expert orientation in PRIP-led development. This new approach shared the PRIP model's emphasis on activity: *"It is the activity that is taken as a main target for development, not only a technical system"* (ibid, p. 11). User participation was revised. It was now the information technology professionals, not users more generally, who were participating in the development activity. This emphasized that it was no longer the technical experts who had control.

After the PRIP committee, Piispanen worked in several governmental bureaux. She tried out the PRIP profession in practice. During these "experiments" she learnt that the technical terms and technical expertise could easily take over the work activity terms, even in organizations that in principle wanted to follow the committee's PRIP approach. Based on this experience she wanted to strengthen support for those involved in the work activity within the process of technology development. Piispanen and Pallas suggest that there should be *"two parallel lines, the line of activity and the line of technical design"* (ibid, p. 81) in the development process. In the activity line, people should be able to talk about their work solely in terms of the work activity. Then, later, the two lines would meet.

The core of this approach is a socio-drama that is played out around the work process to be developed. All workers that have tasks in the work process take part in the drama and play their own part in it. All players gather around one table or in one room. Each task and its performer become visible to and heard among the whole community of those involved in the wider work process. Voices from all hierarchical levels and from various positions are equally present in this drama. Even those tasks that are not normally articulated can be performed and hence receive attention. Thus even bodily knowledge (i.e. writing signatures, nodding for approval) can be presented.

In comparison to the PRIP model the socio-drama approach shapes agency and equality toward a polyphonic form. In other words, each worker has a role in the play. The approach comes closer to situated and bodily knowledge by allowing performances in addition to verbal expressions. It also recognizes that some groups, such as workers in their relation to technical experts, need special support in order to gain equal agency and hence influence the development process. The socio-drama model has developed a long way from the mainstream approach, where equality exists only among information technology professionals. Yet, even here there is a scriptwriter who directs this socio-drama play and her role is not discussed at all. There is once again a new expert – the person who organizes and leads the meetings. Although there are useful experts, and not all experts are equally powerful, the contradictions relating to the relations between experts and other workers should be acknowledged in an approach that seeks equality.

5.   National Information Society Strategy

The worldwide development of information societies has brought the expertise of information and communication technologies to the front stage of societal development. The 1990s information society strategies do not leave the development of information technology only to the specialist groups. Generally, the information society strategies in Western countries presuppose that it is the duty of all citizens to develop skills in new information technologies in order to gain equal access to information and technologies. A Finnish national strategy, *Quality of Life, Knowledge and Competitiveness* (1998, p. 10), aims *"to provide equal opportunities for the acquisition and management of information and for the development of knowledge"* and *"to strengthen democracy and opportunities for social influence:"*

> The information society offers all people better opportunities for personal development and active interaction both at work and leisure-time pursuits. The progress in ICT creates better opportunities for individuals, families and different communities to cooperate and interact, regardless of the distance between them. As citizens, people have better tools and channels for realising their freedom of speech and influencing social decision-making, as well as acquiring information needed to this end. (ibid, p. 11).

The strategy has many other objectives, too, but it clearly sets out to strengthen democracy and equality. Equality is meant to apply to all people. Experts are not mentioned at all.

Upon closer inspection, this agency turns out to be the agency of individuals and of liberal citizenship. The society promises to make services and basic skills as well as easy-to-use products available to everyone and then leaves the responsibility for using them to individual people:

> *People themselves have responsibility for their own choices, as well as for making their needs known or for putting their personal data at the disposal of the markets. (...) To be able to avail themselves of the opportunities opening up, people must have new skills as citizens, consumers and employees. The skills are gained in everyday interaction and in work tasks, as well as training offered in different sectors. The decisive factor is the individual's own initiative. Different communities must support their members in seizing opportunities available and developing competencies* (ibid, p. 11).

The welfare state provides opportunities for all and each active citizen needs to take on individual responsibility for developing her or his expertise in and usage of information technologies. Agency and expertise are meant to apply to everyone, but the nature of the social order and differences intertwined with people's everyday practices, although a central condition for agency, are passed over in the document. Some differences, such as age and region, are mentioned later in the strategy text. But even these are not thoroughly discussed. They are only labels for special services to be provided for individuals in elderly groups and those living in peripheral regions. The social world and an analysis of people's activities are not at the agenda. This means that the expertise to be acquired is not anchored in people's daily practices. It is not based on people's situated knowledge. Rather, it is an entity, defined in terms of objective knowledge, which needs to be achieved. This makes the expertise of technical experts the norm. Technical experts, and most importantly Nokia engineers, have been forerunners in the development of new technologies and they have been remarkably visible in daily newspapers and other media. This led to people talking about the need to monitor technical developments and the way forward being shown by these experts at the end of the 1990s (e.g. Uotinen *et al.*, 2001).

The strategy for all defines, paradoxically, people's agency and equality in a technically mediated society, called the information society, in terms of the expertise of technical experts. It provides equal rights to all, but the equal agency is not spread equally to all. It does not question the relations between experts and citizens and it ends up esteeming expert groups. This is not entirely different from the mainstream definition of user participation and equal agency. The information society development has been broadly run in terms of technical artifacts and economic relations – instead of the everyday practices of citizens.

6.   North Karelian Regional Information Society Strategy

The development of the information society as such need not deterministically put technical expertise at the center. An alternative approach was developed in North Karelia, a region on the Russian border, with vast open distances, high unemployment and relatively good support from EU structural funds. The North Karelian information society strategy for the years 1999–2006, *By Joint Work Party to the Information Society* (1999), put local everyday practices and communities first:

> *So, the information society is coming – but on whose terms? When people talk about development, they are often enthusiastic about technology, but, still, we are talking about a society for human beings, which is meeting new challenges and a new kind of action environment caused by technical development. (...) From the citizen's perspective, the people themselves affect what the information society in which they will act will be like. Then technology will serve as a helper and is shaped by its users. The information society is not only an isolated sector just for professionals but a natural and useful part of people's everyday life, leisure and work.* (ibid, p. 1). (...) *The information society is an entity of interactive communities built by North Karelians, in which information technology is exploited for one's own needs. Not using information technology must not lead to social exclusion, but basic services and rights have to be guaranteed for everyone* (ibid, p. 5).

The North Karelian strategy considered the information society as being a society that is developed by the inhabitants themselves, from the starting point of their everyday practices. It supported the development of local citizens' net, electronic village archives and experimental training programs that aimed to approach information technology from the point of view of people's everyday lives. Universal rights to equal access are also present in this strategy, but they were embedded in particular situations and local practices. Furthermore, it was not the choices of individuals that were to be the "driving force" in North Karelia. Instead, the information society was to be developed as a communal effort, together. Individuals had a choice not to take part in the development and they were able to say "No" to particular technologies. But it was not the individuals who were responsible for use and development.

The developers of the North Karelian approach had used actor network theory and other social shaping of technology theories as a resource. That enabled them to make more concrete references to the social world compared to many other information society strategies (Cronberg, 1999). There was a special emphasis on everyday practices, which also gave room for the located and situated knowledge of various groups as well as taking into account social hierarchies and differences. The agency of citizens was at the very center of the strategy. Equality became defined as a situated equality.

Although this strategy managed to define the situated agency, it was not easy to put it into practice in concrete development projects. Several development projects took up the challenge and aimed to build their activity on the situated knowledge of North Karelian inhabitants. Some of them managed to implement their aims in their concrete activities, but most others failed, at least partially. The citizens' center and its net café in Joensuu, in the regional capital of the North Karelia, were able to prioritize people's own activities and their continuous negotiations. The net café – instead of being furnished in a stylish manner in a separated area as is usual – became one organic part of the space and activities within the citizens' center. Computers and net connections as well as free user support were available, often arranged by the voluntary workers of the center, for anyone who wanted to have it. Nobody was under pressure to use them and people were all equally welcome to have a real live chat with their fellow visitors (Uotinen, 2003). Another project, followed by our research, appeared less successful. It started, and got its funding, by referring to everyday practices. Very soon it turned into information technology training packages in the spirit of the national strategy type of liberal agency. Everyday practices and social differences were no longer addressed in the project work (Vehviläinen, 2002).

The citizens' center workers in Joensuu, in a different manner from the institutional actors in the latter project, actually reflected consciously upon their practices. They were careful not to bring in their own ideas, not even supplying fixed training packages in information and communication technologies. Instead, they were ready to facilitate the grassroot activities of the people themselves. For them, the situated agency started from the daily practices of people. It was co-operation between a number of societal actors, starting from the frameworks of the European Union structural funding, national and regional authorities, local institutions, organizations and groups of inhabitants.[1] All these actors worked hard to adjust their practices to support situated agency (Uotinen *et al.*, 2001).

7.   Discussion

In this chapter, I have discussed four approaches that have been used in the development of technology. Each of them has goals related to agency and equality. They aim to support the participation of people – users, workers, citizens – in the development of technically mediated practices, and thus, to promote equal agency in society. They all aim to challenge the previous mainstream process

---

[1] By 2003, the European Union funding framework had changed and the focus of the development projects had also changed remarkably. A technically oriented mode had taken over the development projects instead of one reflecting a citizen's perspectives.

of information technology development where the technical experts had power. The understandings of equality and agency, however, vary considerably from an individualistic liberal agency to broader understandings of the social world, including the one of situated agency and knowledge.

The first approach is based on the activity theory and work research and it aims to shift the focus of expertise from information technology to work practices. Another one is a national information society strategy, a rather hegemonic approach in all Western societies, which aims to develop equal access to information technologies. The first one makes a scientific analysis of work processes and their histories. Equality and agency are understood as embedded in socially constructed and collective processes. The latter defines equality through individuals and their responsibilities. In spite of the differences, both of the two approaches are based on the understanding of universal knowledge detached from the practices of actual people. In contrast to these, the other two approaches seek forms of situated knowledge. The socio-drama approach debates with the activity theory approach and builds room for voices from situated positions through socio-drama scripts and plays. The North Karelian approach engages with the liberal approach and is also based on situated and located agency.

According to my four examples, the approaches to technology seem to acknowledge agency and equality in a rather unsystematic manner. The understanding of equality has not evolved or developed in a linear line from one decade to another. The two first approaches, the PRIP education and the socio-drama model, succeeded in challenging the expert power of information technology professionals. Then, again, the information technology experts once again acquired a new kind of powerful position within the turn of the millennium information society strategy. The 1980s approaches understand human activity as a socially organized process. In the 1998 information society strategy any understanding of the constraints of the social world is limited and the actors are individuals within a liberal citizenship framework. It treats, for example, low-income and minimally educated single mothers in rural areas similarly to technical experts in their responsibility to develop information technology skills and uses. Thus, it is not always the latest approaches that have the most elaborated views of equality. It is useful to look back and recall the practices that have been developed during previous decades. The memory of scientific communities tends to be short and the wheel is invented again and again – and sometimes it does not get invented at all.

The socio-drama approach, although it never became broadly adopted, is a particularly interesting case because it provides people in different social positions with a forum to gather together and discuss their common work and development processes. This forum is a ground for communal, not only individuals', activity. The groups in non-privileged social positions are given the opportunity to have a voice and their performance is seen and heard in a common space. Socio-drama plays strengthen these groups. Not only does it provide them with an equal opportunity, but also directs attention to the daily practices of people, so that technical terms do not take over the whole development process.

Comparable facilitating forums have been arranged in accordance with the North Karelian information society strategy. Women's groups studied information technology in women-only groups supervised by women teachers in order to break the nexus between masculinity and the expertise of information technology. Local citizens' networks have also been built. People need support as workers in organizations and as citizens in society. In particular, the expression of situated knowledge has proved to be demanding. Technical terms tend to pass over people's everyday practices as a starting point for technology development. Situated equality is a difficult form of agency. The North Karelian strategy makes a good start, but more societal discussion, development and research are needed. To begin with, societal actors should learn to distinguish situated agency as a valuable form of equal agency, as an alternative to liberal equal access agency. The situated agency would provide equal access, too, but it would pay attention to people's actual chances in reaching it. Furthermore, institutional actors should reflect upon their practices – to be able to assist (and not to lead from above) the situated agency of concrete projects and people.

Equal agency necessarily includes the possibility to say "No." The North Karelian strategy provides this option. In the concrete "project world" of the regional EU funding, all active citizens are, however, supposed to take part in the common project of societal development. The strategy does not take into account resistance nor alternatives for those who want to live without technical tools. These are all topics for further discussion.

In sum, the understandings of both "equality" and "agency" vary in the different approaches. Moreover, people whose practices are organized through various social differences do not face the agency provided in these approaches in a similar, "equal" manner. We have seen how the practices of equality and agency get defined in four different ways and this further intertwines with the understanding of expertise and knowledge.

Although they all aim to strengthen equal agency, the different understandings of equality and agency make the various approaches support different groups of people – instead of providing agency and equality evenly to everybody. The approaches that ignore the social relations of expertise give priority, especially, to technical experts, in spite of, in theory, providing equal rights to all citizens. The approaches that take the social world and its practices seriously begin to give the agency related to technical practices to the people themselves, but they easily replace the technical expert with other experts without questioning this. The understanding of situated knowledge, together with an understanding of the social relations of agency, finally make a sufficient theoretical basis for situated equality – where agency is to be defined for citizens experiencing various social differences – to apply to everyone equally.

References

Cronberg, T. Pohjois-Karjala tietoyhteiskuntaan: Alueelliset toimijaverkot ja syrjäytymättömyyden rakentaminen (North Karelia towards information society: Regional actor networks, building non-displacement, in Finnish). In Eriksson, P., Vehviläinen, M. (Eds.), Tietoyhteiskunta Seisakkeella: Teknologia, Strategiat ja Paikalliset Tulkinnat; 1999. SoPhi, Jyväskylä: 215–230.

Finnish National Fund for Research and Development. Quality of Life, Knowledge and Competitiveness: Premises and Objectives for Strategic Development of the Finnish Information Society; 1998. Sitra, Helsinki.

Haraway, D. Simians, Cyborgs, and Women. The Reinventions of Nature; 1991. Free Associations Books, London.

Joint Work Party to the Information Society. The Information Society Strategy and Action of North Karelia 1999–2006; 1999. The Regional Council of North Karelia, Joensuu.

Lister, R. Citizenship: Feminist Perspectives; 1997. Macmillan, London.

Piispanen, E., Pallas, K. TOTO, Tietotekniikalla Tulosta Hallintotyöhön (Information Technology Improves Profits in Administrative Work, in Finnish); 1991. VAPK-kustannus, Helsinki.

Smith, D.E. The Conceptual Practices of Power: A Feminist Sociology of Knowledge; 1990. University of Toronto Press, Toronto.

Suchman, L.A. Plans and Situated Actions. The Problem of Human Machine Communication; 1987. Cambridge University Press, Cambridge.

Tietojenkäsittelyn kehittämisvastuuhenkilöiden koulutusohjelma (An educational programme for Persons Responsible for Information Processing, in Finnish), Komiteamietintö 1986:7. Valtion painatuskeskus, Helsinki

Trist, E., Bamforth, K.W. Some social and psychological consequences of the Longwall method of coal-getting. Human Relations, 1951; IV(1): 3–38.

Turner, B.S. Contemporary problems in the theory of citizenship. In Turner, B.S. (Ed.), Citizenship and Social Theory; 1993. Sage, London: 1–18.

Uotinen, J. Involvement in (information) Society – The Joensuu community resource centre netcafé. New Media and Society, 2003; 5(3): 335–356.

Uotinen, J., Tuuva, S., Vehviläinen, M., Knuuttila, S. (Eds.). Verkkojen Kokijat Paikallista Tietoyhteiskuntaa Tekemässä (Local Information Society in the Making, in Finnish); 2001. Suomen Kansantietouden Tutkijain Seura, Helsinki.

Vehviläinen, M. Living through the boundaries of information Systems expertise – A work history of a Finnish woman systems developer. In Adam, A., Emms, J., Green, E., Owen, J. (Eds.), Proceedings of the IFIP TC9 WG9.1 Fifth International Conference on Women, Work and Computerization: Breaking New Boundaries – Building New Forms; July 2–5, 1994a, Manchester, U.K. Elsevier, Amsterdam: 107–120.

Vehviläinen, M. Reading computing professionals' codes of ethics – a standpoint of Finnish office workers. In Gunnarsson, E., Trojer, E., (Eds.), Feminist Voices on Gender, Technology and Ethics; 1994b. Centre for Women's Studies, Luleå University of Technology, Lulea: 145–161.

Vehviläinen, M. Gender, expertise and information technology. A Ph.D. thesis; 1997. Department of Computer Science, University of Tampere A-1, Tampere.

Vehviläinen, M. Gendered agency in information society: On located politics of technology. In Consalvo, M., Paasonen, S. (Eds.), Women and Everyday Uses of the Internet: Agency and Identity; 2002. Peter Lang Publishing, New York.

Chapter 14

COMMUNITY–TECHNOLOGY INTERFACES IN PARTICIPATORY PLANNING: TOOL OR TOKENISM?

Somya Joshi

1.   Introduction

... it is in the confrontation between technical objects and their users that the latter are rendered real or unreal. (Akrich, 1992, p. 208)

In recent years, there has been a great deal of reflection on the role of technologies within participatory decision-making. The avenues being opened by technical mediations to enhance discussion and information dissemination have been challenged by criticisms regarding the shortcomings of those same technologies to facilitate any genuine communication or knowledge-sharing between groups. Thus, on the one hand, emerging interactive technologies have been hailed as empowering and enabling, whereas on the other hand, they have been alleged to reinforce the very power divides that they have set out to bridge. The problematic being addressed within this chapter is not one of deciding whether a technology should be seen as an instrument of progress or a new method of subjugating people. It is rather an examination of the processes of technical mediation (looking at visualization and interactive technologies in particular) and their attempts to challenge divisions of power within the context of local participatory planning. The framework for this analysis is that of Activity Theory, which offers a critical lens both for the dynamic nature of community networks and for the role played by technical tools in mediating relationships of power.

In this chapter, I will begin by providing the reader with a detailed view of the context of this research, which will be followed by a description of my methodology. I will then proceed to examine critically the emerging frames

Leslie Haddon (ed.), Everyday Innovators, 218–232.
○ 2005 *Springer. Printed in The Netherlands.*

of participation and community–technology engagement in the light of the tensions they face.

2. Context

2.1. The VULCAN Project

The Virtual Urban Laboratory for Computer Aided Networking (VULCAN) was set up as capital grant project. Its remit extended beyond the research and development of augmented reality technology within a laboratory setting. Instead, the aim was to use this technology in the significantly less-controlled setting of an engagement with the local community in Salford, in Northern England. As articulated in its initial bid statements, the project had from the outset this aim: the design and deployment of virtual and mixed reality technology, from a multi-disciplinary perspective, as a means to improve the quality, effectiveness and efficiency of urban regeneration processes through enhanced participation of all stakeholders. In order to bring together these distinct frames of expertise and knowledge, the project brought on board a team of experts whose collaborative goal was to design an interface that would allow disenfranchised community members to participate in local level decision-making.

The three main thematic streams or goals that emerged from this project were:

1. The technological mediation of physical and symbolic space to assist communication, participation, decision-making and evaluation.
2. The development and use of augmented and mixed reality systems for modeling urban regeneration schemes.
3. The integration and management of complex information flows.

As a project, VULCAN had built into it certain "wish-lists" that reflected the uniqueness of its intentions. At one level, it aimed to develop a cutting-edge technology by researching innovative applications of virtual and augmented reality systems within a multi-disciplinary setting. At another level, it was to act as a platform via which local planning participation could be mediated. The local community context within which these aspirations were set was that of a Regeneration Project in Salford. In many respects, the characteristics of this changing physical and social environment, along with the prior decision to enhance participation in local planning, made an ideal test-bed for the VULCAN project. In Section 2.2, I will explain in a little more detail about this regeneration initiative.

2.2.   Chapel Street Regeneration Project

The Chapel Street Regeneration project was a major integrated urban initiative aimed at the economic, physical and social renewal of the historic core of the City of Salford. The project was overseen by a Partnership Board, which had representatives from the following bodies: Salford City Council, Northwest Development Agency, Government North West, University of Salford, Manchester Training & Enterprise Council, Greater Manchester Police, the Chapel Street Business Group and Manchester Chamber of Commerce and Industry. Thus, the stakeholders in this initiative ranged from the community residents to the local authorities (e.g. councillors), from the business communities to the planners, architects and development workers. In terms of aspirations, the following would broadly sum up the stakeholders' articulated needs:

1.   Strengthening a sense of local "community".
2.   Resource mobilization – allocating funds for immediate basic local needs (e.g. health, education, crime, transport, services).
3.   Genuine participation in local decision-making – to counter what was aptly termed "consultation fatigue."
4.   Bridging the "skills-gap". The anticipation here was that inclusive interfaces (as promised by the Virtual and Augmented Reality systems) would enable non-specialist stakeholders to participate in an informed and equitable manner.

Before I begin my analysis of the extent to which these initiatives were able to realize these anticipations and the challenges they met with, I will examine my choice of conceptual framework as well as the methodological tools I employed, in Section 3.

3.   Methodology

The theoretical lens through which I have analyzed my research findings is that of Activity Theory. As a framework, this seeks to understand how cultural tools and symbols mediate the relationship between human agents and the objects within a given environment (Engeström, 1987). It offers an effective methodology for critically analyzing the design ideologies that underlie technical systems. In this framework it is argued that an individual's creative interaction with his or her surroundings can greatly influence the production of tools. The theorists within this school of thought (Blackler, 1993; Engestrom, 1996) argue that the processes of *objectification* or *manifestation* of internal insights (tacit knowledge) takes place, making the external artifact more accessible and therefore more useful in some ways for social interaction. It is this

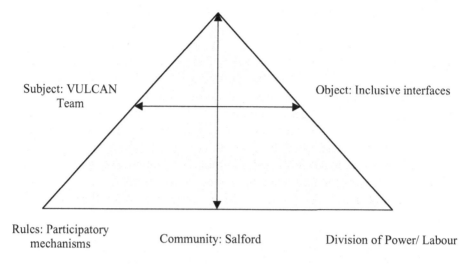

Figure 14-1. The VULCAN Project

process of transformation from tacit knowledge to inclusive technical interfaces that forms the focus of this chapter.

Furthermore, the principle of tool mediation plays a central role within this approach, with a significant emphasis being placed on social factors and on the interaction between agents and their environments. It is argued that tools are created and transformed during the development of the activity itself and carry with them a particular culture – the historical remnants from that development. Taking this point further, one could argue that within the use of tools itself lies a means for the accumulation and transmission of social knowledge.

To clarify the two points raised in the last paragraphs, let us first look at how the model offered by this framework applies to our case (see Figure 14-1). What we have here is a network of activity, undertaken by human agents (VULCAN and the Regeneration team) who are motivated to solve a problem or motivated by a purpose (to make the local decision-making process more inclusive), and mediated by tools (VR/AR Interface) in collaboration with other stakeholders (the Salford community). This structure of activity, the way these interact, is further constrained by cultural factors. These include conventions (e.g. technical know-how, the consultation mechanisms) and the divisions of power (hierarchies within VULCAN and within the Regeneration body) (see Engeström, 1987).

At first, this method of framing the activity networks might appear to be too rigid or flat. But if we bring into consideration the two arguments raised above regarding the recognition of the role played by tacit knowledge and the translation of this into the external mediating artifacts themselves, then we begin to appreciate the dynamic nature of this conceptual framework. In Activity Theory, the basic unit of analysis of all human endeavors is "activity," a broader more embracing concept than individual goal-oriented actions. What this means is that there can, at any given time, be multiple activity systems with interactions and mediations between them. In the case of the empirical data that I draw upon for this chapter, the activity system of VULCAN is in direct interaction with that of the Salford Regeneration Project. Each has its own set of anticipations or notions of desired outcomes (often with internal contradictions and conflicting opinions about what the outcome should be). Brought together by the over-arching desire to deliver an inclusive platform on which designers and users alike can make informed decisions, this interaction was, then, not without its own set of tensions and inherent contradictions.

In Section 4, I will discuss the emerging challenges when the two frames meet.

4.   Analysis

4.1.   *Differing Perceptions on Desired Outcomes*

> *The outputs of the project will be used, in the first instance, by the participants in the Regeneration Project, in order to help them evaluate the long term environmental and social impacts of the various strategies being put forward, thereby making the decision making process more inclusive.* (VULCAN Mission Statement)

The two set of anticipations articulated in the above statement, namely the desire to create an inclusive decision-making paradigm of development and the hope that technology could facilitate this transition toward sustainable outcomes, struggled to make the leap from discourse into practice. One reason for this concerned the belief held by many in the VULCAN team that this would strictly compromise the creative freedom of the technical designers who were seeking to lead the innovation process with regard to a cutting-edge technology. A (board) member of the VULCAN team expressed this discrepancy in the following statement:

> *While I do think the community should perhaps have the power of veto in some way, I don't think they should be allowed to design or lead the process . . .*

Thus, we see the first instance of contradiction with regard to the level of community involvement in the project. According to Gibbons *et al.* (1994, pp. 3–16), change occurs not only through producing new knowledge but also through taking existing knowledge and reconfiguring it so that it can be used in new contexts or by new sets of users. VULCAN provided the ideal platform for this. Its novelty lay in the innovative application of a technology that had not been used within such a context before. While Virtual Reality (VR) Technology itself had been researched, its application in the field of community participation in planning was not only unique but also it was promising in terms of challenging entrenched power structures within local planning and policy making. However, not all members within the project shared this view.

One of the key arguments on the basis of which VULCAN justified its push toward technical innovation was the intuitive interface of its VR model. This was supposed to make the entire process of community–technology interaction more transparent and accessible. These transparency and access aspects, it was argued (by the VULCAN technical design team), would be enabled intuitive tools that made explicit the most complex and specialized information. For instance, a lay member of the community within Salford would struggle to understand fully, and thereby relate to, an architectural drawing or plan of his/her area, drafted by an expert and put forward for consultation. It was argued that with the aide of a three-dimensional model – simulating the very urban environment under regeneration – the experience would be more immediate and visual. This would then enable all the stakeholders alike to make informed decisions about the proposed changes.

However, once again the seeds of doubt as to the promises made and the outcomes desired began to surface. A member of the technical design team expressed his concern:

> *I think the idea of an intuitive interface is disingenuous. To me it is nothing but a label that a lot of technology projects are using these days because it gives the false impression that we're doing something which communicates with people in the real world.*

Perceptions of a "real" world here are as thinly defined as the virtual interface itself. There existed within VULCAN differing views as to what exactly the "reality" that had to be captured was and if there existed one single defining reality to be represented within the model. This contributed greatly toward a number of members feeling some disconnection between their actual work and the context that they hoped to be working within (as is reflected in the statement above).

4.2. *Object-Oriented Activity – Embedded Assumptions*

When technical designers define the characteristics of their objects, they necessarily make hypotheses about the entities, sometimes people, that make up

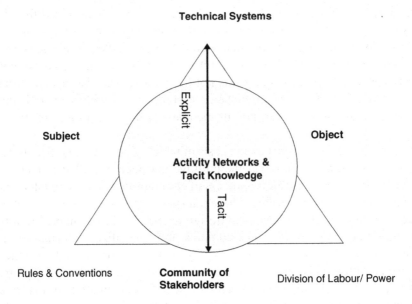

Figure 14-2. Activity Theory and Technical Systems

the world into which that object has to be inserted. In other words, the technologists build into the technical artifact certain assumptions about who will use it, how it will be used, and hence its very functionality. In doing this designers, thus, assign the "community" of users with motives, competences, aspirations, political prejudices, and so on.

Activity Theory recognizes that there are two kinds of objects: real, physical (material) objects and ideal (mental) objects, present in the subject's (designer's) mind. These set of tacit assumptions play a significant role in informing the technical interfaces as well as the platforms designed for user interaction (see Figure 14-2) To illustrate this point, we have the object (desired outcome) of involving and engaging community members in local decision-making. But the manner in which these participatory exercises are carried out and the tools employed can themselves reflect rather strongly the assumptions made on the part of the designers of this activity. This is reaffirmed in the following statement by a frustrated community representative:

> *When they consult they're not doing it because they are really interested in what we have to say. They're only doing it because its part of the process outlined by the government now. They don't consult us in order to better inform us or get our views. It is simply a question of telling us what they've already decided is best for us.*

It becomes vital to evaluate in what sense a particular technology has a distinctive or cumulative impact, an impact that can be traced through the various social contexts in which the technology became embedded. It is, therefore, not just the mediating artifacts that need to be taken into account but also the socio-cultural contexts within which they are developed. This dynamic is addressed by Activity Theory, as it lays significant emphasis on the active nature of the subject of an activity. It recognizes that people bring with them a whole range of biases that will affect how they approach the activity: previous experience, personality, skill/aptitude and culturally determined traits. These will continue to evolve as the person undertakes the activity.

The technical realization of a designer's beliefs about the relationships between an object and its surrounding actors also reflects the myriad divisions of power within that context. And the assumptions might prove to be wrong. It might be that no actors will come forward to play the roles envisaged by the designers. Or, alternatively, users might define different roles of their own. In the case of VULCAN, this was beautifully illustrated. The assumption made on the part of the designers was that given their lack of familiarity or knowledge of high-end technical systems, users would want to adopt a passive role and thus only navigate through – not interact with – the model. When the consultation exercises were carried out, it emerged that the users from within the Salford community were more receptive and open to the idea of actively participating than had previously been imagined. This led to the further development of another more interactive model that would allow the users to play a more constructive and consultative role.

4.3.   Community – Who are the End Users?

Within complex hierarchical systems such as VULCAN and the Salford Regeneration Initiatives, there is the implication that multiple communities of practitioners exist. These considerations, in turn, justify describing communities of technological practitioners as being composed simultaneously of individuals and collectives, such as organizations. While there is considerable debate and discussion regarding the end users of technical interfaces, there is relatively very little clarity as regards who exactly comprises this group. Often projects such as VULCAN find themselves in a "Catch-22" situation where they cannot design a system until they have a neatly defined set of user-needs. Yet, they cannot begin to collect these without an interface or model to take into the target community of users in order to get this feedback and allow consultation.

The confusion and lack of clarity regarding who the stakeholder community was, who the end-users for the VR/AR model would be, is reflected in the following:

While one member of the Regeneration Planning team said:

> *Personally, my vision is it's (the end user is) the architect, the strategic people, the people who need to authorise to pay the projects, and so on. So I'd say it'd be*

the influential people in the local government. I don't really see members of the community using what we're developing.

A technical designer from VULCAN reminded us of the tension that exists between the perceived lack of technical knowledge of the lay-community and the complexity of the technical artifact itself:

I would say the main 'users' are the people who live in the area. However, what has been said is that because the technology is so difficult to understand, we might look at the Planners as the users.

Hence, we are given a clear understanding of how contested the domain is when it comes to the "end user". Not surprisingly, then, I argue that the pre-suppositions regarding who this user group is, what their competencies, skills or attributes are and how they will use the technology, all become enmeshed in the artifact itself. As a result, the final technical tool opens doors of possibilities for some while pre-empting, and clamping down barriers for, others.

4.4.   The Role and Nature of the Subject

Bijker and Law (1992, p. 17) observe the age old idea that an individual tech-nology moves through a natural cycle: from pure through applied research, it then moves to development, to production, to marketing and maturity. They argue that this view needs to be challenged as it has proved to be inadequate. There is nothing inevitable about the way technologies evolve. Rather they are the product of what we might call "heterogeneous contingency" – i.e. there are many factors at work, including elements of chance.

In this section, I explore the varying outlooks on the role of Chapel Street within the domain of VULCAN. At one end of the spectrum, there existed the view that there was a desperate need for sensitivity to context, for reflecting on the specific nature of the situation and people involved in this community. At the other end, there was the view that VULCAN was essentially setting out to create certain generic technological tools and Chapel Street was nothing more than a test-bed from which certain generalizable lessons could be learnt. Illus-trating this, a technical designer of the VR model responded in the following way:

I see VULCAN as a set of generic tools, approaches and methodologies, within which Chapel Street is just a case study.

While another team member articulated his concern regarding this "case study:"

Chapel Street was seen to be as just incidental, any context sensitivity to it just didn't matter. Apparently objectivity means having nothing to do with the understanding of context. Generalisability was what they meant by transferability. And for me a piece of technology cannot work unless you understand the context in which it is to work.

When we speak of a nebulous term such as "community," the obvious question that arises is what does this term signify for the subjects concerned? Should one be classifying a group of people according to spatially defined boundaries, saying that a certain area counts as a "community"? Or instead should we be conceptualizing communities as being based on shared interests and practices, around which people mobilize and interact? These questions are highly relevant because unless we have some clarity as to whom exactly we are referring to as our subjects and stakeholders within the activity of planning, we cannot assess their role or the extent to which they are mediated by technical tools.

Wenger (1998) talks about communities in terms of a "social landscape defined by the boundaries of various practices." In addition, he acknowledges that one can be a member of several communities of practice simultaneously. He articulates this point in the following statement:

As communities of practice differentiate themselves and also interlock with each other, they constitute a complex social landscape of shared practices, boundaries, peripheries, overlaps, connections and encounters. (p. 118)

However, regeneration programs generally target resources to spatially defined areas rather than communities defined by common practices. The choices made regarding the allocation of funding are further defined by the limitations of external funding criteria. For example, these state that the area in question not only needs to demonstrate characteristics of widespread deprivation, but it also needs to show signs of possessing the capacity to benefit from regeneration resources. The danger here lies in the fact that some groups become favored and receive widespread attention while others become nobody's priority.

The short timescales available for consultation, coupled with the fact that plans are often pre-defined by external criteria such as the one above, have often meant that community groups have found it difficult to participate. As a consequence, they have had little real influence on the development agendas. Unlike other partners, local people often do not come to the table readily equipped with the appropriate skills for participation. Of course, skills related to negotiation, presentation and time management can be learnt with the appropriate support and training. Yet, community representatives often find they do not come to the table with the same resources backing them and with the organization as their other partners. Therefore, some stakeholders carry less "clout" even before the negotiations begin. A member of the Chapel Street Community expressed her frustration regarding this practice:

> *The way they go about it is like this: they tell us the plans have been submitted and everything, then they tell us in the community – you have 14 to 21 days to put something in by way of feedback. Now how many ordinary people can figure something out, let alone frame it in some organised format in that length of time?*

In order for communities to become genuinely involved in strategic partnerships, local authorities and their partners may need to make substantial investment in terms of developing the community capacity's to do so, before the parameters of strategic programs are set (Craig and Mayo, 1995).

This Activity Theory model of hierarchy has two significant messages here for us. One is that focusing on the whole activity, and not just individual actions, may facilitate genuine dialog between the different stakeholders. For instance, once the cross-disciplinary boundaries within VULCAN have been transcended, the overall purpose behind the need for engagement with the community comes into better focus. Secondly, it is important to understand the interplay between the levels of actions and operations in order to design more usable and transparent technical systems. The aim in interface design should be to allow users to engage with the model in question and to allow their tacit understandings of its use to better inform the design of the tool itself.

4.5.   Mediating Tools

In the VULCAN project, there were models of the mediating tools that were to be used between the various stakeholders. The first of these was a navigational model using VR. The other was interactive in only two dimensions – e.g. via a computer screen – and therefore relatively more easy to access, for example. These different types of interface reflected different conceptions of the world being represented. For instance, the overall purpose of the navigational VR model was to allow for a "fly-through" of the projected redevelopment sites. The depictions of the community space here were often reminiscent of computer games, where a sanitized view of the community was presented. A community representative responded to this by saying:

> *The 'wow-factor' is overwhelming in this model. But I don't feel as if this is the area I live in. It's too clean.*

However, according to the chairperson of the VULCAN project, who was in many respects the person who conceptualized this initiative, the benefits far outweighed the "unreal" feel of the model:

If you can use VR to elucidate, clarify and demonstrate things that you want to do, it is a major advance. I think a major part of this whole exercise is to build trust, to build confidence in the community by bringing them together. Visual references are always integrating mechanisms. They bring people together because everyone can share the same experience.

The assumption here, that everyone involved in the activity without exception will have the "same experience," demonstrated the somewhat naïve belief, on the part of VULCAN decision-makers, in the role played by the mediating tools. While visual models can facilitate the sharing of knowledge and experience, the degree to which people chose to share, communicate and subsequently build trust is dependent on several variables other than the tools employed. As was demonstrated in the actual engagement of "the community" within the VULCAN case, the almost blanket reliance on the technical tools to accomplish what negotiations and dialog could have done – in terms of building trust – proved to be counter-productive for the overall aim of the project.

5.   Conclusion

The processes involved in the design and creation of technical artifacts involve co-operation that crosses group, professional and subcultural boundaries. More specifically, when the desired outcome of a project is to draw on the myriad reserves of knowledge and activity, to transform the tacit meaning-systems, rules and motivations into an explicit participatory system, then it becomes imperative that the actors or subjects involved transcend the boundaries confining their role. The VULCAN Project was no exception. The difficulties of working in situations where several groups have different practices, traditions and working objectives are well known. Different groups, professions and subcultures embody different perspectives. They communicate in different "jargon." Much of this cannot be translated, in a satisfactory way, into the terms used by other groups, since it reflects a different way of acting in the world (a different ontology and epistemology).

My critique of the way in which this process was handled in the above project relies on the centrality of *interpretation* in the conduct of this work activity. Clearly, the development of technical applications requires the collaboration or involvement of a variety of distinct communities – workers with different skills, analysts, developers, programmers, etc. This necessary heterogeneity poses a number of problems, which cannot be removed simply by ensuring good "communication" between the differing groups. The issue is more fundamental. It arises out of the different practices of the groups and the essential inconsistencies of their worldviews and language. Hence, the emphasis on the need for mechanisms through which these cross-cutting interpretations can take place.

When we turn to the specific modeling process used in this project, a distinction needs to be made between the nature of *description* and that of *interpretation*. Models can then be seen as interpretations, as constructions, which for some purposes, under certain conditions, used by certain people, in certain situations may be found useful. But it is not a question of whether they are true or false. Thus, I see the modeling process as one of reframing rather than of describing or abstracting. The artificial world of VR simulation is centered precisely on this interface between the inner and outer environments; it is a form of interpreting the world. This is central to the process of design itself; there is a real tension between the pre-suppositions and aspirations of the designer working on a simulation or representation (internal) and what the final technical system (external) means for the users and communities of stakeholders that engage with it.

Activity Theory offers us a clear lens to examine the phenomenon of internalization and externalization. It explains how, through activity, individuals and groups internalize meanings, views and methods arising from the encounter between different stakeholders in projects. At a later stage, these become externalized in the design and deployment of the mediating tools. It is now possible to make some final observations about this theoretical framework. An activity system does not exist in a vacuum, as we saw in the project above. It interacts with a network of other activity systems. For example, it receives rules and instruments from certain activity systems (e.g. VULCAN management) and produces outcomes for certain other activity systems (e.g. Salford Regeneration clients). Thus, there are outside influences on any particular activity system. Yet, such external forces do not provide a full account of surprising events and changes in the activity. We have to appreciate that such outside influences are first appropriated by the activity system, that is, turned into and modified to form internal factors.

Furthermore, there are various dynamic processes at work. There is a constant process of construction and renegotiation within the activity system. Coordination between different versions of the object must be achieved to ensure continuous flows within the operation. Tasks are often reassigned and redivided, just as rules are often bent and reinterpreted. There is also incessant movement between the various nodes of the activity. What initially appears as an object may soon be transformed into an outcome, then turned into an instrument, and perhaps later into a rule (Engeström, 1996). In the case of VULCAN, the object, which was to create an inclusive interface for participatory planning, became the mediating tool or instrument while the communities of stakeholders kept evolving in terms of membership.

While the above might suggest a simplistic, neat transition from one axis to another, the very process of change is often problematic. Polanyi (1962, 1966, 1969) makes a strong argument concerning the difficulty in "capturing" the tacit aspect of knowledge in explicit forms. This is not to suggest that there exists a simplistic process of transformation from the tacit to the explicit. In fact, if anything the capturing of tacit knowledge within explicit systems is highly problematic (see Polanyi's (1962, 1966, 1969) seminal work on tacit knowledge). The argument being made here is that through consultation and consistent, genuine engagement with the various stakeholders, this tacit knowledge can be made explicit and through this process invaluable resource consisting of their knowledge and experience can be learnt from and applied in making tools more enabling.

Despite the conflicting interests, leading R&D institutions have already begun to identify public participation as a core value and a large and growing number of NGOs have done likewise. In effect, participatory development proposes and gradually imposes a new paradigm of decision-making on all sectors of society. It entails a new perspective on present-day issues and challenges. And it requires a better appreciation of the complex interconnections between the various activity systems based on economic, social and technological factors. Adopting an activity perspective amounts to looking at current problems through a new lens that broadens our vision from a singular focus on only the economic, technical or social aspects of an issue to an integrated consideration of all three.

In this chapter, I have critically examined the potential of a technical initiative such as VULCAN to facilitate and enable participatory local planning. However, in order to realize this potential, I argue that greater attention needs to be paid to the interactions within the various networks of activity. This bridge between the various differing perspectives on outcomes, between the differing subject groups and communities of stakeholders and between the changing rules, conventions, and divisions of power can be provided only through dialog and consistent negotiation of meanings.

References

Akrich, M. The de-scription of technical objects. In Bijker, W., Law, J. (Eds.), Shaping Technology/Building Society: Studies in Sociotechnical Change; 1992. Routledge, London.

Bijker, W., Law, J. (Eds.) Shaping Technology/Building Society: Studies in Sociotechnical Change; 1992. Routledge, London.

Blackler, F. Knowledge and the theory of organisations: Organisations as activity systems and the reframing of management. Journal of Management Studies, 1993; 30(6): 863–884.

Craig, G., Mayo, M. Community Empowerment; 1995. Zed Books, London.

Engeström, Y. Learning by Expanding: An Activity-Theoretical Approach to Developmental Research; 1987. Orienta-Konsultit, Helsinki.

Engeström, Y. Interobjectivity, ideality, and dialectics. Mind, Culture and Activity, 1996; 3(4): 259–265.

Engeström, Y., Escalante, V. Mundane tool or object of affection? The rise and fall of the postal buddy. In Nardi, B. (Ed.), Context and Consciousness: Activity Theory and Human Computer Interaction; 1996. MIT Press, Cambridge, Massachusetts: 325–374.

Gibbons, M., Limoges, C., Nowotny, H., Schwartzman, S., Scott, P., Trow, M. The New Production of Knowledge: The Dynamics of Science and Research in Contemporary Societies; 1994. Sage Publications, London: 3–16.

Polanyi, M. Personal Knowledge: Towards a Post-critical Philosophy; 1962. Harper Torchbooks, New York.

Polanyi, M. The Tacit Dimension; 1966. Routledge and Kegan Paul, London.

Polanyi, M. Knowing and Being; 1969. Routledge and Kegan Paul, London.

Chapter 15

CONCLUSION

The tone of this book reflects the background of its contributing authors: whatever their disciplinary training, many have worked in some capacity within companies developing ICTs or for those firms. The same is true of the editors. The remaining contributors have usually been involved in or studied other design projects or innovation processes. Hence, a number of the chapters reflect on these authors' own experience of the design process, and sometimes the difficulties encountered, as well as on the experience of users. The authors draw upon a diverse range of theoretical frameworks, but they usually do so not in the sense of critically evaluating those approaches. Instead, they ask how theory can act as a tool and provide insights for practioners – like themselves – as well as for other audiences in academia, design education, those interested in relevant ICT policy issues, etc. Even if questioning some process or concept or other limitation within the innovation process, they usually provide implicit or explicit guidelines as to how better to deal with this in the future. In sum, much of the book is about sharing experiences of research and of the innovation process.

In the early 1980s there were some books within British sociology on what might be called the politics of research (Bell and Roberts, 1984; Roberts, 1981). Here, a number of researchers reconsidered studies that they themselves had conducted some years earlier and reflected on such matters as how those studies were shaped. This included what they may have missed, why they asked the questions they did at the time, what frameworks they had used, the problems involved and how they might do things differently now. Such writings are noteworthy because they are rare. In fact, when people report their research at conferences, certainly ICT conferences, it is more common to hear of examples of how to do something, what positive things can be learnt from a particular approach, a theoretical framework or a methodology, rather than to hear about any reservations.

This book is novel to the extent that many of the contributors raise issues. This is very clear in the chapter by Mallard and the one by Limonard and de Koning, thinking through the dilemmas faced by social scientists working in and with ICT companies. Mahé and Rantavuo, in different ways, reflect

Leslie Haddon (ed.), Everyday Innovators, 233–236.
© 2005 *Springer. Printed in The Netherlands.*

on the role of artists', but also on the limitations that constrain them. Gilligan questions rurality, one of the concepts used by social scientists when mapping ICT use, while Sarkkinen presents a critical evaluation of one small part of the design process, the test scenario. Joshi indicates the problems of involving end users in a particular ICT community project, whereas Vehviläinen shows these limitations on a grander scale, within different understandings of user participation.

But these authors also show a certain optimism and offer practical advice. Thinking first of the innovation process, sometimes one aim of these chapters is to provide a kind of checklist or guidance for practioners to think about. Mallard's chapter and that of Limonard and de Koning both do this for the social scientist. Mahé suggests what positive role artists could have in the innovation process and what relation they could have to team members, while Rantavuo argues how companies could benefit from involvement in art exhibitions. Tuomi encourages designers to rethink the design process and provides a way of conceptualizing the social role of ICTs in everyday life. Sotamaa outlines the lesson that the games-industry learns from its fans, which may well be applicable to some other fields. Gilligan does not throw out the concept of rurality, but suggests how we might approach this in future, and, in the same spirit, Sarkkinen suggests what a revised test scenario could look like – one which would do justice to and empower the user. Joshi raises a related issue of how to support potential users, but this time in the context of community consultation, while Vehviläinen provides a wider vision of what community participation could mean.

A central theme of this book is that of how people have been involved in ICT development, but also what roles they could play in future innovation. The writers share a common view – that the users should be involved – and that there are benefits to be gained from this involvement. One important idea going through the chapters is that products become useful and meaningful through their use and in relation to the social practices in which they are embedded. The authors develop various ways in which the relationship between these practices and the design of products can be better understood and taken into account in the development process. Since people are the designers of and experts as regards their own lives, their everyday life practices, they also invent new ways to use the technology all the time. An interesting starting point for applying these ideas in design, as suggested by our authors, is to see products as platforms for the development of new practices, rather than as strictly pre-programed tools with fixed uses.

In reality, products and practices co-evolve, influencing each other. This appears to be the main source of innovation available for developers from users, but it has not been as well exploited as it could have been. ICT products, however, have the kind of dynamic qualities that make it possible to design in a way that enables and empowers this kind of user innovation. This requires both new design ideology and changes in the design process. The chapters of this book discuss a number of issues in this respect, showcasing interesting practices and providing new insights. But as always, it remains the developers' responsibility to apply these insights within concrete work.

If these are some of the shared themes it is also clear that this book covers a diverse set of topics. Admittedly, the camera phone is examined or touched upon in four of the chapters, given that it was an innovation that was in the process of being researched at the time of writing. But even then, the way in which different authors analyzed this technology varied.

We would argue that diversity can also be a strength in that it serves to demonstrate at multiple levels and in multiple contexts the key themes noted in the introduction. The different chapters reveal, in different guises, related forms of analysis that try to address those developing ICTs in a progressive way, that try to move things on. At the very least, the contributors provide an introduction to a range of concepts and frameworks with which some practioners might be less familiar.

However, there are two particular dimensions of diversity that deserve further attention. One is that this book is unusual in that is covers both the field of design and users studies. There are examples of research that follow particular innovations across these domains (e.g., Du Guy *et al.*, 1997, on the Walkman). But on the whole it is rare for books to consider both fields. And yet if innovations are to be by some criteria "successful" then the writers in this book have collectively, and sometimes individually, made the case that it is important to consider both the processes taking place in the design stage and in the social world of end users. If more publications were to extend over both domains in this way, it would reinforce this message.

The other dimension of diversity of particular note is that presence of writers from different disciplines. Admittedly social science, and in particular sociology, is over-represented among both the contributors and editors. That said, at least the social science contribution is counterpoised against voices from design and from art, which is again seldom the case in most edited publications. While being wary of overstressing interdisciplinary boundaries, as noted in the introduction, this juxtaposition allows us to appreciate the types of contribution from, but also the constraints acting upon, the participants in design who are representing different disciplines. Such an understanding helps to pave the way for a better dialog, perhaps indicating how one culture can work within the other culture. It is apparent from the chapters that this collaboration is not straightforward – while people are adaptive and can always work with each other, various authors have shown ways in which this is problematic. However, they have also suggested strategies that can move towards a more inclusive and transdisciplinary development process.

Of course, one can always question the particular claims being made within this book. For example, how accurate are some of the characterizations of the design process? How workable are some of the visions? Many authors suggest aspects that we could in principle be more sensitive to, but how difficult is it to implement this as a research process? What new problems emerge if we try to follow up some of the suggestions about the way interdisciplinary teams could work or ways in which potential users could be involved in the design process? Clearly, too, while the chapters often provide examples, they cannot always claim to be exhaustive. There are probably many other parts of the design process that could be investigated in more depth and many other dimensions of user innovativeness – or its limitations – that could be followed up. Yet, although inevitably building upon work that has gone before, these writings provide one starting point for practioners to reflect upon the way in which they approach innovation in the field of ICTs.

References

Bell, C., Roberts, H. (Eds.), Social Researching: Politics Problems and Practices; 1984. Routledge & Kegan Paul, London.
Du Guy, P., Hall, S., Janes, L., Mackay, H., Negus, K. Doing Cultural Studies. The Story of the Sony Walkman; 1997. Sage, London.
Roberts, R. (Ed.), Doing Feminist Research; 1981. Routledge & Kegan Paul, London.

Index

Activity theory 218, 220–2, 224, 228, 230–1
Actor network theory 3–4
Affective computing 104
Akrich 4, 43–5, 47
Appropriation 44, 46–7

Bijker 7, 47, 86, 168, 226
Bricholage 100, 102
Bricholeur (see Bricholage)

Callon 4
Camera phone 9, 13, 20, 57, 61, 67–9, 71–80, 86–101, 136–48, 235

De Certeau 46, 100, 124, 134
Cognitive economies 49
Communities of practice 11, 18, 23, 29–32
Configuring the user 4, 175
COST269 1
Decoding 5, 68
Deconstruction 134, 153, 187–97
Derrida 188–9
Dewey 7, 33–4
Domestication 4, 11, 47, 60–2
Double loop learning 6

Encoding 5, 68
Engeström 25, 220
Equal agency 210, 204–16

Fandom 70, 111–14

HCI (Human Computer Interface) 17, 22, 69, 104–5, 107
Hoogma 6, 53, 56

Inscription 4, 44–5
Interdisciplinary collaboration 1–2, 6, 8, 12, 152, 173–4, 177–8, 235–6

Latour 4, 45, 177
Law 4
Lead user 44, 51
Long waves 32

MacKenzie 3, 86
Minitel 40–41
MMS 45, 67–9, 71–82, 87–101, 136–48
Multimedia messaging (See MMS)
Mutual construction 32

Network externalities 11, 19, 48, 52

Pinch 4

Remediation 96, 135
Rip 168–9

Schot 6, 53, 56, 176
SCOT (Social Construction of Technology) 3–4, 152, 156, 168–9, 174–6, 178
Script (see inscription)
Silverstone 4, 45, 61–2, 86
Situated knowledge 10, 210, 204, 216
SMS (Short Message Service) 40, 42, 56, 59, 68–9, 82, 91–3, 96, 98, 100, 134
Social learning 7, 18, 28, 30–7, 169
Social shaping of technology 3–4, 68, 86
Structurationalist 47
Subject-centric design (see user-centred design)
Systems effects 19

Texting (see SMS)

Usability 6, 9–10, 49, 70
User-centered design 17, 21–3, 27, 36, 104,
   185
User-centric design (see user-centred design)

Vygotsky 30
Von Hipple 18, 41, 114

Wajcman 3, 86
Willams 86
Woolgar 4, 86, 188